BIO OF AN OGRE

By Piers Anthony

Bio of an Ogre
Chthon
Phthor
Anthonology
Macroscope
Prostho Plus
Race Against Time
Rings of Ice

Triple Detente
Steppe
But What of Earth?
Hasan
Mute
Shade of the Tree
Ghost

Series by Piers Anthony

THE APPRENTICE ADEPT SERIES
Split Infinity • Blue Adept • Juxtaposition • Out of Phaze

INCARNATIONS OF IMMORTALITY SERIES
On a Pale Horse • Bearing an Hourglass • With a Tangled Skein • Wielding a Red Sword • Being a Green Mother

BIO OF A SPACE TYRANT SERIES
Refugee • Mercenary • Politician • Executive • Statesman

THE MAGIC OF XANTH SERIES
A Spell for Chameleon • The Source of Magic • Castle Roogna • Centaur Aisle • Ogre, Ogre • Night Mare • Dragon on a Pedestal • Crewel Lye • Golem in the Gears • Vale of the Vole

TAROT SERIES
God of Tarot • Vision of Tarot • Faith of Tarot • Tarot

THE CLUSTER SERIES
Cluster • Chaining the Lady • Kirlian Quest • Thousandstar • Viscous Circle

OF MAN AND MANTA SERIES
Omnivore • Orn • Ox

BATTLE CIRCLE SERIES
Sos the Rope • Var the Stick • Neq the Sword

Bio
OF AN
Ogre

The Autobiography of
PIERS ANTHONY
to age 50

ACE BOOKS, NEW YORK

BIO OF AN OGRE

An Ace Book
Published by The Berkley Publishing Group
200 Madison Avenue, New York, New York 10016

The name "Ace" and the "A" logo are trademarks
belonging to Charter Communications, Inc.

Copyright © 1988 by Piers Anthony Jacob

Book design by Ernest Haim

First Edition: May 1988

Library of Congress Cataloging-in-Publication Data

Anthony, Piers.
    Bio of an ogre.

    Bibliography: p.
    1. Anthony, Piers—Biography. 2. Authors, American—
20th century—Biography. 3. Science fiction—Authorship.
I. Title.
PS3551.N73Z463   1988   813'.54   [B]   87-33461
ISBN: 0-441-06224-5

Printed in the United States of America

10 9 8 7 6 5 4 3 2 1

CONTENTS

INTRODUCTION

Most of this volume is self-explanatory, but some few things should be understood early. First, the term "bio" is not merely a contraction of "biography"; it relates also to "biopsy" and "biology" and ties in with my series of science fiction novels, *Bio of a Space Tyrant*. This volume is more than a narration of *what;* it is an attempt to grasp *why.*

Second, I am not really an ogre. In the 1970s a story was circulated that I was making an ogre of myself at fan conventions—but I had never even attended any. I suspect this was a confusion with another genre writer of this region who suffered a stroke and did on occasion become unpleasant in public. Since I had the reputation, I decided to make something of it, so I wrote a novel with an ogre as the hero. I titled this *Ogre, Ogre,* and it was the fifth novel in the popular Xanth fantasy series. It did phenomenally well, commercially; in fact it seems to have been the first original paperback fantasy novel ever to have made the prestigious New York *Times* best-seller list. Since it was published in October, I rechristened that month OctOgre: the Month of the Ogre. Then I started playing with the other months of the year, and finally developed a full Xanth Ogre Calendar characterizing the months as the ogres perceive them: JamBoree, FeBlueberry, and so on through NoRemember and

DisMember. But it all started because of that false story about me. That in itself says something about the way I am, and why I seem to be loved in some circles and despised in others. I intend, as any good ogre would, to show that the former circle has the right of it, and to smash the latter into well-deserved smithereens. Thus this Antho-bi-Ogre-phy: violence with a trace of humor.

Third, though this text is to be hard-hitting in places, it is not no-holds-barred. It is not that I am shy about telling the universe my secrets, but that some of them involve other people who would suffer unfairly if certain revelations were made. Thus there will be nothing here about skeletons in the family closet or illicit affairs or similar things; this is not a nefarious exposé. For those who are curious about what I might be concealing, I will just say that there are some items, but that on the whole I have led a scrupulous life, and am reasonably clean. The reader need not feel that he is missing out on the best parts; the best parts are here.

Fourth, this is not totally comprehensive. My memory for names and dates is like a sieve, but my memory for events is excellent, as befits a writer of fiction. Were I to cover everything I remember, this narrative would become encyclopedic. Thus I have to be highly selective, and since I earn my living by entertaining readers, my bias here is of that nature. Everything I say herein is true, but it is highly subjective, colored by my intensely personal bias, and crafted to be easy and sometimes thoughtful reading. In short, somewhat like one of my novels.

I have divided my narrative into five major segments, each one covering exactly ten years of my life. Thus Part One takes me to, but not through, my tenth birthday; Part Two to my twentieth, and so on. One might protest that lives are not partitioned in that manner; well, mine is, for this purpose. The first fifty years of my life are now complete; that seems to be a reasonable segment. Herewith, my Antho-pology (Greek: *anthos*, flower; *po*, abbreviation for pole, a measure; *logia*, to speak): my story of the measure of the flowering of my life.

PART ONE

A Cake Made of Sawdust

1.

ENGLAND

I was born on August 6, 1934, in Oxford, England. Both my parents graduated from Oxford University, and both later went on to PhDs. Both knew several languages. There was obviously intelligence in the family, but as it happened, I did not show it. I was to set some kind of record for backwardness in formal education. So much for heredity.

I was not named immediately. My mother, Norma Patricia Sherlock Jacob, could not make up her mind about the proper names. There was a family friend named Anthony, and an interesting character in a series of novels named Piers, and of course it was good to draw on one of the family surnames, such as that of my paternal grandmother's side, Dillingham. Which to choose? Finally, as the deadline was upon her, she went to the office and registered me as Piers Anthony Dillingham Jacob. She confessed to a notion that if I should grow up to become a famous musician or something (I had long fingers), I could draw from one of the extra names as a pseudonym. Mothers can be foolish that way.

My father, Alfred Bennis Jacob, became head of the British Friends Service Council mission in Spain, feeding the hungry children who were the victims of the Spanish Civil War of 1936–39. Spain had had a democratic government, but its own

army turned against it and waged a war of conquest that was
eventually successful. Nazi Germany aided the army, using
Spain as a kind of testing ground for the new weapons it could
not display openly. Idealists throughout the world were appalled, and many volunteered to aid the Republican side against
the attack of the notorious "Four Insurgent Generals," about
which there was even a popular song. It concluded "They'll all
be hanging!" Among the volunteers was a later science fiction
writer, Ted Cogswell, who drove an ambulance.

This meant that my parents were away much of the time. I
remained in England, cared for by a nanny in London, and I
was happy enough. You see, I really didn't know my parents,
so didn't miss them. I had a younger sister, Teresa Caroline,
but until she became ambulatory I hardly noticed her. I remember seeing the doubledecker buses of London, and visiting
the park where one of the little birds was hopping about as if
unable to fly. We notified the keeper, who picked up the bird
and stretched out its wings. The wings extended phenomenally, and it seemed to me that nothing remained of the original bird; it was all wing, merely a construction of folded feathers.
The keeper set the bird down, concluding that it wasn't injured, and it hopped away. But the image remained with me;
could it be that living birds were nothing more than folded
wings? Could I fold a piece of paper in such a way that it could
come to life as a bird? Much later, in my fantasy novels, I was
to play with that concept, with functioning animals and machines fashioned from folded paper.

I remember going to the hospital. Since I knew I was born in
a hospital, I assumed that this was the occasion, and told people
so. Only later did I learn that I had actually been born some
years earlier; this time was to have my tonsils out. Ah, well;
close enough. I don't remember the operation at all; I assume I
was put to sleep for that.

Not all my memories of England are pleasant, but even the
unpleasant ones are not the stuff of horror. My worse experience I do not remember at all. It seems that when I was in the
pram one day, I stood, and the pram overbalanced and pitched
me forward. My face came down on the front bar, and my four
upper teeth were smashed back into my jaw. They were baby
teeth, of course, but it took about fifteen years for the damage
to clear, because the permanent teeth had trouble growing out
when the baby teeth were so messed up. One grew out sidewise

through the gum. Eventually I had one tooth pulled, in addition to the four wisdom teeth, leaving me with twenty-seven permanent teeth and no gaps between them.

I was in bed once, and my nose started to run, and I didn't know what to do, so I called for help. The adults were in the next room, but they ignored me. My nose ran and ran, and I called and called, but they paid no attention. When at last someone came, my nose had flowed all the way down to my stomach; it was quite a mess. Why hadn't anyone come when I called? Yet minor as that episode was, it is one of the few things I remember of that period, and it may represent the first of a series of incidents that caused me to become militantly independent. I do not like to be dependent on anyone else for anything, today; I prefer to wipe my own nose.

Another negative memory concerned my sister. I had a trike, a little tricycle, that I could ride about the property. One day they said I should give my sister a turn on it, for one loop about the room. Giving turns was not something I understood at that age, but I acceded, and she got on and peddled her circuit. But when it was complete, she refused to get off; she continued circling the room, while I followed, asking her to get off. The adults who had required me to give her a turn seemed to have no interest in requiring her to end it. Naturally she rode to her heart's content. But this was an early lesson for me in the penalties of generosity: one has to have the means to enforce the agreed limits. More than one publisher has failed to grasp my attitude on this, and there has been considerable friction because of it. When I make a contract, I honor it, and I expect the other party to honor it; when the other party does not, I get angry, and I neither forget nor forgive. There will be much more of this in Part Four.

Another memory was neither positive nor negative. It is the concept of Tomorrow. The future was difficult for me to grasp. I came to think of it as a street with a row of houses, some distance from my own location. Some day I would go there. Tomorrow.

When I was four, and my sister three, Tomorrow abruptly arrived. We were told that we would be going to Spain. That sounded nice. "Are you going too?" I asked the nanny. "No," she said. "Then who are we going with?" I wanted to know. She told me that it would be with two other people. Now I knew those people, but they were not that close; I was disappointed. Those two people were my parents.

And so we left England, and I left the one adult I had really cared for. I know nothing about her, not even her name; she was just the girl hired to take care of the children, after the British fashion. My mother says she believes the girl was named Bunty Stewart, but isn't sure, and agrees that she was a marvel with the children. My father mentions that more than one person took care of us, so it all remains uncertain.

But to this day I feel a pained nostalgia when I look at an old-fashioned dime. You see, those dimes had a symbol on the back that looked to me like the end of the street where we had lived, with a column marking its termination, and the vines growing on that column; and near it, just off the picture on the dime, to the right, I know the house remains, and that is where I was happy. Of course nostalgia distorts impressions, but it seems to me that I have not been that happy since. A folk song also relates: "I only saw her passing by, and yet I love her till I die." I love folk songs, and I wish that nanny could have remained with us. Echoes of this rather pained nostalgia are to be found in my writing, as in *Chthon,* wherein a child encounters a lovely woman in a glade, who isn't there thereafter. That, too, relates to a song—"The Girl in the Wood"—that I heard only once, and never again, in 1957. I never did become the famous musician my mother fancied, but I do feel and respond to the power of music on a daily basis.

When I left England I never returned. Today I don't like to travel, and I think it is in part because that fear remains that travels do not necessarily have returns.

Now I don't mean to have this seem like condemnation of the members of my family, or to suggest that I harbor any outrage at my situation. My sister, in the episode of the trike, was acting as any two- or three-year-old would. If there was an episode in which I treated her similarly, my selectivity of memory has erased it. I suspect there were such episodes, and that I remember only what cast me in favorable light; this is the nature of human subjectivity. Self-image is treacherous stuff.

Similarly, I understand the situation of my parents. The world is as it is, and compromises have to be made continually, of greater or lesser magnitude. Children were starving in Spain. It would have been easy for my parents to righteously condemn this, as others did, and to let that suffice—as others did.

Such righteousness is worthless. My parents elected to do what they saw needed to be done, and that was to go there and feed those children. There is no way I can fault that. But this was the late 1930s, with the world building toward World War II, and Adolf Hitler looming like a deadly plague in Europe, and Spain already a war zone. It would have been folly to bring small children to that region. So a sacrifice had to be made, and the unity of the family was part of that sacrifice. My sister and I were left with our grandparents and the nanny in England, where we were safe and comfortable, while my parents went, in their Quaker fashion, to war. I don't see what else they could have done. But there was a cost, for all of us.

I should clarify, also, that the anecdotal nature of this bio should not to taken as the whole story. I like to use single episodes to illustrate the points I make; I do not pretend that the episodes *are* the points. The straw is not the wind, it is merely a signal of the wind's nature. The straw does not *cause* the wind; you cannot change the wind by abolishing the straw, you can only blind yourself to reality. So here I am grasping at straws in an effort to understand and to clarify for others how I came to be what I am. It is possible that I shall grasp some of the wrong straws, or will misinterpret those I examine. I daresay that some psychologists or psychiatrists (psychology relates to the mind and behavior; psychiatry relates to mental disorder) will differ with my interpretations. Indeed, it is a free country—but there is a colossal amount these folk do not know about the subject, and I regard their science as no more valid than astrology. (Yes, that statement can be taken two ways. More anon.) Meanwhile, with these cautions, I offer my anecdotes to illustrate the truth as nearly as I can approach.

2.

SPAIN

I understand that my sister Teresa and I went to Spain twice (see my mother's discussion in Appendix A), but I remember only the final trip. It was, I think, mostly by train. When we crossed into another country, men would come through the coaches to open the luggage and inspect for forbidden things. I remember one lifting out a small wrapped package, and my mother explained that it was only a fan, making a fanning motion with her hand, but he unwrapped it anyway. It was a fan. And this is just about all I recollect of the journey.

Thus, by the time I was five, I had traveled Europe: England, France, Spain—and I don't remember France at all.

The Spanish Civil War was over in March 1939, and World War II had not yet begun, so there was no fighting going on. That did not last long; in September Germany invaded Poland, and in April 1940 Denmark and Norway. In May Germany invaded the Netherlands and France. I understand it was a horrendous experience, being in Spain as the German blitz-krieg swept south through France, stopping short of the border. But at age five I was unaware of any of this.

I remember what must have been the capital, Madrid, because we got to go to the hills nearby, which were tunneled for military emplacements, but it seems that that was only a passing visit. I remember a place called Tossa, which was about forty miles up the Mediterranean coast from Barcelona. The house was atop a hill, with a steep road leading up to the front; we were amazed once when a man on a motorcycle made it all the way up.

But for most of the time we were in Barcelona. The name of that city obviously made an impression on me, because later, in America, when we drove by some road construction and I saw one of those two-spouted water pumps spewing out muddy water I popped out with extemporaneous verse: "Barcelona shakes about, and all the water comes out!" For some reason my parents seemed to think that my sister had crafted that poetry; it was almost as if they were unable to recognize the odd type of creativity that I have evinced all my life.

The cellar of the house in Barcelona had a cell with a barred gate that could be locked. Once when my sister and I were down there with the woman who was taking care of us, a young man named Jorge (which sounded like Hor-hee, with a guttural in it) locked the gate on us as a joke. The woman screamed at him in Spanish and he let us out. Jorge was a lot of fun.

Teresa and I spoke English, of course, so could not follow the Spanish. Since English was spoken in the house, that was all right. Our parents were mostly busy with their work, so we were in the hands of the house staff, and I really don't remember much of that either. In 1940 we finally began learning Spanish, I think because we liked Jorge. It was the only language besides English I ever spoke; I was a dunce at languages, and nearly flunked my senior year in high school because of my problem with German. Ironically, the one language I was interested in learning, Spanish, that high school did not carry. So when I left Spain it was lost, and all I retain are a few stray words, like those for "hot water" and toilet functions. I doubt that I ever spoke Spanish at all well.

I really don't remember how our days went. There are only glimpses. In the morning the sun would shine in my window and cast the shadow of a palm tree against the wall. I watched that shadow as if it were a motion picture, excited when the frond dipped unusually low, blown by the wind. Once it went all the way off the wall, to the floor, and I was amazed.

I also remember being punished in what I presume was the European way: Teresa and I were sent to the garden in back with bandages across our mouths. I suppose we had talked too much.

Once we were out in the city, walking along the streets and through a park. I looked about, and realized that my mother was gone. Somehow I had lost her. I was with strangers. I didn't know what to do, so I just kept walking. I believe I was with a Spanish woman and some other children. She bought us some peanuts. Later my mother reappeared. In retrospect, I conclude that my mother had had some errand, so had put me in the charge of a baby-sitter and slipped away covertly so that I wouldn't make a fuss. I believe that is considered standard procedure. I have never done it to my own children. Indeed, my wife and I did not use baby-sitters.

Teresa had a pretty Spanish dress. I think the Europeans have better taste in costuming their women than the Americans do. I also remember wearing sandals whose soles were made of coiled string (hemp). They were called *alpargatas* and worked well enough, though I don't think they lasted long.

Once I met an old man who gave me a little square of candy wrapped in opaque paper. He had one himself, and I think gave one to another person, so that there were three wrappers left. Then Teresa came, and the old man told me he would play a joke on her. He wadded up one wrapper, and wrapped it in the second, and wrapped that in the third, so that the finished product looked just like a wrapped candy. This he gave to her. I was in a titillation of expectation, waiting for her to unwrap it and discover nothing. She took off the outer wrapper and found the second. She removed that, and found the third. So she opened that—and there was another candy, just like the one I had had. The joke had been on me!

I went to my first motion picture in Spain. My mother had mentioned going to see a book that had been made into a movie, and I was perplexed. I visualized a big screen with the pages on the book projected on it, and a theaterful of people reading the pages as they turned. It seemed to me that it would be easier just to read the book directly. But when I went myself, I began to understand. They didn't show the pages, they showed the story itself. In fact it was a cartoon: the Three Little Pigs. The Big Bad Wolf was after them, and the most amazing things happened. I don't think I have ever seen a more phenomenal cartoon since. It is possible that I have seen that same one, as a re-re-rerun on television, but didn't recognize it. Certainly I have seen that story since, but as an adult, and the magic was gone. That of course is the fate of all children: they grow into adults, and the magic departs.

I remember swimming in the Mediterranean. Well, not exactly; I was too small to swim, so I was on a rubber raft, floating. Suddenly I banged into another raft, and toppled off, into the water, and sank. It was a horrendous experience; that water must have been all of two feet deep, and salty too. But I survived.

It must have been Easter, for one day I was given a huge wooden egg. It opened at the equator, falling into two halves, and in one half was a model sailing ship, and in the other were half a dozen chocolates. They don't make Easters like that anymore.

And an unpleasant memory: I got sick, and they were worried about me. Finally a doctor came. He looked at me, then asked for a spoon. He took the spoon, turned it over, and poked it in my mouth, back down in the throat. I vomited immediately, on the bed. Satisfied, he departed. To this day I don't know why he did that, but it rather colored my impression of the business of doctors. Later experiences with needles confirmed that impression: they existed to hurt children. Indeed, Teresa told me of a worse experience she had, in which a doctor put a knife down inside her throat and cut it so that it bled. Years later I discovered the adult version of that horror: she had needed to have her tonsils out, and they had no safe anesthetic. The Spanish doctor said an anesthetic wasn't necessary; they would do it without. "Not to *my* child!" my mother protested. But they took the child and did it anyway, just like that. A horror, certainly; yet to us children it was merely another evidence of the inhumanity adults practiced on children. Do those adults ever think of what this does to those children, emotionally?

Then, abruptly, we were told that we were going to America, across the big ocean. We took a train (I think I remember) across the country to Lisbon, in Portugal, where the ship was. We stayed in a hotel, which was fun, and rode in a taxi that had child seats that unfolded from the floor. I believe that my mother had quite a different impression of that hotel, which was overrun by vermin, but I never noticed. I remember riding in pedal-paddle boats, which moved along roped channels. That was fun; I don't think I've seen them in America.

There was a lot more to the matter of our departure from Spain than I knew at the time. My father disappeared, and my mother didn't know what had happened to him. She asked the authorities, but they said they didn't know anything. For three days she was frantic. Then she received a note: He was in prison.

Apparently he had been in an area that was preparing for a visit by Adolf Hitler, and security provisons were tight. They simply arrested anyone they didn't trust, no questions asked. Thus my father was abruptly in a cell, simply because he had been in the region at the wrong time. No charges, no phone call out; dictatorships don't bother with such free-world foolishness. He was incarcerated with a number of other men, and the sanitary facilities consisted of a trench. Women were confined in another cell, but that one lacked the trench, so periodically the women were brought to the men's cell to squat, while the men stood around to see what they could see. Finally he managed to smuggle a message out inside the thermos used to bring daily drinks to a fellow prisoner, and that was the notice that reached my mother. He had also sent her a card at the outset, but I don't know whether that reached her.

Armed with the note, she got the authorities to admit that they had indeed arrested him. Since he was a British subject (naturalized from America), this was awkward; you don't treat foreign nationals the way you treat your own citizens. Naturally the Spanish government could not admit to making a mistake. So they compromised: they would let my father go on condition that he left the country.

Thus we left, going to join my father's relatives in far America. It wasn't safe to try to return to England; in August the Battle of Britain was commencing, and the authorities in England might merely have put my father back in jail as a war resister. It's amazing how subversive average folk consider peace to be, when their country is at war. The relief mission in Spain was shut down, and presumably the supplies of food were confiscated. What happened to that food thereafter I don't know, but it seems unlikely that it went to the hungry Spanish children. Fortunately (?) the stocks had just about run out anyway.

I suppose it was just as well that we were leaving Europe, for the next five years there were to be as ugly as any it has known. Perhaps General Franco had done us a kind of favor; yet I have an implacable enmity to dictatorships. I wonder why?

3.

SHIP

The ship was the *Excalibur,* which was perhaps a fitting vessel for a future writer of fantasy. The original Excalibur was the sword of King Arthur; accounts differ, but it was either presented to him by the Lady of the Lake, whose arm rose from the lake bearing it, or he found it embedded in a stone and drew it forth, vindicating himself as the destined king. For the present purpose, I'll accept the Lady of the Lake version, as the *Excalibur* was to carry us across the water to fabled America, land of the rich and free.

There is another story relating to this voyage. When I was barely two, King Edward VIII of England abdicated. He had taken an interest in an American divorcee, and that was too much of a scandal for the Crown to tolerate, so he left the throne and married the woman the following year. He was now in Portugal, on his way to the Bahamas, where he was to serve as governor for the duration of the war. The Germans had a notion that he was sympathetic to their cause, so they planned to kidnap him and have him make a statement on their behalf. But they bungled the job, and in any event his sympathy was less than they supposed, so he boarded the ship without event. That ship was the *Excalibur.* That's right—the same ship, and the same voyage we were on.

I don't believe I ever saw Edward, but I saw his car as it was unloaded at Bermuda, swinging at the end of the line of a crane. From there we went northwest to New York, and I presume he went southwest to the Bahamas.

I remember being seasick on the ship. My father helped me lean over the rail so I could vomit into the water. I remember how they set up a swimming pool on the deck: a huge canvas enclosure filled with water, which leaked. My father reports: "I have never seen a child so happy as you were with that intermittent splash that burst through the canvas . . . with the ship's motion. It sent you into peals of delight." Well, splashing water is a lot of fun for a child; my own child, Penny, evidently inherited that delight. She wanted the water running constantly in the tub. "Mustn't waste water," I cautioned. "Waste water! Waste water!" she exclaimed eagerly.

I had my sixth birthday at sea. This was wartime, and they were short of supplies of the festive type, so the galley made me a cake from sawdust; it was, they explained, all they could offer. As I recall it was nicely covered with icing, with candles burning. But when we started to cut it open, things halted, and it was taken away. I didn't understand why, then. When my own children were that age, I told them of that experience, and at one time I'm sure my daughter Penny was jealous: *she* never got a cake made of sawdust. But in another way, that cake seems like an analogy to my early life: the solid foundations of it turned out to be made of sawdust.

I received a gift, too: a harmonica. I was delighted. I played it endlessly for the rest of the voyage, walking up and down the deck. In later years I was to wonder whether in some stateroom the former king of England was gritting his teeth and muttering, "Can't somebody shut that brat up?" But I'm sure a little music was good for him. I have retained a certain affection for harmonicas ever since; I own a good one, and they appear in my novels. In fact, I retain a delight in music, which also shows in my fiction, though I am not skilled with any instrument.

In due course we landed at New York, America. Life in the New World had begun.

4.

AMERICA

My grandfather, Edward H. Jacob, was a wealthy man. He had made his fortune growing mushrooms, starting with a cellar operation and eventually expanding to a million-dollar operation. He was known as the Mushroom King. In 1929 he decided that the time was right to retire from the business, so he sold it. Two weeks later the stock market crashed. Jacob's Mushrooms eventually became B&B Mushrooms, and I believe the brand is still marketed today. But his impact is more than that. He trained other people, who then set up similar mushroom operations of their own next door. Thus half the mushrooms of the nation were for decades produced in just two counties of Pennsylvania. The King still reigns, in his fashion!

He owned a fine house in West Chester, Pennsylvania, and a cottage at Seaside Park, on the coast of New Jersey. I remember my delight discovering the little circular staircase in the West Chester house that led down to the kitchen. That was the maid's stair; we were expected to use the main stair, but as a child I preferred the child-sized one. There was a vast sloping lawn out back, leading down to a highway, and across the highway was a golf course. There was even a fish pond with goldfish. And decorative columns with reflective metal balls; I could see my distorted reflection in them. All in all, sheer delight.

My grandfather was hard of hearing, so he used a hearing aid. In those days these were relatively big and clumsy. His sat on the table and looked like a toaster; my father joked about putting a slice of bread in it.

The food of course was excellent, with plenty of bread and jam. I suppose there were dull things too, like potatoes and spinach, but my memory has erased them. America certainly seemed like a fine place.

My father had left America to go to Oxford University, and I understood he had been somewhat distanced from his father, my grandfather. When my father married an English girl, he notified his father by mailing him a newspaper clipping that summarized the event. My mother was, perhaps understandably, uncertain about her reception here. But it happened that my grandfather, twice a widower, had married a third time not long before, and so I had a stepgrandmother, Caroline Nicholson Jacob, who I think was a prominent woman in Quaker circles. She welcomed my mother and made her feel at home. That was the beginning of a lifelong friendship.

This was of course the Philadelphia region: the Quaker City. "Quaker" is the colloquial name for the Religious Society of Friends, founded in England by George Fox in the seventeenth century. It was bestowed derisively when Friends spoke of quaking before the Lord, but they made it their own. Friends are known for their silent meetings, believing that no spiritual intermediary is required between man and God; each person is guided by his own inner light. Friends wore plain dress and spoke the "plain language" typified by the use of "thee." They have always protested war, and have been persecuted for that. They also object to the use of oaths, preferring that a man's word be his bond at all times. In the larger world, two things seem to distinguish Friends: they are pacifists, and they are good businessmen. There is a joke: The only person who can buy from a Jew and sell to a Scotsman and make a profit is a Quaker. I don't believe this is intended to be derogatory to any of the three parties named. At any rate, William Penn was a Quaker. Thus we have the state of Penn-sylvania, (Penn's Forest), and the City of Brotherly Love. The city and state governments are no longer run by Quakers, so they suffer the corruption and violence of other regions, but at least the memory is there. Certainly my grandfather was a good businessman, and he supported Quaker causes. Thus the American influence on me related to pacifism, simple devotions, integrity, and good business sense.

I was born in the time when my mother was changing her religion from Church of England to Quaker; thus I fell between the cracks and belonged to neither. When I grew up, I elected to join no religion. I will have more to say on that later. But certainly I hold no objection to the Religious Society of Friends, and I sincerely respect its precepts, and honor them informally. I believe particularly in the principle of honesty; to me a lie is an abomination. I am not, however, a pacifist.

We spent some time at the cottage in Seaside Park. This was another delight. There was an endlessly long beach, and the cabin sat at the edge of it, with a telescope mounted on the porch so that we could look at the ships. This was fascinating. I remember seeing a tiny blob on the horizon, but when the telescope focused on it, it became a yacht with girls running all about its decks and splashing into the water. It seemed like magic. Up the beach a way was an amusement park with a penny arcade; put a penny in, wind the handle, and see a cartoon run as the pages of the book flipped over. More magic!

But good things do not last forever. Somewhere then I got sick with German measles. I was under some sort of quarantine; my mother took care of me in another cottage in Pennsylvania while I wore through it. The main thing I remember is a special kind of bread she found: the slices were huge and delicious, and one of those with butter was wonderful.

Then we moved to a type of adult school community called Pendle Hill. I was given a scooter there, and I loved it. I rode it endlessly. But this had a consequence: I always pushed with my right foot, and in time this caused that leg to be longer than the other, so that I stood crooked. But it was years before this was realized. My father took me to a chiropractor; he looked at me, then brought out two scales. I stood with one foot on each. One read sixty pounds, the other forty pounds. I had to have a corrective shoe for a time; this solved the problem. Some folk speak disparagingly of chiropractors, but this one caught what the regular doctors had missed.

5.

SCHOOL

I have a curious memory of this period, which perhaps illustrates the manner that fantasy could interact with reality in my life. I dreamed that we went to a fancy wedding, but instead of gifts for the happy couple, they were given to the visitors. An enormous wagonload of brightly wrapped packages was brought out, and each of us got to take one gift. Mine, when opened, turned out to be a set of ceramic bowls, perhaps six of different sizes and colors, nestled inside each other. I was delighted—but of course it was only a dream. Nevertheless, we used those bowls for years, and gradually lost them to routine breakage, until only one was left. Oh, I'm sure we could work out some mundane explanation for the origin of those bowls—but let's not meddle with the memory.

Meanwhile, I was six years old and eligible for school. That was to be a trial. I was enrolled in the first grade at the school in Media, Pennsylvania. It was a nice enough school, but somehow the teachers weren't satisfied with me. I thought I was doing the work they asked, but it seemed that wasn't so. They said my work was messy and not good enough.

In retrospect, I suspect that I suffered from what is now termed L-D, Learning Disability. The insight came when my own child, Penny, encountered similar problems in school, and was so diagnosed. Quite a number of otherwise bright children are to a certain degree L-D. In extreme cases it prevents them from achieving any education; in mild cases it can pass unnoticed. Sometimes a case is fairly extreme, but the child is uncommonly intelligent, so is able to compensate sufficiently to get through. How often do we hear of a teacher saying to a child, "I don't understand why someone with your potential doesn't try to do good work!" The child *is* trying, but there is an interference along the line.

I think the best way to clarify this type of problem is a case I read about a dyslexic child. Dyslexia is a related complication, in which the child has trouble grasping the meaning of what he reads. He may be ambiguous about right and left, and that can be disastrous when he is expected to distinguish the letter *d* from *b*, *p* from *q* or *g*, *j* from small *t*, or to read the word *no* instead of *on*. To him *god* may be the same as *dog*, *bee* the same as *dee* or *eeb* or *eed*. He just can't tell what the teacher wants. In this story, a man brought his dyslexic son to an optometrist, a doctor who specializes in problems of vision, under the impression that there was something wrong with the boy's eyes. The father told how no amount of encouragement, cajoling, or punishment had been effective; the boy just got more perverse. The doctor assessed the situation, then asked the father to participate in an experiment. The father was to use a device in which he traced lines on a reversed image. He took the pencil, and when he tried to move left, the image line moved right. "Idiot!" the doctor chided him. "I said *left*." The man tried again, and overcorrected, messing up the line. "Not that way!" the doctor snapped. "Can't you do it right?" Nettled, the man tried again, but was again betrayed by his reversed reflexes. "You just aren't *trying!*" the doctor exclaimed. At which point the man jumped up, ready to punch him out. "That is what you are doing to your son," the doctor said calmly. And the father, understanding at last, sat down and wept.

No one wept for me. I was adjudged perverse and/or subnormal, and it took me three years to get out of first grade. I simply couldn't learn to read or write. I swore that if I ever grew up, I would not forget what it was like to be a misunderstood child—and I have not forgotten. When my daughter encountered similar teacher insensitivity, I was on the case immediately, militantly, at times coming on very much like an ogre. I was determined to protect my child from the horrors I had endured, and I believe I succeeded. She grew up to be not at all ogreish.

However, there were other factors that may have contributed to my failure. We seemed to be constantly moving, so that I found myself in five different schools, in five different states, in the course of that first grade. Pennsylvania, Vermont, New Hampshire, New York, and Maine—each time I began to be familiar with the new situation, it changed. Each time it seemed I was required to start over. Also, they had different ways of doing things, so that what I had learned before did not apply. Even my English accent interfered. I had learned the alphabet, and the last letter was zed. I discovered to my surprise that the Americans thought it was zee. At one school they labored to correct my sloppy pronunciation when I managed to read a word. I pronounced the word "grass" in proper British fashion, "grahs," but it seemed they wanted it rendered "gr-ass." That was a problem, because I had learned that the American "ass" was their version of "arse," a dirty word, and it bothered me to align my pronunciation with that. So while they drilled me in dirty pronunciation, the business of actually learning to read languished. I remember being envious of a fellow student's ability to read the immense word "apartmenthouse." It was too complicated for me.

Perhaps the strongest influence on me was social. I have tried to analyze this in retrospect, but can only approximate the truth. There was an immense but nebulous emotional gulf opening under me that wrought havoc with my equilibrium. Think of it this way: You are standing on a mountain, massive and firm and solid. Then the mountain shakes and moves and drifts, and you realize that it is actually an iceberg, which breaks off and floats into the ocean. But it is still pretty solid. Then it melts, and you see it shrinking, but there is nothing you can do about it, for you can't turn off the sun. It becomes no more than a plate of ice, rocking precariously in the waves. You can see the shore, but it is far distant, and you don't know how to swim, and there are sharks in the water. Then the ice cracks in half forming two platelets, each just big enough for one foot. You are still standing, but your situation is precarious indeed. Then the platelets drift apart, so that you are unable to use both. What do you do then?

My original mountain was England. Then my situation broke off and became the iceberg of Spain. Then it shrank to the plate of America. Then it became the two platelets of my parents—who were now in the long, difficult process of separating. It would be another decade before they divorced, but the marriage was over years before that, and the first cracks were developing now. I had no control over what was going on, and indeed had no comprehension of it, but I felt its effect, as my only remaining emotional fundament sundered. What was the point in laboring hard in school to please quixotic teachers, when the gulf was opening out beneath me?

I see no point in going into detail about the individual schools. They ranged from good to bad. I will just touch upon spot memories.

For Christmas when I was at Media I was given a sled. It was a Flexible Flyer, and it was fast. When I raced against kids on other sleds, I always won. It went with me, a year or two later, when I was still in first grade at a private boarding school in New York State. During the Christmas holiday break, the "old" kids took the sleds of all the "new" kids and threw them in the river. Thus I lost my wonderful sled. The adults running that school paid no attention; it seemed they didn't care. That school had a gym, but we were not allowed in it; our chief delight was the neighboring dump, where all manner of fascinating things were to be found. My sister was there with me, also in the first grade; she had had the good fortune to be sick with tuberculosis when her turn came to enter school, so had been in bed for six months, and my mother had taught her to read. Thus when she entered school, late, she tested at the sixth-grade reading level. Children would hurry up to me, exclaiming, "Aren't you lucky to have a smart sister like her!" I just wished that *I* had been sick then, so that I could have avoided all the failure in reading. But things were not necessarily delightful for my sister, either; I was wandering around outside one day, and a girl asked me if I wanted to see my sister, so I said sure. So she went inside, and I heard a scream and thud, and in a moment my sister was down, disheveled and I think scratched. This was just the way it was, there.

In fact, that school was a horror from the outset. When we arrived, the adults were solicitous enough, in the presence of my mother, but the first student who spied us exclaimed in disgust, "Oh, a new skug!" I think that was the word. I was put upstairs with the other first-graders. One of the bigger second-graders told me to go into a room on his floor, so I did. They blocked the door and told me to take down my trousers. I did. Then my underpants, so I did that too. But about that time I began to catch on that this was not an entirely friendly encounter. I said I wanted to go. They wouldn't let me. Terrified, I hauled up my pants and lunged for the door, scrambling over the guard and managing to win my way free. I escaped to my own floor. It seems to have been a routine initiation, and perhaps a deliberate terrorization of a new, small student. Children are like that, when adults are not alert—and the adults were never alert when needed. That evening there was some kind of program on that region, and I was sitting on the floor with the others watching, when from nowhere came another boy. He slammed into me, kicking, punching, shoving. I scrambled to my feet and fled the building, not knowing why I had been attacked or what I could do about it. Naturally the adults paid no attention. I ran around the building and into the dusk down the road, and hid behind a tree. No one pursued, but I knew that a massive pursuit was imminent, because I could see the wooden wall of the building, and from the other side came shouts and crashing noises, and the wall vibrated as something slammed repeatedly into it. What rage was there!

At last things settled down, and I dared to leave my hiding place. Later I was to realize that the ground floor of that building was the gym. Older boys had been playing basketball or something similar there, and I had heard the ball and/or their bodies slamming into the backboard. They had not been after me at all. I crept up the stairs to the third floor and got to my bed. I had not been missed. I think, but am not sure, that the boy who attacked me was the one I had scrambled over when I escaped the initiation; he was angry about that.

Thus first grade. But I did, finally, learn to read. This was not a positive thing. Since I was subject to getting beaten up when with other children—that situation was eventually set to rights not by the adults, but by other children, who finally decided that enough was enough, brought my oppressor to me, required us to shake hands, and informed me in his presence that if he touched me again, they would beat *him* up—I came to prefer the classroom. I developed a very positive attitude about the effort of reading, and so made progress. My efforts were halting, and it took another year or so before I really got into it, but when I did I became a readaholic. The first book I read on my own was *The Last of the Mohicans,* and the second was the huge *The Cloister and the Hearth*. They took me months of almost full-time effort, but they were moving experiences. The words of the books were better than the world I knew. I have been a reader ever since. But a slow one; I was required to read aloud, and my pace became set; today my silent reading is at the same rate as my aloud reading, and I pronounce every word subvocally. I'm a pretty good proofreader, though, because I take no shortcuts.

Yet even the hell of boarding school was not all evil. I learned some pretty songs there. My mother remarks on a picture I drew for her, to illustrate the refrain "Then at last my weary footsteps lighted on the way,/And each print behind me brightly seemed to say:/'Cheer up, weary traveler—after darkness comes the day.'" I had drawn the shining footsteps. I still love the concept of day following the dread darkness, and find it echoed elsewhere, as in the song "Nicodemus," about a black slave: "There are signs in the sky that the darkness is gone; /There are tokens in endless array/That the storm which had seemingly banished the dawn/Only hastens the advent of day." How I longed for that new day!

It was there I made a friend. He was an older boy whose IQ had tested at 180 (I will have somewhat to say about such tests in due course) whose mother was white and whose father was black. His name was Craig Work; others thought it wonderfully original to come to him and say "Craig—work!" He sort of took me in hand, and my life improved considerably thereafter. I suspect he had something to do with the manner the other boys brought a settlement with my attacker. He was an extremely sociable, coordinated individual, universally liked, and a godsend to me. Later he and his mother visited my home, and it was a great occasion. It has been the custom of racists to claim that some of their best friends are black, making a mockery of the term "friendship"; my best friend really was, and racism is anathema to me. This, too, was to have an effect on my adult career.

I skipped second grade, and later I skipped fifth grade, finally catching up to my peers. For schooling, the worst was over.

6.

BED

When I was six, perhaps seven, I began to wet my bed. I had been "dry" overnight for some years, but now I regressed. My parents did not understand. Why should a child who *can* get through the night start wetting his bed? They questioned me, but I didn't know; it just happened. They chided me. Eventually I was required to wash my own sheets every day. The water was cold and my hands felt raw. Perhaps this was not intended as punishment, but the message was plain enough: If I insisted on doing something as thoughtless as this, I would pay the penalty. Punishment is as you perceive it, in the absence of understanding.

The bed-wetting continued for several years—four or five, I think—and led to a number of additional complications in my life. I believe it was another aspect of my shrinking iceberg. The time I had spent in England had been, as I understood it, happy; back at the beginning I had been taken care of, all my needs met—and at the beginning I had wet my bed. I think that I craved a return to that state, so that at night, when I was asleep and my rational defense down, I simply did return to it. I became a baby again. Perhaps this made no sense in the real world, but it made sense emotionally. It was my deepest need, for comfort and security, crying out. Rebuke or punishment only made the present world worse, intensifying my need to escape it, if only temporarily, if only by illusion. I suspect that something like this is true for other bed wetters; the roots are not in their biology but in their emotion. I could not cure the real problem, which was the separation of my parents and my confinement to an alien land, so I tried to escape it internally. I don't want to be too free with conjecture that may not be valid, but it is tempting to relate this to my lifelong affection for fantasy: the crafting of a better world inside than exists outside.

I had to have a rubber sheet on my bed, to protect the mattress, and this held the urine so that I lay in it the rest of the night. On warm nights I would roll over and kick off the soaking sheets, and work my way out of my pajamas; it was more comfortable. Once at the boarding school other boys, not friendly ones, marched in and lifted off the top blanket. There I lay, naked and soaking. They left without comment. Later, one approached me privately. "When I go pee at night," he said, "sometimes I wait, and after a while a little more will come, and then a little more. Maybe if you waited, you could get it all out." He was trying to be helpful; he now saw me as so pitiful a creature that I was not worth bullying, and he never bothered me thereafter. On cold nights—and when we lived in Vermont, in an unheated, uninsulated house, they could get very cold—the wetness would chill my legs so much that my feet turned warm again. They felt as if they were on fire, and that was better than the other. I knew from that time on that if hell was hot, I had no fear of it.

Those cold mornings, I would wrench myself up, dripping, dance on the floor, which was too cold to tolerate straight, and run naked to the bathroom. There I would break the ice on the pitcher of water, pour it into the basin, dip my washcloth, wad it up, take a breath, and start rubbing it across my chest. By the time I worked down to my stomach, the edge would be off, and I was able to complete the washup. In summer it wasn't bad at all, of course. In the afternoon, after school, I would wash the sheets, wring them out as well as I could—that was the part that made my hands feel raw—and hang them up. It was a routine, and I was able to cope.

Eventually I was put in a hospital for observation, to discover whether there was a physical cause for my bed-wetting. That was a horror of its own. They stuck me with every type of needle; to this day I hate needles. There was one qualification about my condition: I never wet down a strange bed. I think I had some tension about the unfamiliar that prevented me from relaxing enough, even in sleep, to release my bladder. So in that hospital I did not wet down. One day they "forgot" to bring me the bedpan; after almost twenty-four hours I was about bursting, and finally screwed up courage to ask for it. They concluded that there was no physical cause for my malady. But two things associated with that stay made a lasting and negative impression on me. The first was the morning when I woke and discovered a group of nurses huddled just outside my door. They were whispering excitedly. I heard one say something like "I don't tell them; I just wait and *shove it in!*" I was terrified; I assumed it was a knife she meant, and that I was to be the target, and for the next two days I existed in terror of that assault. But it never came; others might get sliced up in a hospital, but they let me go. I suspect that those nurses were actually talking about giving someone else an injection, or taking temperature anally (I have always been suspicious of the medical establishment's fixation on the anus, though there was one very pretty nurse there and I really didn't mind when she had at my posterior) or perhaps even a sexual experience. I just wish they had not chosen to whisper about it right by my room! The other thing I learned about later: The hospital wanted to be sure it was paid. I was covered by insurance, but just to be certain, they refused to let me go until the money was guaranteed. So my three-day stay became five days, and I suffered that extra isolation and fright because the hospital was more interested in money than my health. Today I recognize hospitals as necessary things, but I can't say I love them; they have not changed their nature.

I was taken to see another doctor. His prescription was simple: No fluid after four in the afternoon. No water or milk or juice, just solids. From that day on I had a new horror: thirst. One of my favorite songs is "Water": "All day I faced the barren waste without the taste of water, cool, clear, water." To this day I hate to be thirsty. It is ironic that after my kidney stone, at the age of forty-seven, I was required to drink great quantities of water. Today I drink a cup of it every half hour during the day, except when I have to travel or be in public. It can be a problem, running to the bathroom every hour. But in my study in the pasture, no problem at all; I water down the little cedar trees, and they flourish. Sometimes I wonder whether the genesis of that kidney stone lies in this period of thirst in my youth. But water every half hour is far more comfortable than none for fourteen hours every day. Desperate, I used to suck a few drops from my washcloth as I washed my face. No, of course this regimen had no effect on my bed-wetting; it was merely another punishment.

There was a worse aspect to bed, however. That was the horrors of the night. Generally my dreams were neutral or pleasant, for they were my escape from the mundane world. But it was always a struggle to get to sleep. I was terrified of the dark, with reason: Monsters lurked therein. I had to have a light in the room. So a kerosene lamp would be left where I could see it, turned low, and after I was asleep an adult would come and take it away. Even so, it was a terror. The monsters of the dark loomed right up to the very fringe of the light. I would bury myself under the blanket, even if it was a hot night, leaving only an airhole for my mouth so I could breathe, and a peephole for my eyes so I could see the light. I remember when, after perhaps half an hour, an adult came quietly to remove the lamp, and I cried out: I was still awake. So it was left, and half an hour later the adult came again—but again I protested. I think I remained awake on the third call. Then, at last, I made it to the relief of sleep. I don't think others ever really understood that I was not resting, I was struggling for my sanity against the demon of Fear.

Yet sleep was not universally joyful. On rare occasions I had nightmares—and they were the worst horrors of all. Once I dreamed of a picnic scene, with children playing on a pond. There was a baby, but the baby somehow fell into the pond and got hurt. We picked it up, but its foot was leaking some sort of goo or pus and we had to throw it back. That dead baby remained under the water near the edge of the pond as we played, and we did not dare to use the water too near it, for fear of the pus. I think then that I did not know the true structure of the human body; to me it was a container that, if punctured, would leak its innards, in the manner of a squashed caterpillar. The memory of that leaking foot haunted me for some time thereafter. Later I learned more about human anatomy, but for a long time I wondered how and why the food we ate got separated into solid and liquid wastes. Today I wonder how many sinister memories are buried beneath the level of consciousness of the average person, ignored because they cannot be abolished but are too horrible to be approached. Dead babies . . .

But the worst nightmare of all concerned my mother. One day my father took me to an amusement building. It was a fascinating place, with all manner of marvelous activities. There was a slide about three stories tall. There was a huge figure in man shape, with circular stairs inside; people went inside, and every so often the figure would roar "Ho Ho Ho!" and wiggle a little on its mounting, and all the people inside would scream. That seemed stupid to me; it only wiggled a little bit. But I suspect that to the folk inside, it seemed as if it was falling over: a momentary terror. My father went through that route alone, and reported his experience: It led into a chamber with a table of attractive watches, with a sign saying FREE—TAKE ONE. But when he touched one, he found it was tied down, and he got an electric shock. There was more, but that's all I remember. Then he took me on a horror ride. The carriage started moving on its own, down its track, and passed through swinging doors. Inside it was dark—except for illuminated monster figures that leaned over us as we passed, as if to grab us. I was scared and thrilled, exactly as I was supposed to be. Then suddenly a bright brick or stone wall appeared ahead, and we were cruising right toward it. Just as we were about to hit, the cart dropped an inch or so to a lower track and swerved aside. It seemed very like a crash. I was wrung out by the time that ride was over, but I loved it. I retain a liking for that sort of ride, and made sure that my children had the chance to experience similar—but always with warning, on a voluntary basis. I regard that sort of thing as the kind of education every child should have, along with solitaire card games and whoopee cushions. As I said, I never forgot either the tribulations or the joys of childhood.

But that evening I had a dream. I suspect it was triggered by the excitement of the day, but I do not blame the day; it had been a great day. I blame the underlying situation. I have described this dream in my fiction, as I have some of the events of this period of my life, but I trust that those readers who are conversant with my fiction will bear with me for this repetition. It consisted of four still pictures. The first was of myself with my sister and my mother, walking down a city street. That of course was drawn from life; there was nothing remarkable about it. The second was of my mother in a telephone booth, unable to get out. This too was drawn from life; at some point she had sought to make a call, and the door did not operate properly, and she had difficulty getting in or out, and I worried momentarily. That had been about the time that she was scheduled for some sort of operation. I knew nothing about it, but had the impression that it involved cutting her open. I had a horrible mental picture of her lying on a table while some man cut into her abdomen with a knife. Thus that phone booth was associated with a lurking horror. The third picture of the dream was of a forest glade, with an altar of some kind in it, and upon it a lightly clad woman, as it were a sacrifice. At the edge of the glade stood a man, and beside him was a lion. Now that glade was familiar; it happened that I had recently seen a county region, with fields and forest interspersed, that served as a pasture for cattle, and there I had spied the huge, bleached-white, hollow-eye-socketed skull of a cow, lying on the ground. I knew what it was, and was chilled: This was the tangible manifestation of death. Now that region was in my dreams, as well as I can reconstruct it, more than forty years later. The fourth picture was of the same glade, only now the woman was gone and the man was lifting up the lion in his arms, as though to heft it for weight. Obviously the lion had eaten the woman. Symbolically, the woman was my mother, forever lost to me. The man may have been my father, but I had not recognized him as such; I think it more likely he was the anonymous surgeon destined to carve up my mother. I may have interpreted details differently, in prior renditions of this dream, titled "Four Pictures"; I have searched and re-searched for the truth of it, and different aspects manifest at different times. That dream was *the* event of my early life.

I woke screaming. I think I rousted the whole household. My mother appeared, and tried to comfort me, but in my dream I had seen her die, and that dream was in its fashion more telling than the reality. The dream related not so much to literal death as to the loss of my mother because of the sundering of the family, and *that* was a true vision. That was the vision that haunted me every night for the following three years: the death of my mother. The corpse would manifest, and I would try to banish it, but it would reappear as a skeleton, more horribly dead than before. I tried to make it move on, leaving me behind, and it became like a train passing in the night, one coach following another rapidly, each one a version of that corpse. There was simply no escaping that horror.

Well, there was one way, and that was the way I eventually took: alienation. The loss of my mother would not hurt so much if her presence meant less to me. So when I began to need her less, the dream faded, and finally it was gone. I lived, emotionally, without a mother. She might be there as a person, though for long periods she was not a member of our household, but she was pretty much like other people, without strong emotional attachment. I had succeeded, in my fashion, in ridding myself of the horror—but I regard the manner of it as another horror. When I had children of my own, I did my best to ensure that they never suffered anything like this.

Sometimes I would daydream, trying to convince myself that all this life in America was merely a dream, and that in the morning I would wake and find myself back in England, the nightmare over. But I knew it wasn't so, and in time I came to terms with that reality too: my life was in America. Another of my favorite songs is "America, the Beautiful." I pictured the purple mountains and the shining seas. But I think it was never as good as what I had left behind.

7.

HILLTOP

During my stay in first grade we moved to a farm in Vermont. It was four miles from the nearest village, atop a mountain, and we called it Hilltop. We had goats there. That became my home for about four years, and a summer home for a number of years following; I even brought my fiancée there once. We had goats there, and strawberries and blueberries growing wild, and we ate from wooden bowls. There was no electricity, and my sister and I had to walk two and a half miles each way to school every day, through the forest. In winter the snow would pile up three feet deep, and until we managed to tramp down a path it would be a terrific chore to plow through. Sometimes we used snowshoes. You might think that all this would be another horror for me. Not so; I liked it. The blueberries were good, and we could pick and eat all we wanted; the goats were excellent company. I retain a deep liking for the forest, and it shows in my fiction. Weekends the adults would gather for folk-singing—and though I did not participate, I loved those songs, and memorized them (memorization was an awful chore for me, which shows how important this was to me), and today I still sing them to myself when I am alone, and they also color my fiction. Today our horses take the place of those goats, in my emotion; horses are about the same size for me now as the goats were then. For many years—well over a decade—I wrote my novels in pencil and typed them on a manual typewriter, preferring to be independent of electricity, as we were there.

But there was stress there too. My father liked the country; my mother did not. She was more a creature of the city, preferring not to exist, as she put it, "like troglodytes." I believe this became the final stress upon their marriage, this difference in preference for lifestyles, and this too is reflected in my fiction. In whole series of novels, such as *The Apprentice Adept,* there is the way of the city, with its technology, convenience, and pollution, opposed to the way of the country, with its forest, its animals, and its magic. I wished the two could be merged, so that my family could be reconstituted, and that carries right on into my present existence, wherein we live literally in the forest, but have electricity and all its attendant benefits. We have a good wood-burning stove for heat in the winter, and a forty-foot television tower that brings in a dozen stations from all parts of the state. We have farm animals, and computers. We have merged city and country—but the root of that mergence was here at Hilltop Farm, where it was not to be.

Of course my view of the farm is limited by my horizons of the time; I was a child. For an adult view of the farm and the philosophy behind it, read my father's essay "Reclaiming an Abandoned Farm," in Appendix B.

Memories abound, but let me settle for a mere sampling. An artist—as I recall his name was Cliff Bennett—painted a picture of the house, on a wall in the kitchen, virtually a mural. It was beautiful, and below was written the legend "Let not the seeds of war be found on these our premises." Surely a fitting sentiment for the cooperative effort of pacifists. But later the legend was painted out; the seeds of war were to be found even here.

One good memory was in winter: There was a freezing rainstorm in the night, and next morning as we went to school the forest had become a fairyland. Every branch of every tree was coated with ice, and icicles hung from every projection. Branches were bowed low with the weight of ice, forming arcades over our path. I can't remember a more beautiful sight—and we passed through miles of it.

One day I was standing at the back door—there were times when the children were not permitted in the house, to give the adults some relief—doing nothing, idly chewing on the latch chain there. Suddenly I realized that the chain was green, and remembered that it was one of the items that had been painted with a substance called Paris Green, intended to poison animals like porcupines who were ubiquitous and chewed our wood indefatigably. Now I had eaten it, accidentally. I walked away, wondering what it felt like to die. No, nothing happened; perhaps that was a disappointment.

One weekend morning my sister and I slept late—a luxury! —and proceeded to entertain ourselves by discovering what noises we could make by putting our open mouths against our arms and blowing. It sounded like voluminous flatulence, the loud breaking of wind that is so delightful to the young. But it evidently bothered the adults, downstairs; my father came to tell us that there would be no more of that. Now this was an unreasonable stricture on the face of it; we had only been having fun. As my father left, I could not resist making one final, faint *bzzz*. He turned about, came back, hauled me out of bed, and whaled me repeatedly on the backside. I screamed; never before had I been beaten like that. The commotion was so great that my sister soon was screaming too. My father left, but in a moment my mother was there, trying to put things right. From this experience I learned two things. The first, obviously, was not to do that again. Physical punishment does make that sort of point, which is perhaps why it is so popular in certain circles: the simple answer to a problem. The second was more devious, but is also a consequence of that sort of discipline, on the societal as well as the personal level. It alienated me from my father. I suspect that had he known how deep and lasting that alienation was to be, he never would have done it. This did not mean that I ran away from home; rather it meant that a certain structural damage was done to our relationship. (For that concept of "structural damage" I am indebted to Stephen King's novel *Pet Sematary;* I read it when he sent me an autographed copy.) For our family did not practice physical chastisement; pacifistic solutions were the rule. In resorting to violence, my father demonstrated quite emphatically to me that his philosophy was seriously flawed. One small act of defiance, in the face of what I still feel was an unreasonable demand, and this pacifism deserted him. His true belief was revealed. Herein is the root of my abandonment of pacifism as a viable philosophy; I had seen that it was not truly honored by those who recommend it. Violence, it is said, is the last refuge of incompetence; I believe it—but there's a lot of incompetence in our culture. I have always reacted negatively to the unreasonable use of force, and I never forgive it. But I do accept force as an option. I don't like all the lessons I receive, but I learn them well.

I became an indefatigable collector. For example, I saved boxes, ranging from matchboxes to big cardboard cartons. I fitted one inside the other, so that about a hundred different-sized boxes took the room of only the three largest ones. I made lists of two- or three-meaninged words, such as meat—meet-mete. Later I collected science fiction magazines. I saved bottletops that I found on the ground, until I had hundreds; I devised a game wherein I would draw them out randomly and make patterns of them, each one set adjacent to another of its type, and the types would try to circle and enclose each other. I was good at devising isolated entertainment; I was my own best company.

We developed a kind of family tradition in the naming of our animals: our name was Jacob, so members of the family began with J. Thus our first goat was Junie, and our dog was Juliette. We finally lost Juliette when we put her in the back of the truck with the goats; when we checked twenty miles later, she was gone. She must have jumped out. We retraced the route, but there was no sign of her. Life is like that; those close to you can disappear, and you never know what happened to them.

One of our neighbors, about five miles away, was Scott Nearing. He was a radical political commentator, for years publishing his views; earlier in his life he had been a communist, and was put on trial for treason, but defended himself and was found innocent. Later he was to become noted for his books on self-sufficient living, such as *Living the Good Life*. He lived to be one hundred. On what I think was my eighth birthday I went with a friend to buy some maple sugar from him. He told me that it was his birthday too, and refused payment. He was correct: we shared August 6, though he was fifty-one years older than I. My adult politics do not align with his; I am liberal but not radical. But Scott was always a good neighbor and friend. This is another lesson I have remembered: It is possible to differ politically, socially, religiously, or in many other ways, yet to be friends.

One bad experience concerned a neighbor, whom I shall call

Mrs. X. This may have occurred when I was ten, putting it technically in the next part of this volume, but it is really part of our farm experience and I think belongs here regardless of the technicality. Mrs. X lived about two miles from us, half a mile from the school, and our route took us past her house every day. One morning my sister and I delighted in the fresh snow, and took turns lying on our backs and moving our arms to make angel figures, and we took hold of saplings and whirled around them, leaving circular patterns of footprints. This was in sight of Mrs. X's house, and when we got near she yelled at us from her doorway. Apparently she hadn't liked our trespassing on her property. It was entirely innocent and harmless, and we had thought it was part of the road's right-of-way, but she was furious, and sent us scurrying on past toward the school. Once again, an adult had spied children having fun, and had reacted with anger.

Later that morning a note arrived at the school. The teacher read it, and told us we would have to go back; Mrs. X had something to say to us. So my sister and I walked the half mile back to present ourselves, not knowing what it was about. Mrs. X stood inside her screen, a huge fat figure of a woman, and screamed at us about ruining her trees and about how I had come into her house and cut a hole in a bicycle tire. I had done no such thing; I had not even been in her house, and I did not practice vandalism. (Her own boys did, so I can guess the source of the mischief; how much easier for a parent to believe a lie about another person's child, than the truth about her own.) But my protestation only enraged her further; she virtually spat at us in her fury. Finally, confused and terrified by her vehemence and the false charge, we returned to the school.

Thereafter we were afraid to pass by her house. But it was the only route. My father had to walk with us to get us safely by—which meant losing perhaps an hour from his day in the morning. In the evening we would walk back with the teacher, protected. On the third morning, Mrs. X charged out despite the presence of our father, repeating her accusations. My father simply said that he would not talk to her while she was in that state, and walked on. His words were polite, but the effect was potent; she was silent. Perhaps this was a pacifistic approach; nevertheless it had teeth in it. But that showed him what we were up against; he knew we were innocent. So he went to a great deal of trouble to make a new route for us to take to school, which went entirely through the forest, never entering the road or going near Mrs. X's house. For the rest of the school year, in fair weather or foul, we used that tortuous hilly route. It was arduous, but it solved the problem; Mrs. X could not get at us. And perhaps most importantly, it demonstrated tangibly that our father was ready to stand by us at need. If there was structural damage in the family, there was also some solid shoring, and this too is not forgotten. I have lent similar support to my own children, sometimes pretty roughly, as will be seen. Eventually Mrs. X calmed down, apparently having realized her mistake, but I have remembered her only with horror and anger. She had borne false witness against her neighbor. I shall never forgive that. And when anything of that kind happens elsewhere, I become an ogre indeed. I am no longer relatively helpless, but the old emotions remain. Anyone who seeks to bear false witness against me or my children—and there are those who have—had better be prepared to defend himself. But I always make certain I have the right of it before I act.

PART TWO

Bare Feet Don't Stink

1.

HABITS

This section properly begins in Part One, while the end of the prior sequence properly ended here in Part Two, but that just shows the problem with artificial categorization. Let me, however, mention one thing that does fit here: the atomic bomb. It was dropped on Hiroshima on my eleventh birthday. I am not especially proud of that coincidence.

My problems of the night continued, and in due course spread into problems of the day. I became compulsive in various little ways. I counted: footsteps, phone poles, number of seconds it took to urinate—anything that was there to be counted. Indeed, I never stopped being compulsive in that way, and I still count all manner of things automatically, all the old ones plus number of chins I do on the rafter of my study in the morning, number of words of first draft written per day, how long it takes me to run three miles, and so on. Harlan Ellison recently chided me for my supposed meanspiritedness in keeping a list of the publications of other writers; he assumed it was some kind of hit list, but actually it was only part of the pattern of counting I do in all aspects of my life. I like to know exactly where I stand, and that means I have to know not only how many books I have had published, but how many other writers have published, and how each is doing. I have accurate lists of all payments received for each of my novels, and I track the progress of each book on the best-seller lists with great glee; all part of the pattern, and if that makes me a neurotic, I confess to it. When I computerized, I discovered a fundamental compatibility with the machine: the computer likes to count things too! It watches and lets me know constantly exactly what line and what column my cursor is on, and how many kilobytes' worth of space I have filled, and it never forgets. A thing like that can't be all bad!

But the counting went mostly unnoticed, because it was internal. Other habits didn't. My hair grew long; I was never eager to get it cut, because my father always made remarks about how long it was when cutting it, and sometimes accidentally pinched my ear with the scissors. Ears sort of disappear under hair, and you forget they're there, until abruptly reminded. Sometimes I was mistaken for a girl. When my hair flopped in my face and obscured my vision, I would give my head a toss to fling it clear. Natural enough—but that motion became a fixation, so that even when my hair was short, I still tossed my head every minute or so, the same way.

Once after I washed my hands, there was nothing to dry them on, so I gave them both a short, sharp shake to eliminate most of the water. I liked the feel of that, and thereafter I shook my hands every minute or so, though they were dry.

This continued for years. Naturally it made me the subject of ridicule among peers. Why didn't I stop? Ask a smoker why he doesn't stop. Or try not scratching an intense itch. If you don't scratch a mosquito bite, it won't be as bad, and you know that—but you find yourself doing it unconsciously, even in your sleep. So when others asked me why I did it, I simply replied, "It's a habit." That generally sufficed. I got some kind of emotional satisfaction from performing those motions, and I was unable to stop. It may have been as simple as the momentary relief of not having hair in my face, or not having water dripping from my hands; for the sake of that illusory relief, I repeated the actions. It was, I think, very much akin to the bed-wetting.

I mentioned smoking. This relates, in a reverse manner. Back at this age, around ten, other boys told me how they would sneak behind the shed and take puffs of cigarettes. Okay—if smoking was the thing to do, I would try it. I went to my father and said I wanted to try smoking. Now you might think that this would have landed me promptly *in* the woodshed, not behind it. No, our family did not operate that way. My father agreed that this was the type of thing boys tried, and he cooperated. There weren't any cigarettes in the house, but we could get around that by making our own. We had bags of "goat tobacco"—used to worm the goats. It wasn't intended for smoking, but it *was* tobacco, and could be put in a pipe. There wasn't any suitable paper to roll cigarettes, but we had toilet paper. (Here I wonder, because we didn't use toilet paper; the outhouse was stocked with old Sears and Ward's catalogues, whose pages served the function. But my memory says toilet paper.) But how to make a rolled cigarette stay together? No problem: we had blackstrap molasses. So we rolled goat tobacco in toilet paper and stuck it together with molasses, and it worked: serviceable cigarettes. Of course this tobacco lacked the agent that makes commercial cigarettes continue burning when not being puffed, so it was necessary to draw on it constantly to keep it alight.

I had a ball. I smoked five cigarettes and three pipefuls of tobacco. My father warned me that I might feel a little strange if I overdid it, but I was having no problem. Then, I think about an hour after starting, that strangeness came upon me. I vomited where I stood, on the living room floor.

After that, I never felt inclined to smoke again. As the horrendous gradual consequences of smoking have become known in later decades, I remain glad that it happened. It's about the only time I have gotten sick and have been happy to have had the experience, because it cured me of smoking before I ever got started. Someone as compulsive as I am was bound to become a smoking addict, except for such an event. I don't know whether that was the way my father planned it; I think it more likely that, as a matter of policy in a liberal family, he simply felt that there was no purpose in sneaking around to do forbidden things; better to do them openly. I was never forbidden alcohol, either; if I wanted to taste beer, I tasted it openly, and the same for wine or whiskey. I was more cautious about that, though, so have never in my life been either drunk or sick from alcohol. Thus I never developed any forbidden compulsion for it; I can take it or leave it; and I generally leave it, because I don't like to cloud my mind in any fashion when I'm working, and I'm usually working. I'll accept a social drink, as a matter of grace rather than enthusiasm, and that's about it.

But about smoking: my wife does smoke, and cannot quit. Originally I just accepted it as part of her lifestyle. As the evidence of the hazards of smoking has increased, I have become less sanguine about her addiction. But I remember what it is like to be compulsive, regardless of social reaction or personal health, and that provides me with tolerance. When the local newspaper had a feature on smoking versus nonsmoking, and invited reader comment, my comment was published. It mentioned my quarter-century-long "miscegenous marriage" between a smoker and a nonsmoker, and concluded with a fanciful dialogue:

He: Why don't you give up smoking?

She: Why don't you give up sex?

But the roots of my tolerance are deeper than that. I have always tried to profit from my experiences, the bad ones as well as the good ones, and to remember what the other person's situation is like. I understand compulsion, so I can accept it in others. It's a variant of the Golden Rule.

Since I was plainly a maladjusted child, I was sent to a series of psychologists and psychiatrists. Now I may have appeared subnormal, but I was not; I caught on early that these were paid professionals who had little inkling of the true nature of children. So I would talk about this and that, being generally positive, and they would be satisfied that they had done me some good, while never actually touching the real me.

However, in one case, one reached me. It seemed that what he did was this: He told me that my mother felt I didn't like her, and he told my mother that I thought she didn't like me. He did not tell either of us what he had told the other. This had the effect of creating a barrier in communication between us that had not been there before. There was an ongoing process of alienation, but that was a subtle thing, not expressed in any overt dislike and not related to it. I never hated my parents; I merely had to learn to live without them. Perhaps the psychologist thought the effect would be opposite. Since both his statements were false, I regard this as ignorant mischief, and when I learned of it, and pondered it, I developed a cold attitude toward such meddlers. In due course I simply refused to see any more of them, outright. I retain a healthy disrespect for that profession, and I find much of Freudian pretension laughable. Theory is one thing; real people are another.

Yet there can be some value in psychiatry. Psychiatry is considered a science, while astrology is considered fantasy, but I see them as equivalent. The psychiatrist employs largely irrelevant assumptions to unriddle the confusions of the human personality. The astrologer employs similarly irrelevant parallels to the celestial phenomena to fathom the course of human events. It doesn't matter. What does matter is that in each case, a disciplined person gives his whole attention to the problems of the confused person, trying to help. *That attention is what counts.* The client realizes that someone cares. That is not generally sufficient to solve his problems, but it can make them easier to live with. The human mind likes to make sense of things, and any philosophy that seems to provide such sense is valued, even if it is nonsense. Hence we have psychiatry, astrology— and religion. But I don't require any of these in my life.

I have, however, a fond and perhaps irrelevant memory of one astrologer, Marc Edmund Jones. My father worked with him on some projects, and he visited Hilltop Farms once. He gave me a compass, and we used it to help us find our way directly through the forest from Hilltop to Scott Nearing's house, where my father was to give a talk. I fear that cross-country excursion was rough on Marc Jones, but he didn't complain. At any rate, he showed me a poem that continues to delight me:

> *Mary had a pair of skates*
> *With which she loved to frisk.*
> *Now wasn't she a foolish girl*
> *Her little**

For those who don't get it, I suggest reading it aloud, pronouncing the terminal symbol.

From point of my refusal on, my situation improved. I had declared my independence, and had taken the organization of my internal life into my own hands, and my hands were better than the others had been. Gradually my more obvious compulsions faded out. I stopped wetting my bed, and stopped shaking my head and hands. That did not mean that my life was free of problems; I had an immense psychological pit to climb out of, and in some ways I am still climbing out of it today. But it was, I think, the turning point. As I mentioned before: I prefer to wipe my own nose. My father comments that it became evident in time that my compulsive habits were worst when my mother was with us. I hadn't realized that, but it does seem to fit the pattern.

However, at this time there was another factor that may relate. The psychologists were my mother's route; my father had a different one. He preferred a more spiritual approach. Now I never did have much truck with the supernatural, but this may have had its effect. My father said he could write to a group who would pray for me, in that way helping me to get better, or he could take me to see a lady personally, who might be able to help me. I considered, and saw no benefit in being anonymously prayed for, so I chose to visit the woman. This meant a trip to another state, and it became a kind of spot vacation with my father. Right there, there were benefits! The woman was called Mrs. West, and she talked to me for about half an hour, and told me how some things were real even though we could not see them. She used electricity as an example. Then she took me to a bookstore and bought me a puzzle book.

Now the things-real-but-not-seen thesis of course relates to God, and while I retain a halfway open mind about that concept, I can't say I believe it. But the electricity I believe. I regard this as an excellent analogy. But I think more important was the evident fact that my father cared enough about me to use several days to take me just to talk to someone. Of course my mother cared too, but somehow the ignorant psychologists did not impress me the way Mrs. West did. She did not pretend to know the real nature, of things, she only offered a way of looking at things, and that was fundamentally acceptable to me. I have always had more respect for the person who says, "I don't know the answer, but let's consider and see what we can figure out," rather than the one who says, "I know best; you just do what I say." And that puzzle book—what a book that was! Little stories set up the puzzles, and they were intricate, imaginative things. I remember one especially: A boy's dog had gotten its leash all tangled up with the furniture; could you untangle it? That was a variant of a well-known rope-and-rings puzzle, with the dog too big to fit through the rings (in this case, the space between slats of a chair) but with some line to play with. You have to form a loop in the line and pass it back through and around the tangled object, thus freeing it. It is fiendishly tricky, the first time. I spent hours on it, and loved it—and indeed, have always liked such challenges. So my memories of that episode are very positive, and that, too, occurred about the time my tide turned. Perhaps it represented the type of outside encouragement I needed, when I took my fate into my own hands.

2.

ROSE VALLEY

In two years I completed fifth, sixth, and seventh grades at the best school I ever attended, the School in Rose Valley. That was what it was called, and it was in Rose Valley, Pennsylvania. It was private, which meant we had to pay tuition, but as far as I am concerned, it was worth whatever it cost. The teachers were deeply concerned about the education and welfare of the students, and structured the studies around the needs of the students. The nature of their approach can be seen directly in their first report on me, presented in Appendix C. They were concerned about the "too tightly walled little world of his own in which he is living." They were right to be concerned, but I knew what I was doing. That wall protected my sanity.

My first and best flowering in drama was here. The school put on regular plays, which were crafted around the players. Each person had the part that suited him; in fact he might write his own part. The point was not to put on the most impressive show, but to give every student the best experience. We worked on scenery and costumes too, learning everything. In one play, based on a Chinese story about a woman who wanted male babies, I wished to play the part of the woman. The teachers discussed it with the others, remarking that it was generally preferable to have boys acting male parts, and girls acting female parts, but this was no firm rule. The fact was that I was short, having stopped growing at four feet ten inches while my classmates continued; thus, as the teacher also pointed out, my size would enable me to play the female role readily enough.

And so it came about. I played the woman, and a girl who was larger and taller than I played the husband. In the play he (she) condemned me for bearing him only female babies, forcing him to go several times to the river to drown them. So I went to pray for boys, and was rewarded by an instant presentation with five male babies. "*I, er, san su wu!*" I counted in Chinese, having learned the numbers for this purpose. "Five whole boys!" In my delight I dropped one as I dashed offstage, and had to return to pick up the doll that was the prop. Deliberate, of course, and I understand the audience was properly regaled.

Now others may wonder what kind of school this was, to let a boy play a woman seeking children. It was a fine school, without unreasonable inhibitions. I retained a liking for the stage, but had no further inclination to play any female role. I'm glad I was permitted to do this, on this occasion.

One of the things I learned while there was Opic. This was one of a group of "languages" like pig latin that were adaptations of the regular language. To speak Opic you simply added the syllable "op" after the first sound of each syllable, or before the vowel-sound. Thus "Hello, friend" became "Hopellopo, fropiend." My first name was "Popiers." To the uninitiated it sounded like gibberish, but the trained ear could readily understand it, tuning out the *ops*. It was a lot of fun, for a time. Opa lopot opof fopun.

I gained immensely at Rose Valley, and can hardly imagine a better place to have been. Yet there were errors. The teachers watched for a full year while four boys monopolized the best positions in sports at the expense of three less assertive ones—I was one of the three—then dressed down the four at the end of the year for their inconsideration. Why hadn't the teachers acted while they saw it happening, I wondered? Apparently they felt it was their role to observe, not to interfere, and to let things follow their natural courses. Yet when we went on a picnic, and I was one who went early to prepare the grounds, fetching wood and such, and others arrived later and teased me about my dirty hands (I had been working gathering the wood; they had not) and barred me from eating when they did, the teachers required me to honor that, eating after the privileged ones were done. Thus humiliation, for the privileged were smirking. I tried for years thereafter to understand why the teachers had done that, for the teachers had always been fair-minded. Eventually I concluded that the teachers assumed that those of us who had come early had had extra picnic, while those who came later had been helping at school, so should be rewarded. Perhaps they should have made this clear at the time; as it was, I could hardly credit their sincerity about who was inconsiderate of whom. My preference for establishing my own parameters was reinforced; I could not be certain of the judgments of others. I knew then, and know today, that the teachers meant well; but they misplayed that scene.

Love came into my life at Rose Valley. I was eleven, and the girl was twelve. Her name was Herta Payson; I always mispronounced it "Herda." She wore glasses and had long brown braids that reached to her waist, and was athletic. Of course she had no such interest in me; she associated with a boy her own age. She could hardly have been unaware of my devotion, though I could not express it openly; once I walked into a pole in her presence, literally not seeing it, almost literally blinded by her presence. But it was hopeless from the start, as I knew; she was a great girl, while I was nothing.

Puppy love? That's what they call it. But my definition of the ideal in woman was molded by the image of that girl. For many years I required my wife to wear her hair long, to her discomfort, and my daughter Penny has never had her hair cut short. It shows in my fiction: Long hair is what makes a woman feminine. I suppose it was inevitable that eventually I would write about Rapunzel, whose hair was so long that it reached to the foot of the tall tower she was imprisoned in. My favorite female singer is Crystal Gayle. When I see a woman with long tresses, I just have to watch her. Puppy love? I don't believe I have felt a stronger emotion since. As it was, the love of that girl replaced my nightmare of the Four Pictures, and it burned for three full years, and perhaps has never fully left me. No, I do not laugh at young love; its fire can be as intense as any.

After Rose Valley I went one year, eighth grade, to Nether Providence High School in Pennsylvania, a public school where everything was regimented in the conventional manner, students shunted like cattle from one classroom to another throughout the day. I'm sure it was an acceptable school, but to me its province was so nether as to be not far this side of hell.

3.

ANIMALS

In this period I told my family I would like to have a pet. I'm not sure what I was thinking of, probably a puppy, but my father took me up on it: Why not a goat? I liked the notion, and so I became the owner of Marcella, a grown doe. Later we also picked up Ann, a doe that I think someone else didn't want, so I had two, and that was good because goats are sociable animals and like to have company.

Naturally we intended to have milk. But it is a fact of mammalian life that before milk must come offspring. So we got Marcella bred, and in due course she bore kids. We found homes for them, as pets; does grow up to be milkers, and are in demand, but bucks grow up to be studs, and make no kind of pets at all at that stage, as they can be aggressive (though some are gentle) and they smell with an intensity that makes association unfeasible. I petted a friendly buck once, and my clothes had to be destroyed. Often the bucks are simply slaughtered, but of course that was not for us.

Goat kids are the friskiest, cutest things imaginable. They make odd little leaps, and are friendly. I remember at Hilltop, when we had the kids in the house, we discovered little hoofprints in the margarine. We had them in the house because they had to be separated immediately from their mother, so that they would not develop an attachment and would not take all her milk. We taught them how to drink milk from a dish instead of suckling, and then everything was fine.

Some of the deepest lessons of my life came about because of the goats. Once we had a storm, and the outdoors was buried in snow. I couldn't face going out there, so I delayed, though the goats needed to be fed. I think it was almost noon by the time I went, and then, seeing how miserable the goats were, I was desperately sorry I had neglected them. I resolved never again to do that to an animal. Today we have horses, and they belong to my daughters, but I feed them and pasture them myself, because I prefer to avoid the pitfalls of the unreliability of children, however much I love those children.

When Marcella had her kids, and we separated them, we did not manage perfectly. She could hear the kids bleating in the house, and that set her off. When I tried to milk her, which was normally a peaceful process, she would not stand still. I kept trying, and when I was partway through she kicked over the bucket. Furious, I slammed my left hand down on her back. This stung her rather than causing any damage, but she knew it was an attack. She snorted at me. Now this is a sound a goat makes when suffering certain emotions, such as extreme fear or anger or pain. Never before had she directed it at me. I was devastated. Here I had her tied in the stall, and I had struck her—and all she had been trying to do was save her milk for her kids, a completely natural instinct. Ashamed, I apologized to her in what manner I could, and resolved never to do that again. Actually, I have struck animals since, such as when our dog chewed up my daughter's dolls, and when a horse tried to kick me. But it is not a business I like at all, and I do my best to come to terms with animals by other means. Each experience with violence leaves me less inclined for another.

I learned an economic lesson here. We agreed that I would sell the goats' milk to the family for ten cents a quart, and the money earned would be used to cover the expenses. Thus the goats were not only pets, they were a business. At first it worked satisfactorily, in the summer when they could graze. But in winter they had to have hay, and that cost money. I kept track of it all, and slowly the goat account fell behind. Eventually it was $150 in the hole. As a businessman I had not made it. Where had I gone wrong? Well, goat's milk at that time sold commercially for fifty cents a quart. It was true that there were expenses the dairies had that I did not, such as pasteurization, but they also had the advantage of scale: many goats instead of two, housed and fed efficiently. So things might have averaged out. But they made five times as much per quart as I did. Had I received fifty cents a quart, I would have been well ahead. Thus I came to understand this truth: Don't sell unrealistically cheap.

I liked the goats very well. After all, I had been raised on a goat farm! But there were problems. Remember the novel *The Yearling* by Marjorie Kinnan Rawlings? How the cute little deer grew up to be a real nuisance in the neighborhood? We had some of that. We were in the suburbs, not the country, though we did take the goats with us to Hilltop Farm in the summers. We kept the goats tied, but they were ingenious in getting loose, and I was away at school in the daytime. This meant that on several occasions a goat would get into a neighbor's yard or garden, and the neighbors did not take kindly to that, and that upset my mother considerably.

One day I came home from school and the goats were absent. My mother had arranged to give them away, and by the time I had the first hint, they were gone. Surely she had reason—but had not asked me, she had simply made it a fait accompli, an accomplished fact. It was an unethical transaction, as the ownership of the goats had been mine, not hers, but I was not in a position to oppose it.

This is a subject I would have preferred to avoid in this narration, but it is integral to my attitude on integrity and must be covered. It is a Quaker tenet that anything that requires secrecy for its accomplishment is better done in the open. I presume this allows for something like the secret ballot, wherein the vote is open and only the particular selection of a candidate is private. Corruption in government flourishes in secrecy, and I agree that if a thing *has* to be done secretly, this is a signal that it probably should not be done at all. Certainly the secret disposal of my goats was wrong, and contributed to my further alienation from my mother.

How had a Quaker woman come to practice such a device? Obviously she did not consider it to be wrong, merely expedient. Herein, to my mind, lies the truth of the saying that the road to hell is paved with good intentions. It also shows how the philosophy that the end justifies the means is suspect. If one has a good cause, therefore employs improper means to forward that cause, is one wrong?

In Spain the word of Quakers was known to be good. As I understand it, once a fugitive from the military was conveyed to safety by one of the food-transport trucks. The truck was stopped. "Any contraband here?" My parents felt justified in saying no, for if they told of the hidden passenger, that man would have been taken and killed. The end of saving a life justified the means of the lie. I suspect that few people would disagree with that. Thus the truck was permitted to pass uninspected, and the life was saved. (See also my mother's commentary in the appendixes.)

But the principle had been established: The ends justified the means. A lie in a good cause was all right. It then became easier to use suspect means for lesser ends. Thus I learned, through more than one experience, that I could not trust my mother. Slowly, as I pondered such matters, I came to the conclusion that the only place to stop the erosion of honesty was at the outset: Do not take that first step toward hell. Slowly I forged my own philosophy and labored to perfect it and to live by it, and the cornerstone of this philosophy is honesty. As a child I was fallible, and I went through the usual experiences of lying, cheating, and stealing. As an adult I detest those memories. The only thing I value more than integrity is life itself. I have had a horrendous history of conflict as a writer, because dishonesty is anathema to me, and I do constant battle against it, and no living person I know of matches my own fanaticism about this. Many people don't even understand what motivates me, because integrity is only a word to them, not a principle to live by. Most people *say* they believe in honesty; I *mean* it.

What, then, of the case of the life versus the lie? What would I have done in that situation in Spain? Well, I have defined my values here; in the ultimate decision, I would value the life over the truth. But it would be an appalling choice for me, and I would do everything possible to avoid being placed in that situation. Picture it this way: A despot gains power over your body, and gives you a choice: which of your hands do you prefer to have cut off? Faced with that situation, most people would elect to sacrifice their left hand, so that the more versatile right hand could be saved. (Vice versa for lefties.) But most people, similarly, would do their very best to escape the necessity for making such a decision. Not one, I think, would conclude that since he had made the decision once, it was all right to make it as a matter of course thereafter, yielding first a hand, then a foot, then some other portion of the body, indefinitely. The first occasion would suffice to demonstrate the terrible nature of the choice. That is how I feel about the choice between a life and the truth. Every sacrifice of the truth would diminish me in an appalling fashion, and every one would be harder than the prior one.

Yes, as an adult I have been faced with such choices, though never with a life on the line. I do not seek to proselytize; I am aware that each person must determine his own standards, and that those standards differ from mine. Thus I associate with those who are not, by my definition, completely honest, and some have even been my friends. But I will not lie for a friend. Yet what of the shades of gray? Of social niceties, such as when a person inquires "What do you think?" and the truth is that my opinion would ruin that person's day? I don't believe in the "white lie" either, but I am not inclined to go about telling people unkind facts "for their own good." That is a facet of sadism. Generally I do not comment, and sometimes this is socially awkward. I try to live and let live, keeping my uncomplimentary opinions to myself.

There was one occasion when I came up against it squarely. When my elder daughter Penny was three, our beautiful Dalmatian dog developed such urinary complications that five episodes of surgery could not restore him. He had lost the delight of life, and we concluded that it would be kinder to end his life than to struggle further. Yes, I value life—but not when life becomes suffering. So we took him to the vet, who put him away painlessly with an overdose of anesthetic. That dog, Canute, is a character in my novel *Race Against Time;* he was my favorite dog, and I wish I had known what I know now in time to avoid the problem. But what were we to tell Penny? I did not want to inflict on her the horror that an early awareness of death could be; I have tried to protect my children from all the horrors I experienced as a child myself. But the dog was gone. We compromised; we told her that we would take Canute to the vet and leave him there. That was the truth—but only part of the truth, and so by my definition it was a lie. I did the thing that appalls me most: I lied to my child.

When Penny was five, we adopted a stray black cat who had had kittens in our garage. Though grown, she was tiny; I believe she weighed about three pounds. She turned out to be a wonderful creature, housetrained and so sociable that when we took walks around the block, she walked with us. She would sleep on Penny's bed, pouncing on her blanket-covered toes. We called her Pandora, and she was the only cat I ever really liked. She had a thing about dogs: if anything went wrong, the nearest dog was at fault. Once a neighbor's obnoxious dachshund charged onto our yard, pursuing Pandora. They disappeared around the house. Then they reappeared, going the opposite way: the cat was chasing the yipping dog, though he was far larger than she. Penny had seen it happen: Pandora came to a tree, stopped at it, and turned and smote the dog on the nose with her claws. She was a huntress; when she clawed, it hurt. The dog had been defeated. He never chased her again.

One night Pandora was missing, though she usually came inside. In the morning I discovered her body beside the highway: she had been killed by a car. *Oh, no!* I buried her and kept my mouth shut for two days, but on the third, when Penny asked whether I knew what had happened to Pandora, I had to tell her that the cat was dead. Penny screamed, and it tore my heart out. I don't know which was worse: finding Pandora dead, or telling Penny about it. But I could not lie to my child a second time. Nor ever since.

4.

WESTTOWN

From ninth through twelfth grades I went to Westtown, one of the leading Quaker boarding schools, the tuition paid for by my grandfather. My stepgrandmother, Caroline Nicholson Jacob, had been a teacher there for twenty-three years before marrying my grandfather. It was an enormous improvement over Nether Providence.

Two of the students I had known at Rose Valley were also to attend. One was Joan Nicholson, related to me through my grandmother, and the other was Tanis Fletcher, whose name I had noted on the back of her chair when I had been seated behind her during a Rose Valley assembly. (More than thirty years later I teased the excellent genre writer Tanith Lee in an article, remembering the name Tanis and speculating whether Tanith lisped.) There was one more familiar face: that of Teresa, my sister.

But the first year was not terrific for me. I was the smallest person in my class, male or female, and that meant that I got pushed around by other boys. The teachers, as usual, seemed to be oblivious of this sort of harassment. In fact, my family even had to pay for replacement of the door to my room, which a big boy had kicked apart. The average IQ at the school was supposed to be 117, which meant that standards were stiff. Thus physically and mentally I had a job surviving.

Soccer was the game of choice here; there was no football. One of the good things about soccer is that it is not a contact sport, so size theoretically doesn't matter and injuries are few. Nevertheless, when I went out to play, I sat on the sidelines; I could play well enough, having had experience at Rose Valley, but the coach would take one look at me and ignore me thereafter, satisfied that no one that small could play. Joan Nicholson, with similar experience at Rose Valley, was a highly coordinated girl, and so, ironically, the only way I could judge how I would have done in soccer had I been allowed to play seriously was by watching her. She became outstanding, and in her final year was the one deemed to be the most effective female athlete in the school. I have never liked being excluded without trial, and that has colored my career as a writer, of which more anon.

Since I couldn't get into soccer, and of course basketball was pointless for a boy who stood an inch under five feet tall and weighed about ninety pounds, I went out for tennis. But for that I needed a tennis racket. For the racket I needed money. I didn't have it. I was given an old one, but that needed restringing, and I didn't have the money for that either. So I worked at odd jobs, earning money. It took me two years to earn enough to buy the racket—by which time I was two years behind my classmates who were from more affluent families and had the money for equipment from the start. I gained ground, and once in a school tournament I beat the number-six singles player of the school team. But two things prevented that from becoming anything. First, he had been ill for two weeks, and was only just coming back to play, so it wasn't a fair match. Second, the tennis coach at that time was also my teacher in German, and I was abysmal at foreign languages. In fact, I nearly failed to graduate, because I was failing German, and my grandmother had to come and tutor me in the subject so that I could pass the final exam. The tennis coach simply could not believe that anyone that poor in German could be a decent tennis player, and dismissed me much the way the soccer coach did. I believe that had I been able to start playing tennis in ninth grade, I would have been a strong player, and have made the team.

Blocked from effective participation in the formal sports, I settled for expertise in an informal one, where nothing other than my own ability counted. This was table tennis (Ping-Pong).

From a standing start when I came to the school, I became a player to be reckoned with, though not at the top level. One I broke in, my roommate Ronald Bodkin, in due course became *the* player, always winning. He did the same in tennis, winning the school trophy three years in succession. But for me, sports were simply not that great. One aspect of that of which I am not proud was the fact that I was a poor loser in Ping-Pong. When Ronald started beating me, I was grudging, and our friendship suffered. Thereafter I pondered the matter, and resolved to strive to accept both my victories and my losses graciously. I do try, but not with perfect success, as this volume shows.

Academically it was much the same. One year I was an honor student, but then the burden of two languages, Latin and German, bore me down, and I graduated in the third quarter of my senior class. I had started to do well in higher math, but that had to be sacrificed for the languages. Theoretically I had my choice of courses, and wanted to choose math, but was told my choice was between French and German. This "choice" had the effect of destroying my academic record. I resolved that never again would I permit others to preempt the choices that were properly mine, to my detriment. This, too, was to affect my attitude as a novelist; I have taken novels away from publishers who became too pushy about their content, and I will continue to do so.

Grades do not necessarily represent a student's actual performance, because of cheating by some students and the attitude or ignorance of teachers. Westtown had its share of such problems. I don't like cheating, and once I had gotten this straight in my mind I avoided it. (Sometimes this was impossible, as when a sergeant in the army, taking a class with me, demanded to see my test paper so he could copy it. I'll discuss the army in Part Three.) But I had to compete against those who felt that the grade was all that counted. I elected not to compete on that basis. In my last year I had the measles, and that almost killed me; I was on intravenous feeding and my fever ran as high as 105 degrees. Thus I missed classes—and a final exam was coming up in one. With no time to study, I did my best—and made what could be the lowest score on a final exam in the history of the school: 15% on Quakerism. On another occasion I got hit in class by a ball of paper. I threw it back. The teacher booted me from class and reduced my grade for the month from A to C. Naturally the one who had hit me with the paper got off without penalty. Perhaps teachers don't realize what this sort of thing does to a student's motivation. For a time I was an honor student, and grades were my major passion, but by the time I graduated I had lost interest in academic excellence. It was a good school—but I think not quite good enough.

The odd thing was that I generally associated with the top academic performers, not because I cared about that but because I liked them personally. I roomed one year with Ronald Bodkin, one grade behind me, who was always the top scorer, except when he tied with one of my other roommates for top honors. Of course in retrospect I can see that, regardless of my grades, I was one of the brighter students there, and the others privately recognized that. IQ tests, previously misrepresented to me as games, had been relative disasters; now I took one for real, and was rated with an IQ of 131. I took it again in college, and remembered an item that had given me trouble before, answering it so promptly that I scored a bonus point, for 132. Theoretically those tests are periodically revamped, but the same old items remain. This particular item was a paragraph statement whose key element I immediately divined: the multiplication of 8 times 12. On the first test I took a long time to figure out that math, for I had never been good at the rote "times" tables that the test makers assumed everyone knew; on the second I remembered that effort and instantly said, "Ninety-six!"

Now IQ—Intelligence Quotient—is a sadly abused concept. Theoretically it represents the mental age divided by the chronological age, times one hundred, so that a ten-year-old with the mind of an eleven-year-old is rated 11/10, or 110. But in practice it is sadly limited, with only a portion of the true potentials of the mind tested, and the results on those distorted by cultural factors. There are a number of different types of IQ tests, and some are less accurate than others. So, while my score on the Wechsler-Belleview does not compare to the figures of 150 or 160 that get bandied about, it does put me in the top two percent of the population. But my real mental ability, of whatever nature, is shown by my writing, and that is the way I prefer to be judged, rather than by my score on a test whose makers did not necessarily know the nearest planet (it is Earth, not Mars; the test should ask "What other planetary orbit is closest to that of Earth?" and that answer should be keyed "That of Venus") or which side of a tree moss grows on (it is determined by wind and shade, not the compass). Too many schools judge their students by IQ, without realizing that it is largely a chimera, a fanciful figure that relates only peripherally to reality. Nonetheless, it is about all we have as a rating for the mind, and I remain foolishly fascinated by it.

The truth, I believe, is that all of us have about the same amount of gray matter in our craniums, and it operates with about the same efficiency. But the wiring differs, so that some have a greater facility in one area, and others in another. Those who score very high on IQ tests tend, in my observation, to be correspondingly deficient in other areas, often the practical or social or creative ones; thus we see genius professors who can't find their own way home, or nuclear physicists who have little concern about the consequences of the atomic bombing of civilians, as parodied in the movies. There are "idiot savants" who can hardly talk, yet can perform amazing mental calculations. Most people fall comfortably in the middle range, excelling at nothing but also being deficient in nothing, and that is no bad state. Some of those are fans of my writings, and that is no bad state either.

So if I had any superior mental qualities, they were not recognized at Westtown. With perhaps two exceptions. I was interested in art, and was becoming good at it, and my art teacher, George Whitney, encouraged me. (I also had quite a time with a comic series about a cutworm, called Snip-snip the Cutworm. When he said the magic word "Scissors" he became Snip Superworm, a worm of much power.) And, at the very end, my English teacher, who had given me fairly consistent B's, gave me one A, and approached my parents in my presence to tell them that I had such potential in writing that I really should go on to college. I dismissed that at the time as his effort to get a full hundred percent of my graduating class to go on to college; that sort of thing looks good on a school's records, and I was the only one who did not plan to attend college. But, in retrospect, I begin to suspect that he had something. I did, eventually, become a writer.

One of the facts of life of a Quaker school was the Friends' Meetings. We had them twice a week. I had been attending Meetings for two or three years before then, so this was nothing new, but the experience at Westtown disenchanted me, and thereafter my attendance verged from sporadic to not at all.

The Quakers (The Religious Society of Friends), as I have mentioned, believe that no middleman is required between a person and his God. Thus the religious service is basically silent, with no priest or minister. I understand that in some branches there is a ministerial capacity, but I was never exposed to this form. About the only form of direct guidance at a meeting is by a leading person—in this case the headmaster of the school—who would signal the onset of the service by silently taking his seat at the front, facing the majority, and signal the conclusion by turning and shaking hands with his companion.

However, the silent meeting is not literally silent. At any point any member may be moved to share his thoughts with the others, either in the form of an open prayer or as a straight discussion. On occasion, one such expression will lead to a series of additional comments by others. Once a student stood and said, "What can you do with a thief?" He spoke with passion, summarizing the problem of an anonymous thief who was ransacking students' rooms, and the helplessness of the victims in dealing with this. More than one faculty member rose in the course thereafter to address this issue, one going to the Bible to detail the savage punishment described in the Old Testament, which extended even to distant relatives of the thief and to other generations. I believe that by the time that particular Meeting was done, the entire community had a much clearer appreciation of the problem. Though normally the topics addressed are religious, there is no limit, and this consideration of the problem of the thief was, I believe, an excellent example of the proper functioning of the Meeting.

Later the thief was caught. He was a classmate. He was not expelled, and did not choose to leave; he stuck it out, and expressed his regret for what he had done, and made such restitution as he could. When the matter of theft came up in another context, he had input: "I know what thieving is like, because I have done it." There is no more pertinent comment than that by the person who has been there. This, too, illustrates the Quaker principle of the pacifistic solution to problems. Outright condemnation is usually based on ignorance, and it is better to try for understanding, reform, and restitution, making of a thief a responsible member of the community. Of course this does not work in all cases, and this is one reason I am not a pacifist despite my sympathy with the principles of pacifism; I experienced too much of the schoolyard bully, and knew that acceptance led only to further bullying. When I learned to fight, and developed larger size, the bullying stopped. As an adult I fight with my mind rather than my body, but I do fight. I have a good mind, and choose my positions and terrain carefully; I expect to win any conflict I enter. But I retain respect for pacifism, and will generally try to work things out without violence. When that effort is rebuffed, beware. Too many people assume that one who tries to be decent is dealing from weakness, and as an adult I have given some very hard lessons to some of these who pushed their luck.

But two Meetings a week was just too much. I saw that some speakers were more enamored of their own voices than they were of the Will of God, and some had limited perspectives that I doubt stemmed from the principles of God or Jesus. In addition, I do not believe in coercing children to follow the religious beliefs of their elders. If the religion is sound, the children will in due course perceive its merit and join of their own volition; if not, then it should not be forced. About half the students at Westtown were not Quakers, so their attendance at Meetings represented no special benefit for them, as I see it. For my own children, I have neither required nor denied religion; the choice is theirs.

In addition, I did not believe in God, except perhaps as man's notion of the ideal, so there seemed to be little point in sitting silently in quest of some message from the nonexistent. When I learned about Christmas I was told that Santa Claus (Father Christmas in England) was a jolly fat man in a red suit who traveled the entire world in one evening, dropped down the chimneys, and delivered presents to children. I had a rational mind, despite the evidence of my early schooling, and tried always to think things through fairly, exactly as I am doing here. I concluded that the legend of Santa Claus could not stand logical scrutiny, and never believed in him as other than a comic character. Thereafter I was presented with the concept of God: an old white man with a very long white beard who wore elegant robes and sat in a throne high above the clouds, and who looked down on mankind and required its worship. My mind traveled the same course as it had with the concept of Santa Claus, and came to the same conclusion. I never believed in that kind of God. Since it became evident to me that many people did believe, or professed to believe, and that organized religion was dedicated to this belief, I rejected it from the outset. I have never had occasion to change my mind. I think G. B. Shaw, the playwright, said it best: "Beware of the man whose god is in the skies." That's from "The Revolutionist's Handbook," an appendix to the play *Man and Superman.* I was introduced to that play indirectly at Westtown; we were required to study *Saint Joan,* but *Man and Superman* was also in the book, and I have always been as curious about what the teachers don't teach as about what they do, so I read it on my own. I have been glad ever since that I did.

The God of the Quakers is not in the sky, it is in the heart, where it belongs, called the "Inner Light," but my disbelief was firmly established long before I learned of that. I believe that a person's religion should be integral to his everyday existence, and that he should conduct his every moment of life as if God is watching him, and this is how I try to conduct my own life. To me, there is no God, so he cannot be watching, but *I* am watching, and my standards are a good deal stricter than those I see governing the majority of those who profess to believe in God. I need no formal worship, no Sunday church or Meeting; my life *is* my religion. As Shaw also said: "What a man believes may be ascertained, not from his creed, but from the assumptions on which he habitually acts." So I endorse much of Quakerism, but have no formal participation. Richard Nixon, whom I regard as our nation's first criminal president, professed to be a Quaker; obviously he was something else.

My attitude of the time can perhaps best be shown by this: One day, as a friend and I were leaving Meeting, a teacher, Master Charlie, called us aside. He took us to an office, and there he said: "Chess is a fine game. *But not during Meeting.*" Then he dismissed us. There was no punishment, but the point had been made, and I never did it again.

Our class of '52 was an exceptionally able one, with the best and brightest in just about every pursuit. But it was dominated by a clique whose members hardly deigned to associate with garden-variety folk. Recently I saw the movie *Revolt of the Nerds,* and I felt the déjà vu: I had had a nerd's-eye view of school at Westtown. I have observed the syndrome elsewhere. As a general rule, I prefer not to associate with cliques; I just don't feel comfortable with the "We are better than you" attitude. I doubt that many of those clique members have excelled my performance in life; I take pleasure in having demonstrated my ability to succeed when arbitrary distinctions are blunted, and the raw essence of ability and determination comes to the fore.

We nerds had our fun, though. Once when I heard the song "Hark, the Herald Angels sing" I asked my friend Stuart Baker (his father was Phil Baker, a comic of the day) how it would be if we adapted the song to our purpose. We could change the last word to "shout," for example. He got on it, and soon we had developed a song that spread through the school:

> *Hark the Herald Angels shout:*
> *Ten more days till we get out!*
> *Ten more days till we are free*
> *From this penitentiary!*
> *Joyful all ye suckers rise*
> *Throw your notebooks to the skies!*
> *Scream and screech in jubilee*
> *Glad at last we'll soon be free!*

And a repeat of the first two lines. For all I know, that song may still haunt the hallowed halls of Westtown, as the time of holidays approaches. The number of the days changes as appropriate, of course; the song is good for any season. At least it's printable; the one we developed after I saw an anatomical illustration with the "anal canal" labeled isn't, for the most part. "And you'll always know your neighbor, you'll always always know your pal, if you've ever navigated on the Anal Canal." Then, as now, there was a great deal of humor directed at the homosexual element of society. Perhaps the real mark of our success came when I heard Master Charlie singing "Hark the Herald angels song: ten more days and they'll all be gone!"

There are a couple other events I'd like to mention. As I said, our class, clique and all, was a powerful one, forging through the school like a massive wave. When we were eleventh-graders—known as First Class in the nomenclature of the school—we managed to tease the seniors. When there was an assembly, the normal course was for the seniors to be released first, and then the others. This time the student in charge, who was a senior with a sense of humor, solemnly announced, "First Class!" and we charged out, leaving the seniors gaping.

But another matter went the other way. Each year would come the senior-school baseball game, and normally the seniors won it. But this year the game was close. The seniors scored two early runs, and we, the school, scored one. There it remained for about five innings. In the sixth inning the seniors made no score, but when the school came up it tore loose and made hit after hit. The score was tied, and then the school went ahead—and kept scoring. The seniors were unable even to get the side out, to complete the inning. When the score was 5–2 in favor of the school, the coach, who favored the seniors, called the game because of darkness, reverted the score to the last complete inning, and chalked up a win for the seniors, 2–1. So it went down in the record book that way, but of course it wasn't true. I haven't had a lot of interest in baseball since.

So I graduated from Westtown, but not with any great flair, and under my picture in the yearbook there were no credits. I was a nonentity, and the education I received there was not necessarily the one the school believed it gave me. It was a good school; I just had to travel my own course.

5.

DEATH

I had received a terrible shock with the nightmare of my mother's death. While at Westtown I received another, which was to have consequences as far-reaching.

My sister was not the only relative of mine at Westtown. Actually, all Quakers are said to be related; this may be an exaggeration, but perhaps not much of one. Other members of my class indulged in a treasure hunt of family connections, and about half my class turned out to be related to each other in some devious fashion. Eventually the Jacob family was tied in to this, so I was related too. It didn't matter; I was still pretty much nonexistent. Though I was growing, proceeding from the sixty-inch height and 100 pounds that were my final measurements as I concluded ninth grade, until when I graduated I was about sixty-eight inches and perhaps 135 pounds, I remained pretty much a loss in my own estimation. But others of my family were not. Two older cousins had attended Westtown, one of whom was there as a senior when I was in tenth grade, and a younger one was a year behind me. This was Teddy Jacob, the closest of my cousins in age, size, and compatibility, but a world apart in other respects.

Teddy was a good student, consistently. He was sociable, always in the middle of the throng, well liked by others. I remember seeing a ninth-grade squashing match, in which five boys were on a bench, one bracing his feet at each end and pushing inward, the remaining three trying to survive, seeing which would be the last to be forced out. Teddy was in the center, red-faced, laughing, being squashed and loving it. That was the way of him. He was from a relatively wealthy family, so that he had whatever he needed, and he was a nice boy. The contrast between the two of us was stark: Teddy had everything to live for, while I had little.

Then Teddy got sick. It was a rare form of bone cancer. He wound up in the hospital. They told us that the illness was serious, but that he would recover and return to school; that he was keeping up with his assignments so as not to be too far behind. But the time dragged on, and he did not return.

Then he died. I was stunned; at first I could not believe it. They had told us he was getting better! I dreamed that it had been a false alarm, that they had thought he would die, but he survived, and thought that he would never walk again, but he did. But the adults, once again, had seen fit to lie to children. They had known from the outset that it was terminal; in fact the doctors had predicted that he would be dead in two weeks. He actually survived six months, but the end was the same. Teddy was gone.

The shock was terrible, and the lie made it worse. I had had no chance to prepare. But worst was this: It seemed to be that if God (I use him as a convenient fiction) had had to choose between two boys, having to save one and eliminate the other, he should logically have saved Teddy and thrown me away. I could see no reason why he had chosen as he had. Surely this was a miscarriage of fate!

I was sixteen, Teddy fifteen, when he died in 1950. But these events do not occur in isolation. Teddy's family was shattered by the blow, and his little sister, Dotsy Jacob, was especially affected. To try to ease the burden on her somewhat, they invited me to visit, for I was the closet male relative in age. I did visit, and Dotsy and I got along famously. She was a wonderful girl, with blond hair extending almost to her waist, generally cheerful and lovely and expressive. I had never gotten along well with my own sister, who also had long yellow hair; in fact so deep was my social aversion to girls of that hair color that in later years, when I entered the romantic arena, I had no such interest in any light-haired girl. But Dotsy was different, and she became for me the kind of sister I had not had. I loved her in this way, and now, decades later, I remember her with especial fondness as the perfect little sister. To what extent she accepted me as a brother I don't know, but certainly she enjoyed being with me. So, in the sense that Dotsy needed a brother in lieu of the one she had lost, it was good. It is ironic that, a quarter century later, when I met Dotsy and her children at a Westtown reunion, discovering that her hair had metamorphosed to short and brown in adulthood, and reminisced in one of my monthly family letters about the love I felt for her, my sister telephoned my wife with consolation. Apparently she felt that such love could not be other than suspect.

But I was highly conscious of the fact that I stood only in lieu of her brother, and I felt that I was in a sense usurping the life that properly should have been his. I slept in his room, with his possessions about me, bespeaking his interests, and I felt guilty. The experience made me believe, as I wrote in a diary of the time, that I had a soul, for I felt it hurting. It was bad enough that Teddy had been denied his good life; it was worse that I assume it by default. And so I had to try to distance myself from it, to ease the wrongness. My first trip to Florida was at the behest of Teddy's family; Dotsy and I got caught by a Portuguese man-of-war, a stinging jellyfish, and traced sand on the floor of the house trailer in our agony. That miserable experience has, by the alchemy of the larger situation, become another fond memory. Teddy's father let me know that if I ever needed financial help for college, it was there, but I never asked for it, again because of the wrongness. I had taken too much of Teddy's life already. And so my life separated from that of that family, and I deeply regret that, for it was in certain critical respects the very kind of family I had always longed for. And I could not even explain to them; the wrongness was at once too compelling and too nebulous. It still hurts me today; I wish I had been better equipped to manage.

This death, and the emotional complications of it, worked like another kind of cancer within me. My roommate of the time, Ronald Bodkin, says that I never spoke of it then, so that he was not aware of it. That's why I liken it to a cancer: It did not devastate me immediately, it spread slowly out from a hidden nucleus, as I labored to somehow come to terms with the unacceptable. I lived, in lieu of another; a close-knit family had been devastated, while my fragmented family had not been. What earthly purpose could God have had to provoke such mischief? It seemed increasingly that I could not simply let it rest there; since I could not undo the damage, I had instead to prove that in some devious way the decision had been justified. This has become one of the subtle guiding principles of my life. I am not here merely to feed my face and procreate my genes; I must prove myself in some more fundamental manner. Now, through the medium of my writing, I am trying to do this: to make of the world a better place than it would otherwise have been, to bring what small comfort I can to others who suffer as Teddy's family did. I wrote a novel in which Death was the protagonist (and Teddy was a character), *On a Pale Horse,* trying to make death less of a specter to others. I shall be doing other things. What success I may have I may never really know, but I am trying. I owe it to the life that was lost. The immediate awareness of death has never left me; clinically I'm sure that is called depression, but I believe there is more to it than the clinic. I don't believe in life after death, however convenient I may find it in fantasy, but if there should be such a thing, I hope that Teddy is looking on with the satisfaction that I am doing what he might have done.

There was a more immediate consequence. As I mulled the brutal reality of death, I came to the conclusion that I did not like it. Surely it is a necessary thing, and I can appreciate that intellectually, but emotionally I am appalled by it. So I decided that I would not contribute to it any more than I had to. Not instantly, but in the course of the next three years, I became a vegetarian. This has no religious or dietary basis; it is simply the fact that animals must die for men to eat their meat, and I am prepared neither to kill nor to have another person kill for me. If I consume the flesh, I am responsible. This proscription is not total; I do kill mosquitoes, stinging flies, parasites, and the like, and if an animal attacks me, or my family or my possessions, it will be in danger for its life. But I regard those as special situations. I value the life of beneficial insects and animals, and have taught that value to my children, without requiring them to follow in my footsteps. We do not serve meat in our home, but my daughters know they are free to get it elsewhere if they choose; my attitude in this is the same as it is with respect to religion. Children must be free to make their own important decisions.

And so I am the vegetarian writer, and this is why. It has nothing to do with faddism or show; it is integral to my philosophy. I do not urge it on other people, and I prefer that others not try to talk their kind of "sense" to me about the supposed nutritional benefits of meat. I can become quite cutting about the nature of what *they* eat, when pressed.

6.

GODDARD

I had not planned to go on to college, but both school and family wanted me to go. One day I received a letter from Goddard College, in Vermont, notifying me of a tuition reduction, based on need, of eight hundred dollars. That left, as I recall, only about three hundred dollars to make up, and my family could swing that. I appreciated the offer, and became more interested. Goddard turned out to be a remarkable institution, perhaps the most liberal in the country at that time (there was one called Black Mountain, but it was defunct) with no required subjects and no grades given. It seemed that a student went there simply to learn. I liked that. It meant that the tyranny of required languages that had devastated my high school scholastics would be absent. Also, I felt that I needed more time and experience in the social sense, and that this was more important than either the scholastic aspect or the fact of a college degree. I reached puberty at age eighteen, which is about as late as it happens, and had no real experience with girls in the social sense. So I applied to Goddard, and was accepted, and my course was set.

In the summer between Westtown and Goddard my parents divorced. They feared it would be a shock to me, but it hardly made a difference; I had suffered that particular shock a decade before, and this was merely the legal recognition. I feel that the divorce was the best thing for them, as they could not get along with each other, and now did not have to. My father remarried, and that was it. I can't say I like divorce, but not because of any moral scruple; it is because I know firsthand that it represents a failure of a marriage, and that failure can be hell on the children. Emotionally, I had become pretty much independent of my parents, and that process was to continue in college; they had their lives, I had mine.

My life developed a new and positive aspect that summer. My great-aunt Louisa gave me a book for my graduation from Westtown, Peterson's *A Field Guide to the Birds*. Until that point, about the only bird I could identify by sight was the cardinal, because it was all red. (There's one even redder, the summer tanager, in Florida, though.) I used that book to identify the birds of our region of the Green Mountains, and in that summer I learned about fifty birds, from ruby-throated hummingbird to the huge pileated woodpecker. It was a wonderful discovery, and I have been aware of birds ever since, and can still identify the ones I learned then at a glance. But few others.

Goddard was near the capital of Vermont, Montpelier, about fifty miles from the Canadian border. It was small, with perhaps seventy-five students in all. It was housed in a converted farm; the president's office was in one of the old silos, and the main theater was called the Haybarn, because that was what it had been. It was a four-year, liberal arts institution, and I think it was the best place I was ever at, except perhaps Rose Valley. Tanis Fletcher came there, too, making this the third school we shared; sometimes I wonder whether these schools had the impact on her they did on me.

Goddard was very like paradise to me from the outset. The older students were friendly and helpful; there was no initiation, no social segregation. The instructors were addressed by their first names. The college president was Tim Pitkin, known as Tim. Students wore blue jeans. Classes were conducted by the discussion method, with the instructor leading but not dominating. Meals were in the cafeteria, and were a delight for me, for I had a huge appetite, the largest I have known among students. Perhaps this was because I was still growing; I did not achieve my full height of just under seventy-one inches until age twenty. So I would load up my tray, eat everything, and go back for seconds. I could not have asked for a more delightful situation.

Yet I suppose problems could arise even in the real (that is, mythical) paradise. There are pitfalls to complete security and complete freedom. I had come from the restrictive situation of Westtown, where there was an invisible but quite definite line drawn across the center of the campus, passing through the main building, with the boys on one side and the girls on the other, and an unexcused crossing of that line could result in immediate expulsion. Here boys and girls associated freely, and on weekends there would be open houses so that opposite sexes could visit in the rooms. My roommate, Joel Fedder, was two or three years older than I, a great guy, but he wanted to have a room of his own. Later, when I got up one morning and stepped into the hall, I almost collided with his girl friend, who was leaving. Then I realized why he had wanted his own room. I moved in with a classmate, Dick Weissman, who happened to be the later Ping-Pong champion of the state. I was a good player, and I played a lot at Goddard, but I simply was not in his league. When we organized a college Ping-Pong team, and played other institutions in the state, he was our number-one player, and I was number three; he won all of his matches, and I won two of three of mine.

My tuition and board were paid for, but I had very little spending money. I could scrape together money for a science fiction magazine, but not enough for shoes. No problem; I simply went barefoot. The school was so informal that it didn't matter; I attended meals and classes and everything else that way. My feet got dirty, which bothered some people, but contrary to suspicions, they didn't smell. It is the foot that is stifled in socks and shoes that gets sweaty and smelly, not the one that is open to the air. Thus the title of this Part: bare feet don't stink, and neither does an open, honest lifestyle. I have generally tried to be myself, openly, and those who find that to be naive or uncouth have their values inverted.

For three semesters I was barefoot; then my circumstances improved a bit and I returned to shoes. Today I am older and more conservative in my person though not my philosophy; I wear thong sandals instead of bare feet. They still get dirty, and still don't stink.

I was introduced to a cute little girl. Her name was Bunny Leder, and she stood just five feet tall. I liked her, and it was my first such social interaction wherein there was some response on the part of the girl. But it was her notion to have a number of boyfriends, so that she could take turns, an hour with one, then an hour with another. She was attractive enough so that there were boys available for this, but I, inexperienced at this sort of thing, was a bad sport and couldn't handle it. So whatever there was between us, which was mainly a kiss—she was the first to kiss me, woman to man, and I value that—was no more, and we went our separate ways. I associated thereafter with another girl, Barbara Baller, but she seemed blonde, and that meant that I never had any romantic interest in her. Actually, she had bleached her hair, and was growing it out; I even painted a picture of her with her hair half-brown, half-light, and didn't catch on. She liked science fiction, and art, as I did, and we had many common interests; we called it our "plutonic friendship" as in platonic with a planetary slant. We were able to discuss any topic together, sex not excluded, but it did not exist between us. Some people say that true friendship is impossible between man and woman; I believe it is possible, as in this case, when the sexual element is blocked out. One may wonder how such a small matter, that of apparent hair color, could determine my preference for romance; the answer seems to be that once I come to a conclusion, such as that no girl resembling my sister is suitable for romance, it is binding. I am girt about with such conclusions, and they are not jokes. Harlan Ellison termed me a "strange" man; this was intended as a compliment, and I suspect it is accurate. I really am not quite like other writers, or like other people. Or perhaps I am, only the others don't recognize the foibles that distinguish them.

The Goddard community was always a seething caldron of human interaction, with couples making and breaking and one activity following another. There were weekly square dances. I was hauled into the first, liked it, and always participated thereafter. One year we put on a demonstration dance, which was seen before an audience of I think two thousand, and was reviewed in a newspaper as notable for its precision and polish. I may even have donned shoes for that occasion; I don't remember. Most details of college life were governed by the community meeting, in which students and faculty participated on an equal basis and majority vote carried the day; it was a fine education in the political process, for our maelstrom of a microcosm did indeed reflect the nature of politics in the macrocosm.

There was a little clockhouse in the center of the campus, and the clock would bong the hour. One morning it malfunctioned; I counted something like 112 bongs. Another student went in and fixed it. Later when I commented on the number of bongs, he said "No, it was only forty-nine."

"But I counted one hundred and twelve!" I protested.

"No, only forty-nine," he said with quiet assurance.

Any observer would have concluded that I was the wild exaggerator, and he the one who had actually counted. That experience has remained with me as another lesson: Beware of appearances. The person who seems reasonable may nevertheless be wrong.

Goddard was always on a tight budget, and we had work assignments to help out. One semester I was on the noon dish crew. It had three people, while the evening dish crew had four. I maintained that we had as big a load as did the evening crew, and deserved another crew member. But I was unable to make my point, because we were finishing just as fast with three as they were with four. The truth was that we had one crew member who was so facile with his hands that he did the work of two people. His name was Archie Shepp. Years later I became aware of him again; he was making his name as a musician. I bought one of his records, but it really wasn't my type of music. I term it "squiggle music" because it seems to my uneducated ear like a series of musical squiggles. But perhaps my writing seems similar to his perception.

Every winter, during the months of January and February, the college shut down and the students went out for work term. We had to find jobs for those two months, and then report on them, as part of our total educational experience. It was a good idea, but often impractical in the mundane world. Two-month winter jobs are hard for college undergraduates to come by. Some got jobs by misrepresenting themselves as permanent workers, leaving the employer in the lurch when the time expired. Others refused to do that, and so we could spend more time looking for a job than we had remaining to work when we did get it. The liars thus were apt to wind up with better reports than the honest students, and that irritated me. I worked one winter at a clothing warehouse, and another as an aide at a mental hospital; both organizations were associated with Quaker interests, so that my reference from Westown School helped. I was glad of the experience at the mental hospital, but I could not have endured it for a regular job; the pay was seventy-five cents an hour, and when they were short-handed I worked double shifts, so that my whole day was taken by mental patients, and it was becoming hard to know the distinction between them and me. Mental patients are seldom the raving lunatics pictured by the ignorant; they are regular people who can for one reason or another no longer cope outside. One of my co-workers of the clothing warehouse was a patient at the hospital, unchanged.

I got into drama again, signing up for a class in it. But it turned out that new students were expected mainly to work on scenery and costumes, rather than to get acting parts. This was contrary to my experience at Rose Valley, where everyone worked on everything and the greatest benefit for each student was sought. Here object seemed mainly to put on a good play and to reward those students who had come up through the ranks. Some who were really eager to get dramatic experience were severely disappointed to see the parts going to those who had better appearance or who had been at the school longer. As the years passed, I worked my way up until I had the lead in a play scene we put on, *Lilliom,* but I never respected that system. I was disgusted by the "prima donna" attitude of some, too.

Nevertheless, I profited from the dramatic experience. Once I had trouble making myself heard, and the director finally said, "Speak your lines exactly two point five times louder." I did, and had no trouble thereafter; indeed, since then I have always been able to make myself heard in auditorium or classroom. I also learned to conquer stage fright; one does not need many experiences of forgetting one's lines before an audience to develop a strong aversion to such lapses. I have never really suffered from stage fright since. These two talents—self-possession on the stage, and voice projection—have served me well ever since. I suspect as an actor I was of indifferent quality, but I recommend the experience to others regardless of their talent; the skills are useful in life. It would be nice if college drama classes stressed the development of these skills in ordinary students, rather than catering only to those who wish to be actors. It's the old ends-and-means problem again: The ends are education, but the means of putting on an effective play preempt those ends, and reduce the true benefits. This is especially bad in college sports, where winning preempts the value of playing. The educational institutions should be the first, not the last, to appreciate the true nature of education.

I worked hard to improve my dramatic ability and to facilitate the presentations for the good of the whole, but the director never seemed to notice. Finally at the end of a production for a large (for Goddard terms) audience, he came to tell me that the dramatic director for Dartmouth College had been in the audience, and had complimented me on a fine job. I said that was a left-handed compliment. The director didn't understand; he had thought I would be pleased. Well, this is one of the little things that others have trouble understanding about me, so perhaps it warrants clarification here. I had labored years to please him, the director, apparently without success; now he had told me that someone *else* thought I was okay. I call that left-handed.

I made arrangements with two friends, Robert Pancoast and Malcolm Stewart, and we spent the summer of 1954 at Hilltop Farm, cutting wood for pulp, earning money for the following semester. This turned out to be more work than anticipated; it wasn't that any of us were lazy, but that we had seriously underestimated the problem of hauling wood a mile or so to a staging point so it could be trucked away. But this, too, is the stuff of education. And so, sweating over wood, I came upon my twentieth birthday. The muscle I put on, because of the hard work, brought me to a weight of 155 pounds; since I don't put on fat, I have never matched that since, and now run about ten pounds less.

PART THREE

The Monkey's Paw

1.

LOVE

My third year at Goddard there were a number of new students. One of them was destined to be love for me. My first memory of her was when we had a problem with the dish crew on which I worked, and needed a new person, and my friend Barbara said "Cam is coming in," and pointed her out to me: Carol Ann Marble, whose initials formed CAM. She was at the table, at mealtime, and she had a kerchief over her dark brown hair, and I think she looked up with acknowledgment. She was seventeen, and she stood barely one and a half inches shorter than I. It was a good thing I had grown two inches while in college! That was it; no magic, no revelation that my life had changed.

The process of our coming together was complicated, for I was not aggressive about the pursuit of women, and she was going with a different boy. But we worked together on the dish crew, and in a financial connection, for I was in charge of the Student Loan Fund and she became the community treasurer. So we knew each other, and when her relationship with the other boy broke up, I stepped in.

It is said that a woman takes her time about falling in love, but that a man can plunge head over heels in hours. I am in no position to debate that. Never since my crush on the twelve-year-old girl, nine years before, had I become committed like this—and this time it was real. Our relationship had craggy ups and downs, for she was a conventional girl, the daughter of a Unitarian/Universalist minister, while I was an agnostic doubter. The details fall into the category of too-private-for-this-narrative, yet they would be familiar to anyone who has been in love. I may have tens of thousands of words relating to that romance in my diary of the time; I don't know, as I am writing this volume without reference to any of my diaries. Probably the wordage suffered, because so much of my time was taken up with her, leaving little for any other purpose. We didn't date, for Goddard was too informal for that; we just went together. Before the school year was out, we were engaged to be married. Thus another anomaly of my life: The only formal date I ever had with a girl was in ninth grade at Westtown, arranged by lot (as I recall, her name was Nancy Horsefield, and she was a nice enough girl—just about five years ahead of me in development). I never dated the woman I was to marry.

I'm also the only person I know of who made a conditional proposal. Because I was a vegetarian, and I had seen my parents' marriage sundered in part by their difference over vegetarianism, and because while I was tolerant of the ways of others, I wanted no such barrier between us, I said, approximately: "Understanding the conditions existing, will you marry me?" She said yes without hesitation. Taken aback, I said, "Did you understand the question?" I mean, if she had misheard me, and thought I was saying "What a beautiful night!"—but no, she had heard and understood. She became a vegetarian in order to marry me, and while it is true that I would not have married her had she not done so, it is not true that this was because of any defect in my love for her. I intended my marriage to be permanent.

Goddard, however, was embarking on a change of policy. The faculty felt that things were too free, so there was a crackdown. The dormitory lounges were declared to be closed to members of the opposite sex after ten in the evening. Now this was a community matter, and by the principles under which the community governed itself, long established at the college, there was no place for such a decision by one segment of it, the faculty. This was an arbitrary assumption of power. Therefore the students ignored the matter.

Until one night six of us were in one of the girls-dorm

lounges, three boys and three girls. Cam and I, and another couple, and two others. The other couple was having a problem that had brought them to the verge of breakup, and we were trying to help. At the moment the night watchman spied us, at 10:40 P.M., I was talking in one corner with the girl of the other couple, explaining how Cam and I had had a similar difference, but that the pain of the separation was such that we had found it was really better to work it out. I recommended a similar course to her.

The faculty decided to make an example. The girls were ignored as innocents, but the three boys were called on the carpet. The first said, in effect: "I disagree with your position, and feel you lack authority and have no right to do this, but I know you will screw me if I resist, so I'll just apologize and promise not to do it again." They let him off; he had learned his lesson. The second told them that he disagreed with them, and would not admit to any wrong. They suspended him for a week. I, the third, brought in a tape recorder—and suddenly those faculty members refused to speak, even to present their decision. I found that very interesting. The refusal to be put on accurate record is normally a sign of guilt; I wanted everything public, while the "vice squad" (as it was termed by the students) did not. I was in limbo.

Meanwhile, the community was up in arms. The students held a massive meeting of protest, to which the faculty was invited, at which the faculty policy was roundly condemned. Tim Pitkin's response was a marvel of simplicity: If the suspended student, Charles Gassett (later to be my best man at the wedding) did not depart the campus forthwith, the college would be closed. Faced with that ultimatum, the student body gave way; there was simply too much to lose.

A week or so later I worked out a compromise with the faculty members: they would present their decision in written form, and answer a series of questions for the record. Thus I received notice of my suspension for a week. I left, and Cam joined me. But I was angry, because I did not like seeing such dictatorial methods come to the college. When a Latin American country suffers a coup, and a dictator takes over, the people obey, not because it is right or because they like the man, but because they will be shot if they don't. My acquiescence to this decision was of this nature.

Decades later, when my fortunes had improved and I was in

a position to contribute money the college sorely needed, I did not do so, because the man who had been instrumental in having me suspended had become the college president. Only when he left did I start contributing. Then it was many thousands of dollars, for I felt I owed Goddard a lot. But as I have said here, I do not forgive and forget. The college would have had the money years earlier, had it treated me in a way I deemed fair when I was a student there.

Incidentally, when I visited Goddard twenty years after my graduation, with my daughter Penny, they were amazed at my narration of the grounds for my suspension. Now they had coed dorms, where male and female could room together if they chose.

I retain a deep antipathy to the illicit assumption of power. I never liked dictatorships, and I hated seeing that sort of government come to Goddard. It was contrary to the most basic premise of this institution: freedom to choose and grow. But in fairness I must also say that the faculty was not united behind this new policy. My mentor for writing, Will Hamlin, supported me, and so did one of my prior advisers, John Pierce, who could be trusted to be discreet about private student matters. I named Will Hamlin, with his permission, as a character in my novel *Tarot,* and those interested in further detail on this matter may read the two chapters therein relating to college life. It is fact couched as fiction. I regret that my own parents failed to understand the nature of my stand; it was one more item of alienation. No, they did not condemn me or withdraw their support for me as a person; they simply thought I was wrong. Their comprehension of conscientious objection to war was one thing; their comprehension of their son's stand against an arbitrary assumption of power was another. Evidently they did not see the parallel.

2.

WRITING

Meanwhile, life continued. After six years of art courses, I had assessed my talent as an artist and concluded that I would not make it commercially. I had been balked from a promising mathematical development by being required to take languages instead in high school; now I turned away from art. I decided that for me, words should be a better medium of artistic expression and so I would major in writing. Thus the onset of what in retrospect was the beginning of my career in writing coincided with the onset of my serious romance.

I planned to write science fiction. Back when I was thirteen, perhaps fourteen, I had found an old magazine in my mother's office, *Astounding Science Fiction*. I had started reading it, to pass the time until my mother got out of work, and became entranced by the lead story, "The Equalizer," by Jack Williamson. I was allowed to keep the magazine, as it belonged to nobody, and that marked the onset of my lifetime's fascination with the genre. In fact, I credit science fiction with much of the emotional progress I made thereafter, because it provided me with an array of wonderful other worlds, each of which was better than my own. I lived for each new issue of the magazine. Thus I was conversant with the genre of science fiction, and felt I could be original within it. The college faculty may have looked askance on this, but went along.

I started by entering a contest that *Galaxy* magazine sponsored for amateurs. My story, "Evening," concerned a solution to the problem of population: people were dilated when young, so as to live the subjective equivalent of a lifetime in a few years, then had their instinct of self-preservation nullified so that they soon got tired of it all and took one of the painless suicide pills. Thus the protagonist was an old man, ready to die—at a chronological age of twenty-six.

After a long delay, *Galaxy* returned my story to me with the news that it was one of the top ten finalists, but that they had decided to have no winner of the contest. So much for my first effort! I worked on a novel for my graduating thesis. This was *The Unstilled World,* at ninety-five thousand words the longest thesis in the history of the college. I submitted it to *Astounding Science Fiction* (perhaps it was *Analog*—I don't remember when the title changed), but editor John W. Campbell rejected it. I was dismayed, but I really cannot fault him for this; I had many ideas in it, but the writing was not all that good. It actually took me a number of years to improve to the point where I could sell my work.

My writing was sporadic, because there were other calls on my time, but my submission record shows one or more reports in every year from 1955 on. In 1957 I wrote two short stories, "Firebrand" and "Five Billion," and submitted them to *Galaxy*. The first told of a man who found himself in an ideal situation: a happy world, with a beautiful young woman with flaming red hair named Firebrand who loved him and whom he loved (I knew about that sort of thing, now, though I must confess that Cam's hair was only coppery-tinted, not flaming red)—but suddenly that world crashed about him, and he emerged into a hospital operating room. "Cured!" the demonic doctors exclaimed. It had been an insane dream, and they had thought they had done him a favor by hauling him brutally out of it. The implications for our definitions of sanity are plain enough. The second story concerned aliens who abducted and tested a few earthlings to see how smart they were, because if they were too smart they would represent too great an obstacle to conquest. These earthlings were geniuses, so the aliens, knowing that with normal variation the chances of any folk being that smart in a normal population were one in five billion, gave it up as a bad joke. What they didn't realize, on their sparsely settled planets, was that Earth actually did have five billion people; the very smartest had been selected for the alien testing.

From what I had read of magazine submission procedure, a writer was supposed to send in his story, and if he did not have a report in two weeks, he should send a query. Now my memory fogs on the details, but I believe I waited longer than two weeks, and politely queried, and received no response. Finally, after three *months* I got tougher: I sent a special-delivery, return-receipt letter to the editor, H. L. Gold. That way I knew it would be delivered. The letter itself was mild enough, saying, approximately: "On such-and-such a date I sent two stories, 'Firebrand' and 'Five Billion' to you for consideration for publication by your magazine. After a reasonable interval I queried, but received no response. These stories represent a good deal of effort on my part, regardless of the way they may seem to you, and I cannot afford to send them into a vacuum. Please return them to me."

After another two or three weeks I got my stories back, with an arrogant note by Gold advising me that too many hopeful writers thought they could get rich by the flick of a typewriter, and that now that my entries had cooled off I could see that they were not up to *Galaxy* standards in either content or style, and that I should try to aim only a little higher than I could shoot, and not try to compete with the big boys.

Now this was a good deal more advice than I had sought. There was no apology for holding my stories for an unconscionable length of time without report, or for ignoring my query. All I had done was ask for my stories back. I had not been trying to get rich "by the flick of a typewriter" or to shoot for an impossible market. It seemed to me then, as it does now, that Gold had no call to deliver a lecture of this nature when he was the one at fault. How long would it have taken for me to recover my stories if I had not used heroic measures? The average editor will tell you that it would have made no difference; that editors answer in the time they answer, regardless of queries. That is not so. Today, as a best-selling author, I do get reports in weeks (sometimes in days) rather than in months, and when I query I am promptly answered. But once, before I achieved my present leverage, I experimented: I submitted a novel to a magazine then edited by Ted White, *Amazing Stories*, and let it sit on his convenience without pressing him. That was around 1972, I believe. Today, over a decade later, I still have not received a report. So when editors respond to insistent queries with irritation, I think it likely that it is because they don't like being prodded to do their neglected job.

Actually, Gold was right about the quality of the stories. This is an example of being right but wrong. He was technically right, but wrong in the manner he handled it. He should simply have returned the stories with a rejection slip in the first month, or when queried. He had no business lecturing a writer who would in time prove to be more successful than Gold himself ever was as a writer, trying to discourage those whose potential he failed to recognize. He was an arrogant man who seemed to enjoy stepping on faces. He published a good magazine at first, but as time went on his policies alienated him from a number of good writers. I never showed him any sympathy.

3.

MARRIAGE

I graduated from Goddard with my Bachelor of Arts degree in June 1956. I believe my major was Creative Writing, but in practice it is about the same as a straight liberal arts degree, not very useful for getting employment. Since a free-lance writer is not judged by his college credits but by the quality of his writing, a high-school dropout can become a successful writer while a PhD can fail to sell a thing. But I do feel my college experience helped me as a writer, because it gave me the chance to do one hundred thousand words of it and practice the art of revising and polishing with the input of a professor. At one point I had what amounted to a class of one: just me and the professor, Will Hamlin. I still had a long way to go toward commercial success, but my basic training was there, and I remain grateful for it.

Cam and I had scheduled our wedding for three days after my graduation. But the ceremony was to be in Florida, and this was Vermont. So we packed our best man, Charlie Gassett, and our maid of honor, Teresa Jacob, with us into my Volkswagen bug and zoomed on down the coast. Cam was the shortest person in that little car, at five-nine; my sister was an inch taller, and I half an inch taller than she, and Charlie was six-two. We drove much of the way at seventy miles an hour. (The VW was rated at a top velocity of 68.2 mph, but it had just a bit more oomph than that.) Faces in the big American cars turned in amazement as this jammed midget zoomed past them on the freeways. In those days the foreign import was still a novelty, and the big American companies were saying that they would worry about the foreign threat when it took as much as one percent of the market. That showed the idiocy of complacency.

In memory I quail, now, to think how close we may have come to destroying ourselves in an auto accident on that trip. But we made it, taking turns at driving, refilling the ten-gallon tank every three hours.

I never was overly keen on big public affairs. Today I can handle being guest of honor at fan conventions, and I can't say I really mind being the center of adulatory attention, but I can live without it and generally do. Cam had agreed that the wedding would be small. It would be in her father's church, and he would conduct the ceremony, which I thought was a nice touch.

She was a practical girl, which quality I liked. When we shopped for her engagement ring, I told her that I had scraped together twenty dollars and we could use that. She inspected every ring in the store, and then bought a straight silver one for one dollar, plus ten cents tax. I love to tell that story! Years later, when the silver wore thin, she got another, for perhaps twenty dollars, consisting of five intertwined silver rings that made a puzzle. We have never quarreled about money, because she spends only the minimum required, and I spend less than that. She is smart about managing. My mother says that the first thing she heard from me about my fiancée was her IQ. As I have said, I consider IQ a fallible measure of intelligence, but it's about all we have, so I go for the high end. Cam and I made the same raw score in the college IQ test, but because she was almost three years younger than I, her final score was three points higher. I wanted to have smart children, and I knew that the best way to do that was to marry a smart woman. I like to tell people that I obviously married her for her mind, not her appearance. She accepts that with grace, knowing that I was pretty hopelessly smitten by her appearance, too. So there we were, at the small wedding—and there were two hundred people there, only about half a dozen of whom I knew: Charlie, Teresa, Cam, my mother, and Cam's family. "Well, that was a small wedding," Cam informed me blithely after the fact. How glad I am that we didn't go for a large one! What had happened was that we had the entire membership of her father's church attending. It made perfect sense; it just came as a surprise to me. It seemed as if all two hundred of them shook my hand and told me how lucky I was to marry a girl like her. I wanted to protest, "It wasn't luck! I *chose* her!" But I'm not sure; maybe it was she who chose me. Certainly it seemed that I had the best of the deal; she was the popular daughter of the esteemed minister, while I was just a young vegetarian with no special prospects for success in life. Looking back, it seems to me that the Marbles showed admirable discretion, letting their daughter marry whom she chose despite private misgivings. I expect to do the same for my daughters, though I hope they marry better prospects.

In romantic fiction the story tends to end at the wedding, because you know that the couple lives happily ever after, and that makes for a dull story. This is to reassure my readers that there was a good deal more of my life to come. Indeed, for years I was learning new things about my bride. I remember with fondness the time there was a lightning storm at night, and she dashed out with her flash camera to photograph the lightning, and didn't understand why I found that so funny. Or the time when we were walking together, and she pointed to the side. I looked there—and she abruptly turned and walked into me.

"Wha?" I asked as we recovered from the collision.

"But I signed my turn!" she said. Oh. She also had the tendency to say "Go left," while pointing right. She was the original "Well, *I* knew what I meant!" girl. Our daughters had no trouble perfecting that talent.

We drove back to Vermont at a slightly more leisurely pace, stopping to see the Rainbow Springs in Florida and the Luray Caverns in Virginia. I have always liked caves. It was our honeymoon.

Then mundane reality set in. Cam planned to continue college, and I had to get a paying job. We had rented a five-room unfurnished apartment in Plainfield, Vermont, for thirty dollars a month. It was a lot of money, but it was a nice apartment. Our finances were so tight that I kept a detailed account, and one entry for "income" was when I found a nickel in the gutter. I felt I needed to earn fifty dollars a week to support us. Unfortunately, most available jobs didn't pay that much. Finally

I found one with American News: fifty hours a week, at one dollar an hour. I helped pack the bundles of books and magazines, and then drove the truck on a delivery route in Vermont and New Hampshire to drop the bundles off at the various stores. It was a living.

As summer ended, on a Friday, as I was punching out on the time clock, the supervisor approached me. "Don't come in on Monday," he said. "It was a summer job." It had been represented to me as a permanent job. I was left jobless, with no warning and no severance pay. I have never thought much of American News since.

Not much else offered, but I had to try something, so I tried selling insurance. The manager assured me that I could earn at least fifty dollars a week in commissions. So I took the two-week training course and passed the state exam with the highest score that office had had and went to work selling White Cross accident and health insurance. Fifty dollars a week? It was a struggle to make anything at all! Northern Vermont was a depressed area, and though we had leads and many people were interested in insurance, few had the money to buy it. I also handicapped myself by representing the policies honestly; I would not lie to earn a living. Thus I failed to earn a living.

We were in desperate straits, financially; winter was approaching, and we weren't sure we could afford the money to buy fuel for the oil stove for heat. When the cold came, the car stalled. One night I was determined that I would have it running in the morning, so I went out every hour to start it and run it a little, keeping it ready. But around midnight, when the temperature was down under freezing, perhaps under 0°—I no longer can remember—I thought to try the brake pedal. The pedal went down—and did not come back up. The lubricating oil had congealed. I knew then that I could not safely drive that car, even if I had it running. But if I did not, I would make no sales and earn no money.

How did we manage? Well, my grandfather's legacy provided a trust check of $125 every three months. When we ran out of money, and had none for the rent, I went to talk to the landlord to ask for a delay, promising to catch up when the trust arrived. He agreed, but pointed out that his family lived on the money from the rental. I realized that when the cash was low, we were not the only ones suffering; when we defaulted, the landlord was hungry too. But the check did come, and we did catch up. Also, my mother sent what she could spare, twenty-five dollars a week. Except for that, I don't know what we would have done. Today my finances are more than adequate, and I am eager to repay that debt to my mother, whose finances in retirement are lean, but she refuses "to be a burden" on her children and doesn't want it.

One day when I was out running down leads, I wasn't sure of the next address, so checked it as I drove. As it happened, that was the wrong moment to take my eye off the road; suddenly I was at a curve and almost driving off a six-foot bank. I fought to bring the car under control, stepping on the brakes—and the rear wheels locked and spun the car out of control. At forty miles an hour I sailed off the bank.

I remember wondering, as I saw the ground coming at me, whether I would wake again. That was all; there was no time for fear. Then the car struck the ground, and tossed end around end, and rolled over; it seemed to go on forever, and I wondered desperately when it would ever stop. Then it did stop, and I found my head in the back seat, my legs still in the front seat. This was before seat belts were in vogue. You may be sure that the moment seat belts were available, we installed them, and every member of my family uses then whenever driving. I must have been unconscious for a few seconds, perhaps longer; my right shoulder hurt, but I was otherwise all right.

Passersby stopped and helped me push the car back up to the side of the road, but one rear wheel was locked and it was not drivable. I was given a lift to a filling station, where I phoned my wife, and in due course a friend brought her to pick me up. The doctor checked my shoulder; I could not raise my arm higher than my face. It was just a bruise, and slowly recovered. I was covered by Blue Cross, having not yet changed over to the White Cross I sold, and Blue Cross would not pay because I had not spent the night in a hospital. Thus Blue Cross got stuck with many unnecessary hospital stays, because others knew how to make it pay. Fortunately the bill was only eleven dollars.

The car was another matter. It cost six hundred dollars to get that fixed; the entire roof had caved in six inches when the car rolled over. There had been six-inch clearance over my head. My grandmother sent money for that. Later I thanked her with a poem: "Thee helped us save our little car, when our own funds stretched not so far . . ." There was some money left over from that, and that enabled us to live another month or so.

Having experienced poverty, I concluded that I didn't like it. As the winter intensified, we wished we could go to warm Florida. But we couldn't; we had no money for the journey.

Meanwhile, Cam was pregnant. This was of course good news, apart from our concern about how on earth we would afford a baby. For one thing, it rendered me ineligible for the draft. As a resident alien—I remained a citizen of England—I could not enlist in the American armed forces, but I was subject to the draft. The baby solved that problem, because the U.S. Army didn't want to pay support for families. I was technically a father, and would not be taken.

Then Cam began having problems with the pregnancy. We took her to the hospital, and she miscarried in February 1957. It had been a boy, healthy, just born too early to survive, at about four months. Calculating back, I think he must have been conceived just after I had the auto accident. We were hurt by the loss, of course; we never knew our son, but still the expectation had been dashed. I was abruptly eligible for the draft again.

We considered, and decided that if I had to be drafted, it might as well be soon, since we were barely surviving as it was. Get it out of the way when we could use the security of a guaranteed income, rather than later, when it might cost me a better job. So I wrote to the Draft Board, volunteering to be drafted as early as possible. Generations of Quakers may have rolled in their graves, but it seemed to be the best decision in the circumstances. In those days a person might be granted alternative service in lieu of the draft if military service was contrary to his religious doctrine. Since I had no religion, and only opposed the taking of human life, I had no legal grounds to object. My choice was between the military and prison, and it seemed to me that prison was likely to work greater mischief on my conscience, what with the threat of violence and homosexual rape, than the U.S. Army. So, once again, I took a course that was contrary to the expectations of my family. I can't fault that choice, in retrospect.

4.

ARMY

The army was in some respects like a two-year stint in hell. Even so, it was not as bad as I had feared, and it did secure our finances for that period, and in the end enabled us to get to Florida. I like to tell people that I traveled from Vermont to Florida the hard way, via two years in the army. Well, I did.

Again, I must select only token episodes from the monstrous welter of memories. One was my introduction to basic training: We were loaded on a bus with our ponderous dufflebags of gear, jammed in. When the bus stopped, a helmeted soldier stuck his head in and yelled: "Send your heart home, for your ass belongs to me!" Then we piled out into an evening welter of horror. All around were helmeted men screaming at us. "Move it! Fall in! Cover!" We didn't know what the words meant. One person fell on the ground; as he struggled to rise, a helmeted demon kicked him in the rear. We tried taking off our hats, but only got screamed at worse. Finally we got lined up. To fall in is to assume a formation, one line of recruits standing behind another; to cover is to stand directly behind the man in front of you. It has nothing to do with covering oneself with the hat, for this purpose. Thus, the hard way, we learned. Theoretically recruits are not supposed to be struck; so much for theory. I was struck once, later; I had missed the "eyes front!" order, so was still looking to the right, and the sergeant whammed me on the chest with his helmet liner. The sound was horrendous; I think the whole formation jumped. But we were wearing heavy, padded winter clothing, and a helmet liner is very light; I hardly felt the blow, and certainly was not hurt. I'm sure the sergeant knew that; he had done it for the show of discipline. The U.S. Army is not barbaric, despite the impression it tries to foster.

I knew the only way I would survive basic was to obey orders and keep my mouth shut. I did so, and I got through despite illness. One third of my cycle did not. I was ill with something resembling pneumonia or strep throat—the doctor called it a cross between the two—when we had our final marksmanship testing with the M-1 rifle; even so, I was going for "Expert" until my rifle jammed, and then for "Sharpshooter" until the final target came loose in the wind and I had to fire at what amounted to a waving flag at five hundred yards' distance. Then I got five "Maggie's Drawers" and had to settle for "Marksman," the minimum level. There is no justice in the army. However, that did show me that I would be close to expert with a rifle in real life, when well and with a good rifle and target.

Eating was a problem. The main courses were usually laced with meat, so I didn't touch them. They announced that we were expected to finish eating and be out of the mess in just seven minutes. I was always a slow eater. But I made do. I would always take two of the pint cartons of milk, because milk was healthy and a quart of it could be consumed in a minute, and jammed extra rolls into my pockets for later consumption, and ate as much as I could of the rest in the time I had. They didn't really enforce the seven-minute rule, fortunately. Military food is always criticized, but I found it good enough, and there was generally plenty of it. Once it ran low, and the man in line ahead of me inquired, so the cook put him immediately on KP, and me too, simply because I was there. After a couple of hours I got a sergeant who was going through training in my barracks to intercede, and I got off.

I asked to see a chaplain, because I had a continuing concern. I put "No Pref" in the box instead of "Cath," "Prot," or "Jew" because I belonged to no religion. In due course I was sent to see the Protestant chaplain. I explained to him my concern: that I was willing to undergo military training, but knew that I would be unable to kill a man, even an enemy soldier, because I did not believe in the taking of life. He looked at me and shook his head sadly. "I'm sorry that you don't have more patriotism than that," he said. That was all. To the army, patriotism is defined as the willingness to kill when ordered to do so. I had had an open mind about military chaplains; thereafter I had no use for them.

One day I was reading on my bunk during one of the occasional off-duty hours, and a sergeant told me to get in a line downstairs. We were marched to a classroom where we were instructed in the operation of the furnaces. Thus I became a furnace tender, going from one cellar to another in the unit, keeping them going. We were supposed to get time off after a night of that, so as to be able to catch up on sleep, but that wasn't necessarily honored. Once two of us encountered a broken furnace; there was no way to light it or keep it going. We tried to report to the one in charge. "I didn't ask you for no excuses!" he yelled. "Go and light that furnace." Typical army imperative. So we went and lit a twist of paper, threw it in the furnace, and ran. We reported, "It was burning when we left it," and the man was satisfied. Typical army solution.

When we had the final physical exercises, I washed out on pull-ups and push-ups, as I recall being unable to make the minimum to score, but did all ninety-four squat jumps and a good number of sit-ups, and about one point to the run. My score was something like 211 out of a possible 500, which was decent. My legs and stomach muscles had made up for what my arms lacked. In later life that was to reverse, as I worked up to totals of thirty or more pull-ups and seventy-five Japanese push-ups (not the same, but harder for most people than the regular ones), and down to no squat jumps: bad knees. Overall, I was to be physically fitter in my forties than in my twenties, in this sense. Our unit did very well in those exercises, surprisingly well. We hadn't thought we were *that* good. We realized what had happened when there was a little ceremony to award recognition to the high scorer, and the man from the post read off the name of our fattest recruit, who had been put on KP that day. The cadre had arranged to substitute a ringer, who in the name of that recruit had run up a phenomenal score. The army way.

When I entered the second part of basic, which was training for survey at Fort Sill, Oklahoma, I remembered, and having been utterly degraded once, I stiffened my backbone against it thereafter. The training was easier, being mental rather than physical, but we could be taken from class for stray details, which made it hard to keep up. I helped one of the slower students, explaining what he hadn't understood in class, and that pretty well acquainted me with what I had missed that day, so we both benefited. There was also trouble in the barracks, when a "friend" incited a small, young trainee to challenge me to a fight. I knew that if I accepted, I would lose my chance to be an instructor, for fighting is not tolerated in the military. But if I didn't I would suffer worse harassment than before. So on my twenty-third birthday, the least pleasant of my life, with my bunk dumped and the lad challenging me, I agreed to go outside with him.

"You think I'm afraid of you!" he accused me.

"Yes," I agreed, waiting for him to start it. I was not about to throw the first punch, because I really didn't want to fight; it had to be clear that *he* started it. Then I could legitimately finish it. Others in the barracks were watching from the windows. But he lost his nerve, and didn't make his move. That ended that.

Another day I took a shower and returned to the barracks to discover my entire bunk and footlocker gone. Since I had my wallet locked in my locker, with all the pay I was saving for the rental of an off-post apartment to share with my wife, I was alarmed, and reported it to the corporal in charge. They had locked my bunk in a storeroom, but all was intact. The corporal was annoyed: How had they gotten into the locked storeroom?

One matter I remember with less displeasure now than I had at the time was the matter of tearing up bunks. We slept on double bunks, and I had the top one. Trainees were expected to make their beds perfectly, and there was a daily inspection. If there was any imperfection, the cadre ripped out sheets and blanket and stuffed them into the pillowcase, or tied them in a big knot, and left the mess on the bunk for the trainees to do over when he returned. You would think people would learn rapidly, but it seems I didn't. My bed kept getting torn up. I couldn't see that I was making it wrong. One morning the kid on the bottom bunk—the same one who had tried to fight me—was delayed and could not return in time to make up his bunk, so I made it for him. In the afternoon mine was torn up and his wasn't. I went to my trainee squad leader, so next time he made up my bunk for me. It was torn up again, while his own wasn't. It certainly looked like deliberate harassment. But I'm not sure it was; enforcement of bunk standards was erratic, and I may simply have had a run of back luck. It could be hard to know exactly what the army wanted, in this and other respects. I may have run afoul of a difference in posts: the post where I was taught to make my bunk the army way may have had a slightly different technique than the present one.

I was top man in my survey class, and became a survey instructor. My wife made the arduous drive to Oklahoma—I hate to think of that, now, a young woman traveling so far alone—and joined me there. Thus I was able to move off-post, and to live almost like a human being.

I had labored to become an instructor partly to guarantee my assignment in the States, but it was a decent position on its own merits. I now taught the survey I had learned to new trainees, and regarded it as one of the more positive aspects of the army. After a year I asked for a month's leave, so we could visit my family back East. It was denied; I was too valuable as an instructor to be spared.

I returned from a detail one day to learn that an officer had come and bawled out the academic section for poor performance. An immediate freeze was established on promotions. Now it happened that at that time only one instructor was eligible for promotion: Private Jacob for PFC, Private First Class. I had just completed the requisite time-in-grade, and had done my job so well as to be denied leave, and I needed the pay and allotment increase that promotion would bring. Why had a freeze been established right when it affected only me? So I went to the sergeant major, the ranking sergeant of the full battalion, and explained my concern. He listened, and told me he would check into it. That evening one stripe came down: mine. Apparently by that act I had become a minor battalion legend; no other soldier had had the nerve. But I had only stood on my rights, as I always do. Still, I remember that sergeant major with pleasure; he had damn well done his job.

Trouble came with seeming innocence. There was a drive to sign up soldiers for the U.S. Savings Bond program. Five dollars a month would be subtracted from the pay and put toward a bond, with 2.5% interest. Naturally most soldiers weren't interested, and naturally the army put pressure on. It was said that there was the right way, the wrong way, and the army way, and the army way was whatever was decided on high. I didn't want to participate, because we were just barely making ends meet, and five dollars less would put us behind by that amount. So I exercised my right to say no, and declined. This wasn't basic training anymore; I did have rights.

They put the pressure on. In due course all but two soldiers had capitulated. The other was good at sports, and was perpetually on orders for one sport or another, where he could not be touched. (I, as the Ping-Pong champion of the battery, wanted to play him, but somehow it never came to pass, so we don't know which of us was better there.) But *I* could be touched. The first sergeant called me in and informed me that I would never receive a promotion, a pass, or leave time while I was in the army as long as I didn't sign. He summoned me from teaching survey class and put me on a shoveling detail, promising that the job never would seem right to him until I signed. His threats were true; I never did receive passes or leave (though that was supposed to be at the option of the soldier) or promotion beyond my then rank of PFC. Before I was out, I was ranked by a student I had taught. Still I did not sign.

The campaign intensified. The off-post members of the battery were required to come in for early morning reveille. Thus we had to get up early to go on post and be in formation at 5:30 A.M., then wait around until the regular classroom day began. It was a colossal waste of sleep and time. Evidently the sergeant hoped that others would put pressure on me to capitulate. Well, one did approach me, and he was not a friend, just another instructor. He said, "I know we have to go through all this shit because of you, and I hate it, but as long as I know it's because you won't buy that bond, I'm glad to do it." And so it was; many who had signed under pressure were happy to see that someone else was holding out. When the first sergeant called for me, the corporal in charge of our section made excuses, being unable to pull me from the middle of class or something, protecting me. No one in the academic section pressured me. Once one of my students was required to watch a truck while the driver ate; the driver hadn't returned by the time class was to start, so the student called out to me to ask what he should do. I didn't have class to teach at that hour, so I told him to go, and I would watch the truck for him. Time passed, and the irresponsible driver still didn't return, leaving *me* stuck. One of the office sergeants came by, and laughed when I told him that this wasn't a punishment visited on me by the first sergeant; he didn't believe it. Then the captain in charge of the battery himself came out and talked to me in a reasonable manner about my lack of support for the battery in not signing for the bond; I thanked him for his concern and asked him to send me a relief so I could go and teach my next class. Soon a relief appeared, and that episode was over. But though I appreciated the captain's courtesy, the principle remained: He was allowing his first sergeant to use coercive measures to enforce an improper requirement, so that he, the captain, would look good; I could not yield to that.

When I had had enough, I made a formal complaint against the first sergeant. I charged him with extortion: he was harassing me for improper gain. I happened to know he had a bet with another sergeant that he could get one hundred percent participation in the bond program. The first sergeant huffed and puffed but he had no choice; he had to pass me on up the line, to the captain, who also huffed but had to pass me to the lieutenant colonel in charge of the battalion. For an hour and a half the lieutenant colonel talked to me in a surprisingly friendly manner, while it seems that all the battalion marveled outside; PFC Jacob was doing it again, going where any sensible soldier feared to tread. The minor legend strengthened. But in the end I realized that the colonel would not discipline the sergeant; it wasn't the army way. So I had to give up my quest for justice, because I was not prepared to go over the head of the colonel, who had shown that he understood my position and respected it, even if he was on the other side. I had, at least, made the first sergeant feel my minor power; he well knew what I was telling the colonel. I'm sure he received a private dressing-down.

I was transferred to another battery in that battalion, and the pressure was off. So much for their inability to spare me as an instructor; to get one hundred percent by getting rid of me made me expendable. But my reputation preceded me: I was uncooperative. Thus though I did get some passes and a portion of my leave time (the army had to pay me for about forty days at the end, though, that I had never gotten), I never got beyond PFC. The other holdout had been a grade higher; they eventually found a pretext to bust (demote) him, and he finished a PFC like me. Well, I had been told before I started that "there ain't no justice" in the army. But I had my little innings.

When I saw that there was no pressure in the new outfit, I went in and signed up for that bond. I knew that word would spread at lightspeed back to my original battery, though perhaps the message would not be understood there: Treat a soldier decently, and he may be more cooperative.

The new battery handled meteorology. Thus I learned how to send up weather balloons carrying electronic boxes that monitored atmospheric conditions. It was interesting, and it expanded my horizons. The balloons were about four feet in diameter, as I recall, and we filled them with hydrogen. Yes, they would burn explosively if ignited! But I walked into one bad blunder. I was trained on the job by another PFC, and he forgot to tell me one detail. So when I went out to release my first balloon on a windy day, I simply let it go. To my chagrin the box didn't rise; it swung down and crashed into the ground, ruining it. They had to do the job over, preparing another box and balloon; I had cost the U.S. government perhaps a hundred dollars' worth of equipment. The sergeant in charge explained it to me with a diagram: The wind had carried the balloon to the side, so that it was not straight above me but at about a 45° angle. When I let go the box, the balloon rose slowly—and the box swung down below it to hit the ground. It was back to weed pulling for me.

Later I worked a better transfer: to the staff of the battalion newspaper, the *Observer*. We were an observation battalion, with Survey to emplace the big guns, and Meteorology to help guide their trajectories (atmospheric conditions make a difference), and a Searchlight unit for night work. Now I did articles and cartoons for all the battalion. I honored the suggestion of a sergeant back in Meteorology with a cartoon whose caption read, "What happened to that new sergeant?" and in the background, a man being hauled into the sky by one leg, attached to the string of a monstrous balloon. He also suggested another good one: the notion that all the cold weather we were having was because Alaska had recently been admitted as the forty-ninth state. Maybe, it suggested, we should warm things up again by admitting Hawaii, a warm state. In the Hawaii section was a luscious pair of bare female legs. When a revision in the picture was necessary, the sergeant pleaded, "Keep the legs!" You bet.

In my final week there was a program for several battalions about morale: Why was it that it was so low, so that half the soldiers sent to battle were unable even to fire their rifles against the enemy? I got up. "If they concentrated on teaching soldiers how to fight, instead of on chickenshit, they would have better luck," I said, approximately. That set off quite a round of discussion, perhaps establishing another local legend. I was sure that certain personnel would be after my tail, but by the time they found out who I was (naturally those who knew me did not tell) it was too late: I was out of the army.

My wife got pregnant again in that period, and after a very trying time that had her in the hospital for a month, miscarried again. We paid the first twenty-five dollars; the army paid the remaining eight hundred. It was a difficult period, coinciding as it did with my harassment about the bond, but I have to give credit to the military insurance that prevented it from wiping us out financially.

While with the *Observer* I had a bright idea: I would write a song for Cam, who had had her own ordeals of survival as an army wife. I took the tune from one of the songs I had liked in first grade, and pondered putting new words to it. But right at that time I had a bad scene with a fellow artist on the staff, who had been demeaning others behind their backs. I called him on it, and he was furious, and my mood was so poisoned that I could not work on something as nice as that song was supposed to be. My wife never knew. Maybe it hadn't been a good idea anyway, that song. I had written her occasional poems; she saved the ones she liked.

Let's provide some samples. One was for Valentine's Day, 1958, addressed to CAM—short for CAMera

CAMisole

CAMellia

with the first two crossed out, and the penciled words, "That must be it: a flower"

> *I will not write a*
> *Vasty tome*
> *But plant this Valen*
> *Tiny Pome*
>
> *Should I forget my*
> *Flower's name*
> *'Twould be a chloro*

Phylthy shame

Another that I wrote about this time stemmed from guard duty at the post stockade: long, boring hours in a tower overlooking the compound, with nothing for the mind to do. I don't really like or understand free verse, but I do it on occasion.

Thoughts at the Break of Day

Standing guard as the dawn comes up
I watch the morning cloud formations struggle with the sun
Huge red fingers point into the sky
Sunbeams burst out from behind the black cloud mountains
White radiance curls back the edges, but
They are holding back the fire
A long shape, a submarine in air, fleeing
Disintegrating before the atomic burst of light
And fleece, of course—
Carded across the heavens
The cloud kingdoms retreat
The once almighty misty shapes
Dwindle to little twisted goblins in the sky
The knotted shades of fantasy forget their fascination
Vanquished
As the light of reason vanquishes
The magic of ignorance
So cruel
Now, as the molten brilliance overflows at last
Burning back the black
Bleaching the shapes to inert cotton
Half blinded, I think of you
The gap is wrent, the sun pours through, and it is day
The heat comes out and touches me
The shadows come
The morning shadows
Their long length along the ground
Proving the day has just begun
They will be minus-shadows when I return
When I return to you

The army was not a total loss. It did provide security of income, such as that was, and after my work experience in Vermont I really appreciated that. I did play a lot Ping-Pong, being on orders for it for several weeks as I represented my battery and battalion in doubles play (but for an unfortunate combination of events, I think we would have become doubles post champions), and I obtained my American citizenship there. At the court they assumed it was my wife who was applying, because I was an American soldier in uniform: that led to confusion. In the naturalization ceremony there were fifty people: forty-nine foreign army wives and me. That made the local TV news. It may fairly be said that my life as an American commenced in Lawton, Oklahoma, in the army.

5.

WRITING

Also, while I was in the army, I got moving again on my writing. I wrote a number of short stories and the better part of a novel. In 1958 I submitted seven stories to the science fiction magazines. One of these, "The Demisee," was accepted by *If* magazine, then edited by Damon Knight. Joy! My first sale!

"The Demisee" was about an odd reversal of normal procedure brought about by the pressure of population. It was all right to kill someone accidentally; it was a crime for that person to be brought back to life. Thus the victim was the criminal. A motorist had been racing to catch an orange light and in the process had run over a pedestrian; so far so good, but no dead pedestrian showed up, so they knew they had a demisee: a restored-to-life suspect. But they weren't sure of his identity, so they had a lineup and all, where the killer was supposed to identify the victim. It was a cute story, the kind of play on reality that I enjoy doing.

But Damon wasn't quite satisfied with it, and asked for revision. Eager for the sale, I obliged. He still wasn't satisfied, but said he could probably handle further changes editorially. Then, later, *If* suspended publication, and the story was returned to me. I had lost my first sale.

In a later year I sent the story to a critic for a paid critique. He was Thomas H. Uzzle, of Oklahoma residence, coincidentally. He had formerly been fiction editor of *Collier's Weekly*, and was the author of a book on writing, *Narrative Technique*. He accepted the money but claimed that I was playing a joke on him, as the story was unbelievable. He was a mainstream critic who refused to believe that the conventions of the science fiction genre differed from those of the *Saturday Evening Post*, which he seemed to regard as the ultimate in story quality. There are none so blind as those who will not see; you cannot educate a man who thinks he is an expert. Trying to be fair-minded, I went ahead and took his course in writing, which was run by his wife, Camelia. Part of the promise of this course was the exchange of criticism with another student, each of us to comment on the other's story. But it turned out to be an amateur story they had printed up for the purpose; there was no other party. That I think sums up the nature of the course. The Uzzles meant well, but simply could not handle the more imaginative material I related to. I did learn something useful, though: when analyzing the amateur story and a professional one they recommended, I discovered that the amateur one was full of action without style or characterization, while the pro item was full of style and characterization without action. Neither had the secret of real storytelling! But in perceiving that, I was a step further on my way to success. A writer had to put it *all* together, and that is what I try to do. I am amazed by the number of writers who don't, and by the number of critics who evidently don't comprehend the essentials of compelling fiction. Truly it has been said: those who can, do; those who can't, teach. On occasion I have tried to read the fiction of the *New Yorker* magazine; that is typical of what I mean by inadequate.

Later yet I showed the story to an established genre writer, Lloyd Biggle, Jr., along with the paid critique. He read both and proffered his own, more sensible comment, for free, so that at least I would have something for my money. Mr. Biggle understood the story, of course, but doubted that it was strong enough to sell. Well, since I have discussed it here to this extent, and it never *did* sell, I'll put it in Appendix D: Piers Anthony's first lost sale.

6.

CIVILIAN

So we left the army and settled in Florida in the spring of 1959. I was lucky; I landed a job as a technical writer at an electronics company. The pay started at about $80 a week, compared to the $185 dollars a month I had had in the army, from all pay, allowances, and allotments. It seemed great.

In 1960 we tried to get back into square dancing, as we had enjoyed it so much in college. This didn't work out; the local group seemed more interested in the latest fashions in dances, rather than in doing it for pleasure. There was one other complication: when my wife set out to scrub the floor, she came down with housemaid's knee, which is similar to tennis elbow, and was unable to dance for a time. So I wrote her a little poem to commemorate the event, deliberately incomplete:

> There was a young lady named Cam
> Who got herself into a jam
> She hurted her knee
> On a floor-scrubbing spree
> And now she can't dance worth a

But it wasn't perfect. There were constant office rivalries, and my training in writing didn't count for much when I had to do it to the specification of those who knew little about the proper use of the English language. I became in effect a high-paid file clerk. I objected, laboring to get some real work in, but there was resentment and friction, and in the end I knew I had to leave.

My leaving was traumatic. Cam was pregnant again, and having difficulty again, so that she was in and out of the hospital and had to spend much of her time in bed. I handled the meals, dishes, laundry, shopping, and such. Our marriage has always been egalitarian: Each of us does what is necessary, depending on preference and circumstance. Thus Cam does most of the carpentry and I have on occasion done most of the traditionally female chores. I arranged to come to work early so that I could have time to go home at noon and give her lunch, then back to work for the afternoon. In addition I had a mysterious malady, which at first seemed like a relapse of the mononucleosis I had had, but that continued for months. It left me tired all the time. And a bad episode at work had me depressed. Thus I had problems on three fronts.

The episode at work was this: I was abruptly called in to the office of my immediate superior and informed that my performance was below par and that I was in imminent peril of being fired. As a specific example of my neglect, he described a report I had been supposed to do and had not. Now it was true that I had been supposed to do that report—but I had been told by the co-worker who governed my assignments to set it aside, because it was more important that I catch up on a mountain of filing that had developed. Though the report represented the kind of work I was supposed to be doing, and wanted to do, and the filing was the kind I was trying to avoid, I obeyed. Then that same party put in the complaint about my neglecting the report.

No, this was not intentional malice. The other party, as I had been privately warned by another co-worker, was not about to teach me how to do his job, because that would imperil his own job security, especially if I did it better. So he found reasons to have me do anything but that job. I don't believe this was a conscious bias on his part; it was just what made sense to him, given his orientation. We got along perfectly, as long as I was file clerking. So naturally he told me not to do the report, and then forgot he had told me. And the superiors were not paying attention. When asked about the missing report, he naturally blamed it on me. When I hauled him in and confronted him directly, he admitted it. It had been a mistake fostered by his bias. But the experience shook me severely, because I realized that I was vulnerable to being blamed and possibly fired because of bias and error; the superior had not bothered to verify the facts before condemning me. He was a nice enough person, but as an executive I regard him as a fine carpenter. I could not afford to remain in such a situation, and I knew I would have to leave that job.

In retrospect I conclude that it was more than that. I had operated on the assumption that my job was secure as long as I did my work competently. Now I understood that this was not the case. I could be fired because of factors unrelated to my performance. It was a kind of repeat of my problem in the army, where my decision to stand on my rights cost me my position and promotion. It was wrong, in the army and in the company, but this world is not governed by right. Easy to say—but I had been secure in the belief that justice would prevail, and the loss of that belief was like the separation of my parents, years before. I suffered personal complications. I developed headaches when proofreading; my resistance to illness decreased so that for the first time I was out of work owing to illness; I felt a lump in my throat that persisted for days at a time; and there was the fatigue, so that I could not remain on my feet for more than a few minutes without becoming tired. My wife's complications of pregnancy, and my malady itself contributed in a kind of feedback, making it worse. All three factors seemed to be headed for culmination in May 1962, and it was like the approach of the end of the world.

May came—and on one day I lost my job, received the verdict of the internist who was testing me for my complaint that it was all in my mind, and my wife lost her third baby. It was a girl, who lived for one hour before expiring. It was the worst single day of my life I can recall.

Actually, all three things were ongoing, and none were surprises, so the coincidence of their fruition together made no difference. I had prepared as well as I could. I had, with the company's knowledge and permission, shopped for another job, and had one lined up. It was with the Florida Department of Welfare as a state social worker. I have always been a liberal, which means that I am sensitive to the plight of the unfortunate, and wish to help. Now I would help directly. The pay and benefits were much less than they had been at the company, but we could manage, in part because we had no baby to raise. (In fact, the deduction we got for the third dependent—the one-hour baby—nicely covered whatever expenses the company insurance hadn't.) The effort was positive, and it was like being reborn; now I could do some good for others instead of merely for myself.

The loss of our third baby was a deep disappointment. We understood that a woman could lose one, then carry others; it happened. To lose two was more serious, and to lose three meant that she probably would not be able to carry any to term. Thus we faced the specter of being forever childless. Adoption? We were willing, but we knew better than even to apply at an agency. I was a vegetarian, an agnostic, a hopeful but unsuccessful science fiction writer, suffering from neurasthenia (imaginary illness), and was earning a minimal wage; no way we would be permitted to adopt. The fact that we might make genuinely caring parents counted for nothing. Had I been a churchgoing meat eater with a better job and no literary aspirations, adoption might have been easy enough.

The imaginary illness was a problem in itself. I was sure it was real, and had a physical origin, but could not convince the doctors of that. My insurance ridered me for all mental diseases. After ten years of it, I finally had a more thorough physical examination by a more sensitive doctor, and he diagnosed it: diabetes. The early doctors had never given me a five-hour blood-sugar test, which was what was required to diagnose it. The illness had never been in my mind, though surely triggered by emotional factors. Adult-onset, or Type II diabetes, is a nonlethal variant that is largely asymptomatic other than the fatigue caused by the lack of sugar energy reaching the muscles; there is no spillage of suger into the urine. The doctors had branded me a mental case because of their own inability to diagnose one of the more common maladies of our time. Today my insurance surcharges me heftily for diabetes, being unable or unwilling to distinguish between the mild Type II and the devastating Type I, but it's an improvement. For one thing, now I have a name for it, and know the limits; I don't have to worry whether it will kill me before the doctors stop calling it imaginary.

But the social work didn't work out either. I had a caseload of about 150 families, and it was impossible to keep up with them all properly; there simply was not time enough in the day. In addition, much of my work consisted of explaining to needy applicants that they did not qualify for help. In one case I had to verify a twenty-year local residence two different ways to prove the family qualified, checking records and the stubs of old electric bills and such. Since then, the abusive residency requirement has been thrown out by the Supreme Court, but that was the sort of thing I had to struggle with. Thus most of my effort was going to wrestle with the requirements of the bureaucracy, rather than helping people. I suspect a similar alchemy transforms animal lovers into wholesale killers of pets, as with the SPCA. It is an unpleasantly eye-opening process. So in three months I knew that this position was not for me. But what was I to do? Our family had to have an income.

I discussed it with my wife, and she came up with a radical notion: she could go to work, to earn our living, while I stayed home for a year and tried to realize my longtime dream of becoming a writer. This sounds simple; she had worked on and off before, when the complications of pregnancy did not prevent. But it was complicated psychologically. Within the family we shared the work as convenient, but when I married, I had undertaken to support my wife, and I could not lightly abandon that commitment. It was not that I had any competitive urge that required her to be in the home while I was the breadwinner; she was welcome to work. But to depend totally on her work for our livelihood—that seemed chancy at best. Yet the dream—ah, the dream! *Could* I do it, could I at last achieve the breakthrough to professional publication in the field of my devotion?

7.

WRITING

We tried it. My wife went out in quest of a job, and that was no easy thing; it took several months, and our savings dwindled, and it looked as though I would have to abort my effort and return to the job market. She got rejected by one employer for being overqualified. But finally she did get work, winding up at the local newspaper, the St. Petersburg *Times*, and we were secure.

The deal was that I would try writing for one full year. If in that period I did not make the breakthrough, then I would accept the fact that I was not destined to achieve that dream, and I would give it up and concentrate on earning the best conventional living I could. As I learned later, my fifth cousin, Charles Richard Jacob, had tried something similar, had failed, and thereafter become an executive at Sears, Roebuck, doing very well for himself. We have corresponded for years.

So I was, for the first time since my thesis-semester in college, writing full time. I had been writing all along, part time, submitting material to the magazines and getting it rejected. In 1961 I had marketed my major short story, "A Piece of Cake" and my fifteen-thousand-word novelette *Omnivore*. As it turned out, both these pieces were of publishable level, though rejected when written; Ted White, then assistant editor at the

Magazine of Fantasy and Science Fiction (hereafter referred to as *F&SF*) gave it an "A" report, but editor Avram Davidson disagreed and bounced it. Later I expanded each of these two pieces to novel length, and then both were published. But that took time; I knew I had good stuff, but the editors didn't.

Now, as of October 1962, I was writing seriously. In the eight preceding years I had submitted sixteen pieces of fiction; in that one writing year I submitted fourteen, and I sent out each item more often. If volume and perseverance could do it, I was going to do it.

My first piece of that year was "Southern Approach," about a highway bypass that had been planned but not constructed—only the protagonist, via a magical error, got on it and found a superior route home. This eliminated the horrible daily struggle with traffic and revitalized his marriage. No sale.

My second was "Buckwheat Jury," in which a man committed a crime in a field of buckwheat on a colony planet, and the local bumpkins let him go because they hadn't caught him in the mood that had caused him to commit the crime. But then, elsewhere, when he set out to commit a similar crime, the mood came on him—and he died. The bumpkins had known what they were doing after all. No sale.

The third was "Possible to Rue," about a widower who wanted to get his bright little boy a nice pet. But everything the lad chose turned out to be fanciful: a flying horse, a unicorn, a zebra (obviously there is no such thing as a prison-striped horse!) and so on. The fantasy graded by stages into reality, making it fanciful when they looked it up in the big encyclopedia. The words of the title refer directly to the volume in which the final choice of the story was to fall: a roc bird, in POSSIBLE to RUE, as well as to the likely consequence of starting in with birds the same way the boy had done with equines. In due course all birds would be found to be fanciful, too.

F&SF bounced it. I thought I might try it on a British fantasy magazine, but lacked contacts, so meanwhile I tried it on another American market, just to keep it in circulation. And within ten days, in November 1962, I had notice of its acceptance by Fantastic Stories Magazine. I had made my first professional sale!

The editor was Cele Goldsmith, who was fast and good. She later won an award for the improvement in the magazines she edited. She published the first stories by a number of writers

who were later to become better known, such as Roger Zelazny—
and Piers Anthony. The pay was only twenty dollars, which
came to one-and-a-half cents a word, but the significance extended far beyond the money. *I had made it!*

This story, and most of my others, can be found in my
collection *Anthonology*, for those who are interested in the actual
items that launched my career as a writer. They may be of
greater interest as historical markers than as literature.

Buoyed by that success, I continued with a long science
fiction poem, "Strange is the Measure." No sale, though *Galaxy*
said it might have taken it had it been shorter. Then "The
Toaster," and no sale, though that can be found in my collection. So my initial success was not to be followed by further
successes; perhaps it had been a fluke. My animation flagged.
Looking back, it seems to me that just as a long-distance runner
cannot run twenty-six miles on the first day, and has to build
up to it, so also a writer cannot sustain a torrid writing pace at
the outset. He has to develop performance muscles, as it were,
and to learn to cope with the dreadest of all literary maladies,
writer's block. I found myself not accomplishing much, and
wondered why.

I had been working on an index of science fiction book
reviews. As my stories were rejected and my inspiration wore
thin, I spent more time on that, hoping that I could get it
published and so have a useful reference volume to my name.
Indexing is a tedious business, and many, many hours went
into it—hours I now think should have gone to my fictive
effort. That index had a sad history. I could find no market for
it, until years later a fan, Phyrne Bacon, took it in hand and
found a publisher: H. W. Hall at Texas A&M University. I
signed a contract turning the rights to the index over to Mr.
Hall so that he could update it (for the passage of time was
dating it) and publish it. There was no money involved; this
was a labor primarily of love on my part, assisted by a number
of fans such as Ed Meskys and Buck Coulson and Dick Tiedman,
who indexed magazines I didn't have. But when the index was
published, no credit was given to any of us. I queried, and
received a call from Hall: He had set my index aside and
compiled a similar one of his own, which he had sold to Gale
Research Company. I bought a copy of the published index for
forty-five dollars and checked it against my own: true, his was
different, omitting entries I had made, though it covered a

wider range of publications. It was indeed his own work. But there was a smell about this business that I found distasteful; he did have the right to publish (and therefore *not* to publish, or allow to be published) mine, but I consider it unethical. A great deal of my time and effort had been rather cavalierly thrown away. Having no legal recourse, I let the matter drop, but I did not forget it.

Though I did not write as much in that year as I feel I should have—remember, my wife was working to support this effort—I don't feel it was wasted. It was in effect my practice year, during which I gradually learned to organize my writing habits. I learned to conquer writer's block, as I could not afford to have it. I think this as something like conquering stage fright. All people suffer from it at first, but the professional learns how to handle it. I had learned how to handle stage fright in the course of drama productions at Goddard College, and have never been incapacitated by it since; similarly I conquered writer's block in that first year, and have never suffered from it since. So that year, poor as it seemed, set the stage for the really thorough work that was to follow. For those who are interested, I am including my "boilerplate" discussion on writer's block in Appendix F, along with those on other aspects of the trade that my fans ask me about: ideas, writing, and marketing.

At this time I was also in touch with several other hopeful writers. As part of my writing effort I subscribed to and read all the science fiction magazines, studying my market. I also entered formal fandom by joining the National Fantasy Fan Federation (NFFF or N3F), and met by mail Seth Johnson, an uneducated but friendly and active correspondent who put me in touch with H. James Hotaling. Then, also through NFFF, a fan named Alma Hill put me in touch with Robert E. Margroff and George Barr (then a hopeful writer, but later successful as an illustrator; he did a very fine wraparound cover for the Borgo edition of my novel *Hasan*) and others. Margroff put me in touch with Frances Hall, and Seth Johnson then brought in Andrew Offutt. We formed a kind of mutual critique group, sending our efforts around to each other. From this association were to arise several collaborations, as the record of my publications shows. This effort was excellent, and I feel it really encouraged and helped me, and I hope likewise for the others, but it took a monstrous amount of time. General correspondence was ballooning, too; I was doing about forty thousand words of letters per month. Later I cut down on that drastically— but today, as a highly successful writer, I find it back in that league, because I try to answer my mail.

My output continued. "Tappuah," about a young crippled girl who could commune with animals, including some extinct ones, and her love affair with a young man. No sale. "Ship of Mustard," a clever, naughty story of life in the "shack" where women have the sexual drives of men and men are reticent. (The particular variety of mustard referred to is rape. Yes, it is a mustard plant.) "Quinquepedalian," run through the comment network and sent to *Galaxy*, where it bounced, then to *Amazing*—where Cele Goldsmith, with her usual acumen, bought it.

My second sale, seven months after the first, in June 1963, this time of a seven-thousand-word story at two cents a word, $140. My first had been a minor fantasy; this was substantial science fiction. Most important, it showed that the first sale had not been a fluke; I could repeat. I was on my way.

No, not quite. Though I completed and submitted several more stories in that year, and resumed work on the novel I had worked on when in the army, I made no more sales. So my total was two stories, $160. That was not enough to support a family. So, reluctantly, I concluded that though I was technically a success, I was in practical terms a failure, and I would have to return to conventional employment. Breakthrough, yes; career, no.

8.

SF = 100

My writing year was over, only a partial success. But that limited success still represented more than the great majority of hopeful writers ever achieve. I doubt that accurate statistics exist, for no one can know precisely who does or does not harbor a private ambition to be a writer, but in general it is agreed that only one of every hundred people who try to write commercially ever succeeds in selling anything. My own survey, based on some actual tabulation, suggests that of those who make one sale, only half will ever make a second, and only a third will make a third, and so on. My formula is $SF = 100$, which means that Sales times Fellows (or Femmes) selling totals 100. That is, of every 100 published writers, only 25% will have sold 4 or more items, so $4 \times 25 = 100$. Only 20% have sold 5 or more, 10% have sold 10 or more, 1% have sold 100 or more. So though I was by this reckoning one of the 100, and actually one of the 50 with my two sales, my hands still barely grasped the bottom two rungs. I would need to get up into the top ten rungs to complete the remainder of my ambition, which was to earn my living as a writer.

Still, I was now on the ladder. Those first two sales were crucially important, not only as ends in themselves and as steps up toward my goal, but as evidence that I could indeed do it.

Now I believed it was possible, and perhaps as important, the editors were beginning to believe. A published writer has infinitely more credibility than an unpublished one; he is after all one of the hundred. Editors, knowing that he has been published, are more likely to give his work careful consideration. Thus it does become easier. It is like making the cut, like qualifying for the competition for the bigger prize.

This would not have occurred without my year of full-time writing. Oh, possibly I would eventually have sold something—but it was important that it happen while I still had enough of my life remaining so that I could work up to a career of it. I was twenty-eight years old when I made my first sale, already about eight years behind others of my age who had made it, like Harlan Ellison, John Brunner, Andrew Offutt, and Robert Silverberg. By the time I had my first novel published, Brunner had had forty. He had been born in England, like me, six weeks later; he had remained in England and become a real success as a science fiction novelist. In this, as in most things, I was a slow starter. But, thanks to my wife, I had finally entered the ranks of selling writers.

Herein lies my analogy of the monkey's paw. In the story "The Monkey's Paw" by W. Jacobs, an old couple obtains a magic monkey's paw and makes three wishes on it. Each time they wish, it moves, alarming them, and the wish is granted in a manner that makes it cost more than it is worth. First they wish for money—and their son is killed, with the death benefit coming to them. Appalled, they wish him back alive—but he is reanimated as a zombie. Finally they wish him dead again, and are left worse off than before. This, like "The Lady or the Tiger," is one of those truly marvelous stories that speaks to a much deeper level than entertainment.

I wanted to be a professional writer. Had my first three children survived, I would never have been one, because my wife would not have been free to go to work, and I would not have been able to afford a year without income while I tried writing seriously. As it was, it was a nervous business; we just barely got by financially, and I just barely made it as a writer. It was necessary that we have minimum family responsibilities while I made the key effort. So we had lost three children—losses we never would have sustained, had we had any choice in the matter. But without those losses, I would not have achieved my desire. The old couple in the story lost their son for money; I lost my son and two daughters for my first two story sales.

Oh, I know that the one did not cause the other, and this is only an analogy. But it has a disturbing plausibility. If I could relive my life, knowing what I now know, and had the power to change it, would I save those babies and sacrifice my writing career? I value life to an extraordinary extent, but this would be very difficult. For one thing, I now have a much better life than any conventional employment is likely to have brought me, and I have two daughters who would not have been born if the first three babies had survived, and I love those daughters. I think I am glad that I have no power of retroactive choice.

9.

UNIVERSITY

So I returned to the mundane job market, while my wife continued working. I was encouraged to get into teaching, because I was pretty well qualified for English, and it was supposed to be a relatively secure employment. We happened to live behind a private school, the Admiral Farragut Academy, so I walked around the block and talked to its headmaster, Captain Clarke. He agreed that I might do well in that profession, and suggested that I check similarly with the principal of one of one of the public schools. I went to the one he recommended, and he was similarly encouraging. I asked him point-blank: "If I undergo teacher training, and become a teacher, would I be able to get a job at a school like this?" He said yes.

So at age twenty-nine I entered the University of South Florida in Tampa. I could afford to take time for the training, because my wife was still earning our living, and the prospects were good. Perhaps it is becoming a cliché, the story of the loyal wife putting her husband through school so that he can become a successful surgeon or businessman or whatever. It is no joke; many wives do exactly this, and so did mine, and it is literally true that without her I would not have made it as a writer. Today, when asked how a person can become a writer, I am apt to answer, "Have a working spouse."

119

When I went on campus to register, I almost quit right there. There were thousands of students milling about, and I had a handful of papers that were supposed to specify the courses I had to sign up for, but I could hardly figure them out. There were professors there to advise the confused registrees, but all of them were absorbed in helping all the *other* confused ones, and it was evident that if I waited till my turn came for help, the day would end before I got straightened out, and I would lose my classes by default. I stopped right there, and asked myself: Should I just go home now? I was sorely tempted. But I do have an ornery streak and I don't like to quit, so I muddled on through. I discovered that one of the classes I needed to take had been filled and closed out the day before—which day I had not been permitted to register, because of complex schedules for different types of students. But there was an avenue. I phoned the one in charge (I hate to phone; I am jinxed by phones) and he agreed reluctantly to make an exception and allow the class to overregister by one. So, finally, I got all my classes in order. I was set for the program.

Later I based a story on that experience. I converted it to science fiction, of course, and changed the details, so it really doesn't resemble what happened to me, but the essence does remain: the immense frustration a beginning student faces, just getting registered at a university. It was titled "University," and was published as "Getting Through University" (editors have abysmal taste in retitling; this story was about registration, not getting through) in my *Prostho Plus* series of dental stories; it can be found in my collection *Anthonology*. When the readers of *Galaxy* and *If* magazines voted their preferences, it was one of the top stories of the year, and it was the only one of those, I think, that was also on the ballot for the Hugo Award. I conjecture that a great many readers had experienced similar problems at educational institutions, and really picked up on that theme.

So I attended classes for two trimesters. I had to make a seventy-five-mile round-trip drive every day, crossing the bay from St. Petersburg to Tampa. Our Volkswagen got forty miles to the gallon, with that steady driving, as I avoided stoplights or timed them, and did not speed. (Then I had the car in for a routine check, and they told me my coil and plugs were bad, and replaced them, and after that I only got thirty-eight miles per gallon. Such things make me seethe.) The required courses for Education were, in the end, pretty much of a loss; the educators had evidently lobbied for featherbed requirements at the expense of the students. I wrote an essay about some of this, but could not get it published. But two peripheral courses were very good. One was on testing, and it changed my attitude about testing. I had been cynical, having always been able to finesse a multiple-choice exam and do well even when I know little of the subject. Now I saw that a superior multiple-choice exam can be a genuine one. The problem is ignorant testers, not the format itself. And I learned about other types of testing, and became so intrigued that I considered going into testing as a profession. But after interviewing a testing administrator, who did not discourage me but who offered sensible cautions, I decided not to. In retrospect, I think perhaps I should have; it could not have been a worse course than the one I actually took.

The other course was Modern Literature. There I encountered the professor Wesley Ford Davis, a novelist in his own right. He brought insights to the subject that illuminated it for me, and aspects of what I learned there were to affect my own subsequent writing. I remember the experience with fondness.

In one class, the one on structural grammar, there were two major problems. First, it did not relate to what I would be required to teach in high school, where they remained with the old-fashioned notions of grammar. The university, in true ivory-tower fashion, refused to relate to the real situation, and taught an idealized mode that, while valid on its own terms, I had to discard the moment I began teaching. Second, the instructor was a busy man, so would sometimes leave the class to a student assistant, who sometimes told the class the direct opposite of what the professor had told us. I was quick enough to recognize the dichotomy, and at one point challenged the assistant on this in the class. "So if I don't understand your way, I'm just out of luck?" I asked. "You're out of luck," he agreed. The girl behind me, not grasping the irony, whispered to me that I should not feel upset, because many students were having trouble understanding the material. I knew her type: bright, well-meaning students who were perhaps too conformist to avoid getting A's. I said nothing, but it griped me privately. I don't like being patronized, however well intended it is.

Later, when I had qualified for the honor society (I forget the exact designation; it meant I had a B or B+ average) and there was to be a gathering, I figured it would be a waste of time. But I remembered that girl, and I thought of what her expression would be if she saw me, the supposedly dull student, there. So, for the wrong reason, I decided to attend. And it happened just that way. I walked in, and there was the girl. I said hello and moved blithely on, leaving her perhaps somewhat stunned. I saw her go over to the table where the name tags were given out, inquiring; as it happened a classmate who knew exactly how bright I was and that I was a published writer was there at the table. So I know the girl got news that amazed her. It was a small and perhaps illicit satisfaction, but I delighted in it. Apart from that, the gathering was a waste of my time, being merely a kind of pep rally for getting good grades.

I have always been a slow reader, so I decided to take advantage of the university's speed-reading course. I was given a vocabulary test. "Take your time," the supervisor said, and left the room. So I took my time, making sure I had each item the way they wanted it, rather than the correct way. You know—the word "celibate" has to be given as "unmarried" rather than as abstaining from sex. By that definition, a bachelor who has a different woman every night is celibate. When I was halfway through, the supervisor returned. "Time's up," she said. That was when I learned it was a timed test. Thereafter they drilled me on vocabulary, having ascertained that that was the reason for my slow reading. Every word I had done was right—but they assumed I didn't know the other half. They wouldn't listen to my assurance that I knew them all. Thus much time was wasted.

They had little boxes that showed one line of text at a time, moving at set rates. You read a piece, then answered questions on it, then used the answer key to grade yourself. You kept running the machine gradually faster, in this manner accelerating your reading without losing comprehension. Fine; I did all that. But one of the answer keys was mixed up; I rechecked the text and found that my answers, not those of the key, were correct. I took it to the instructor, and she checked and verified that the key was wrong. But would you believe—I was the only one to have discovered that? How had the other students made "perfect" scores, using that key? In the end I concluded that speed reading was illusory; certainly it didn't work for me. I can read rapidly if I have to, but it is a strain, and my retention suffers. Thus I might pass a test given immediately after the reading, but forget most of it the week following. That, to me, is wasted time, unless I'm reading for pure entertainment and don't mind forgetting what I have learned. I suspect the case is similar for most people, except that since the average student cares more about the grade than about the learning, he doesn't mind forgetting it all after the exam.

In the second trimester my status as an achiever was torpedoed. A professor arranged to give me a double C grade—that is, it counted for two courses—for my practice-teaching, which knocked me off the roster. The high school teacher with whom I worked, and who was supposed to be a consultant on my grade for that, told me later that he had felt that it would be stretching it to have given me an A, for I had made mistakes (it was after all supposed to be a learning process) but that he would not have opposed it. The C astonished him; the question had been between B and B+. That, and certain other indications, showed me the lay of the land. A grade of C in an education course was equivalent to one of D elsewhere, in the arena of automatically inflated grades. Later, when I considered going on for a higher degree, and they assigned me that professor as my adviser, I dropped it, telling them that he was unacceptable. I suspect that the professor had been privately jealous that a mere student should have gotten paid for having material published, while he, the professor, had not. This sort of person should not be in the field.

My practice teaching was done at the same public high school whose principal I had queried. It was a horrendous experience, because I learned the hard way that I did not have much of a touch for discipline. But I did get through. A more detailed description of my practice-teaching experience is presented in my essay of the time, "Bastille," in Appendix E.

Then I learned that in that county the ratio of applicants to actual teaching positions was five to one. My chances of getting a teaching job there were not at all good, and indeed I never did get a position at a public school, despite having a teacher qualification test score in the ninety-ninth percentile. I was going to have to make do as a substitute teacher. Already the promise of education was losing its luster.

Meanwhile I had continued to submit stories, and sold two more in the year following my writing year. One of these, "Sheol," was a collaboration with H. James Hotaling, and it sold to *Analog*. That was the former *Astounding* that had hooked me on science fiction as a teenager, and to which I had submitted my college novel. Success there was the height! But I was still far from being more than an occasional writer.

This is a personal narrative, but one national event should be noted here. In the fall of 1963 President John Kennedy visited the Tampa Bay region. He was the first president I voted for, when I got my American citizenship, and I supported him. I know he had his flaws, but he shines like a beacon compared to those who followed him. It was all I could do to keep up with my classes, driving, and homework, so I did not go to see him on display, but I know that our region welcomed him.

Five days later he was dead. He had been assassinated in Dallas. I came to an education class, and the woman next to me asked whether I had heard the president had been shot and was seriously hurt. "I hope it's not true!" I said. But in a few minutes the instructor arrived. "By now most of you know that the President is dead," he said. Then we went on with the class, but it was a distracted experience in the face of that horror. When it was dismissed, I passed knots of people murmuring with shock. Then I passed one student chuckling. The urge to kill took me—but I kept my peace, knowing that it was a free country, that he had a right to his disgusting opinion—and indeed, he might have been chuckling about something else entirely. We jump to conclusions at our risk.

For three days the television was dominated by the murder and the funeral, and we watched with that appalled mesmerization the nation was suffering. My outrage focused on the city of Dallas, Texas, where the foul deed had been done. Opponents had run a full-page newspaper ad there condemning Kennedy; no wonder the assassin had been encouraged. He had not come to Tampa Bay; he would have known that he would have been torn apart there, where the president was respected. He had gone to the place that was hospitable to his inclination. And the manner in which the assassin had been so conveniently eliminated before he could talk, thus covering up whatever guilty traces there might have been. A very pretty piece of mischief.

I call this the Dallas Syndrome. Of course I know that the majority of the residents of Dallas were similarly appalled by the murder. Even if they had wanted Kennedy dead, they would not have wanted the deed done on their own doorstep. At the same time, the region was a hotbed of dissent, where rich conservatives cursed Kennedy's liberal and humanistic policies. So I do condemn Dallas, for generating the climate that led, in its purest expression, to murder. I am sure that many others feel as I do.

But there is a noticeable corollary: many people seem to like Dallas, for the same reason. They sing its praises, they invest money in it, making it a phenomenally successful and expanding region. I submit that conservatives like it for the same reason I dislike it: because it was the site of the murder of a liberal president. The symbolism is as valid one way as the other. Of course most liberals and conservatives do not care to present their real, gut reasons for their biases, so they give other reasons, but I believe there is truth in my thesis.

PART FOUR

Swinehood Hath No Remedy

1.

TEACHING

Substitute teaching was hellish. I never knew what day I would be working; the call would generally come in the morning, and I would hurry out to the particular school to take over one teacher's classes for the day. The students would be primed for trouble, knowing that I did not know them and would not be back—but if anything went wrong, I would be the one to get the blame. Some teachers had things well organized, and those days were all right, but some did not. I found I had to have tough discipline, or chaos would quickly develop. At one school, the students were rough, and I had to hold them down by a constant and immediate threat of sending troublemakers to the office. I did send one, and found he had given me a fake name. I had them work on their assignment, and checked them on it—only to discover too late that I had been told the prior day's assignment, so it was repeat work for them. Naturally not one of them had let on. At the end of the class period, at half past the hour, I tore up the report slips I had prepared—I made them out at first warning, and implemented them when the offense was repeated, and the students did come to understand that—then realized too late that the period ended at three minutes past the half hour. The class went wild, as if school had expired. In those three minutes two teachers came in from neighboring classes to bawl out the class, ignoring me.

Interesting; where were those teachers before, when I could have used some advice on things like correct student names and correct assignments? The situation is loaded against the substitute, and the schools could and should do something about that. I was never invited to substitute at that school again.

Another time I had a number of calls from one school, and had a good month's work, sometimes handling the same classes several days in succession, which made it easier. One afternoon as I was checking out with the assistant principal who handled the calls for substitutes, he talked to me for perhaps an extra fifteen minutes, friendly and informative. He related stories about principals who had taken female students to bed. Later I pondered this unusual dialogue: Why would such a person talk in this way to a substitute?

Perhaps I am forming a picture that is not justified. But several things seemed to fall into place. One was that I was one of the brightest of those who had undertaken the profession of teaching; the tests showed it. Yet I had not been able to get any job in the state system. True, the professor had saddled me with a low grade in practice teaching—but was that all there was to it? I believe that there was, and probably still is, an illicit agreement in Florida, wherein those suspected of being homosexual are not hired, with other reasons always being given. I was a married but childless man. The assistant principal's commentary was in certain respects very like a homosexual come-on. Suppose my name had been placed on the illicit list, and he had seen it there, so was checking it out? When it became evident that I had no homosexual inclinations, his interest in me evaporated. The truth of this suspicion will probably never be known, but I will always wonder.

My personal preference is adamantly heterosexual; I have difficulty understanding how any man, given the choice, would pass up a willing young woman in favor of a man. But that experience, existing largely in my own conjecture, has caused me to consider the situation of homosexuals. I feel, as a matter of principle, that each person's sexual tastes are his own, and he should be allowed to indulge them with other consenting adults. I am sure a homosexual male teacher would be less likely to sexually abuse a female student than a heterosexual teacher would, so I don't see any reason to exclude homosexuals for education. *No* teacher should take sexual license with *any* student, regardless of the sexes involved. That agreement to avoid hiring homosexuals is a blot on the already sullied name of education, and should be abolished. I am sure that homosexuals (and by that I mean male and female ones; lesbians are homosexuals) do suffer discrimination, and feel they should not. I have considered writing a novel relating to the subject, and may yet do so, as a matter of challenge. Two or three problems cause me to hold back, however. First, I really have no taste for it myself, so it would be extremely difficult writing, given my standards of accuracy and feeling. Second, I fear it would brand me a homosexual, and that is not a reputation I would care for. Third, I don't know whether it could be published. So I may never write it. Decisions such as this are not easy ones: whether to tackle a personally distasteful project for the sake of challenge and education, or to stick to the safe material.

On days I wasn't called to substitute, I worked on my writing. My novel, *Chthon*, was making good progress, because more often than not I wasn't substituting. In June 1965 I completed it, after having worked on it erratically for seven years (it was the one I had started in the army in 1958) and submitted it to a $210,000 novel contest of the time. That contest, like the one I had entered in college, had no winner. In fact, the near-winner was announced before the contest closed; but for a veto by one of the sponsors, it would have won. I presume the novels as-yet-unread would have been out of luck. I kept sending the novel off to other markets. Meanwhile, my stories were having better success; in the calendar year of 1965 I sold four more, doubling my total. Those were bright spots in an otherwise pretty dull period.

In the spring of 1965 I got a break: the Admiral Farragut Academy, the school against whose yard we lived, had an emergency and needed an English teacher to fill out the final two months of the year. I took the job, of course; my days of substituting were blessedly over.

That did not mean that things were easy. I retained the job for the 1965–66 school year, and that four-thousand-dollar stipend, added to my wife's earnings, put us in a comfortable financial situation. But I had the heaviest teaching load of any English teacher there, being required to cover all of tenth grade and one-third of ninth grade—a total of about eighty students. This was of course a smaller number than I would have faced in the public school system; one of the things a private school can do is provide smaller loads, so that teachers can pay more attention to individual students. But that ninth-grade class meant I had to do a whole additional preparation, which doubled that aspect, and somehow all the ninth-grade troublemakers had been included. I was not alone in noticing this. It wasn't any conspiracy; it just happened to fall out that way. But it made that class another nightmare, because I had to wage a kind of war just to keep discipline, and it was hard to do good teaching in that situation.

One example: I went to the captain in charge of discipline (that naval rank was higher than an army captain was) to express my problems with some classes. He told me that the thing to do was to draw on the more responsible and committed students for help in maintaining class decorum. I asked who these might be, and he named one of my worst troublemakers. I shut up, realizing that he was out of touch with the situation. Later there was serious vandalism in the school, with some students tearing up school property. They held a room search for evidence, and caught them. One was my troublemaker. He was expelled. If only that action had been taken earlier! I had to put up with things like a rock thrown through my window (now we lived too close to the school!), and a telephoned threat of death, and military salutes that seemed to be performed with a single vertical finger. I was taught to salute in the army, and that may be the only thing the army teaches well; a naval salute can indeed most resemble a cross between a wave and an obscene gesture. But that of course was not the whole story.

Farragut was a decent school, all things considered, and I'm sure it delivers a good education. But I knew that teaching just wasn't for me, and I resolved to retire and try serious writing again when the school year was done. That was just as well, for I was not offered a contract for the next year. I inquired, just for the record, and was told that though my dedication as a teacher was unexcelled, I had too much of a problem with discipline. I have no quarrel with that assessment. Thus, in June of 1966, I retired from teaching.

2.

MILFORD

I like to keep track of things, as I have mentioned. I had been watching the science fiction genre avidly, noting who published what, especially those promising writers like Roger Zelazny and Norman Spinrad who broke into print around the same time I did. It was as if we represented a new breed who might someday dominate the field. Foolishness, of course, but the drive for success in writing had become dominant in my life. I *had* to succeed this time, for I was pretty much washed out of all other employment. So I watched, and also started a daily work record that noted what I accomplished each day: so many words of first draft written, or so many pages read, or letters written, or whatever else that took up my time. The record was brief; I generally squeezed it into a single line for a day.

That list continues to this day; I have many thousands of daily entries. You might feel that it is pointless, for anyone who is not a compulsive counter, but I discovered that it was an excellent way to spot events whose timing I had forgotten. When did I write to a certain publisher? When did I complete a particular story? How long did I spend on a given novel? Sometimes it becomes important to know, and the record represents a ready way to get the information. But perhaps as important, I found that it represented a regular ox-goad of an

133

incentive. I generally wrote about two thousand words of first-draft fiction a day; it bothered me to have only one thousand words posted. Those writers who have difficulty applying themselves to their work might do well to emulate this record; it could make a difference, that daily accounting. I wish I had had the record during my first writing year.

Two weeks after I retired to writing, I received news of an offer for *Chthon*. It had been rejected by three hardcover houses—hardcover outfits have seldom been interested in my work, for what reason I can't say—but a paperback publisher wanted it. A fifteen-hundred-dollar sale! This breakthrough for novels was not only nice for itself, but it meant that I could now earn my living from writing. It was my tenth sale, which put me, by my SF = 100 reckoning, into the top 10% of genre writers. All very nice.

Now that I was back in full-time writing, I thought I should get into more direct touch with the genre. My wife and I visited Keith Laumer, who lived in Florida, and found him gracious and informative. Later he had a stroke that affected his personality, and I decided to let my original impression of him stand without further contact. I made arrangements to attend that year's Milford conference. Milford was a week-long gathering sponsored by Damon Knight, where selling writers brought stories for mutual comment, in the manner of the informal group I had worked with by mail before. But it wasn't just a critique I wanted; I desired the interaction with other writers. I don't like to travel, having done way too much of it as a child, but will rouse myself when the occasion warrants, and this seemed to be the occasion.

The trip from Florida to Pennsylvania by bus was horrendous. Theoretically there is a seat for every passenger, but there was not. After an hour of so of having a black child stand beside my seat, I simply got up and told him to take the seat for a time while I stood. We switched off every hour or so until he reached his destination somewhere in Georgia, I believe. It was wearing on me because of my fatigue, but I simply could not sit forever and watch an unfairness. Whether there is racism on the buses I can't say, but the image of the white folk sitting while black folk had to stand bothered me also. I detest unfairness of any type, but in the American South racism becomes the most obvious type of it. But I would have done the same for any other person in that situation.

Ed Meskys met me in New York and got me around the city. Ed was a fan I had encountered when working on the review index; he had done a lot of work on it, and now was publishing his own fanzine (amateur magazine devoted to the genre), *Niekas*. I understand that's a Lithuanian word meaning "nothing." Ed was in the process of going blind, which I did not realize at the time; later he got a seeing-eye dog named Ned, whom my daughter Penny was pleased to meet. I spent the night at his house, and he took me to a party sponsored by another fan, Charles Brown. Charles later published the newszine *Locus* that was to become the leading newspaper of the science fiction field. I phoned my wife from his apartment, having the usual awful struggle to get through (I really am jinxed by phones), and he lent me a copy of John Taine's *Before the Dawn* to facilitate my research on dinosaurs for my novel *Orn*. I met Poul Anderson there, one of the most prolific and successful science fiction writers ever, and his wife Karen, and Alexei Panshin, later to write perhaps the definitive book on Heinlein. Already my trip was paying dividends! When Ed Meskys's fanzine revived in the 1980s after being defunct for a decade, I remembered the favor I owed him, and contributed several essays. My reputation was by then considerably more potent than it had been when Ed was so kind to me in New York, which perhaps may be taken as a lesson of sorts: Be kind to beginning writers, because when things change they may remember.

Next morning the Andersons and I took the bus to Milford, Pennsylvania. We sat at the rear of the bus, where we could share a seat. Unfortunately this was next to the toilet, whose odors wafted across us. While Poul was the "name" writer, whose work I had admired from way back, I had also been influenced by Karen's writing. She had had a short story concerning little sphinxes in one of the magazines, and when I had read it I had said to myself, "I can do that!" and I had done it, and started selling short stories.

And at Milford I met a score more writers, many of whose work I had known. I don't want to make of this narrative a tedious itemization, so will mention only those with whom I had some special interaction. One was Harlan Ellison, who is about three months older than I am, and in whose famous *Dangerous Visions* series of anthologies one of my more daring stories appears. Another was Gordon Dickson, whose *Dorsai* I had admired; he was a jolly, friendly, totally sociable creature. I remember how he took extra time to figure out how to comment on my story entry in such a way as not to alienate me. The effort was unnecessary; I am not quite as intemperate as many people seem to believe. But the fact that he was that perceptive and careful impressed me, and I have kept it in mind since as a lesson, and do the same for others when I deem it necessary. There was Samuel "Chip" Delany, who became an award-winning writer. And Joanna Russ, later to be known for her strongly feminist writings. And Anne McCaffrey was getting into novels the same time I was, and was I think to become the first writer of the genre to make the New York *Times* best-seller list in hardcover. (I was the first to do it with an original paperback fantasy.) Norman Spinrad, another writer whose fame was to expand considerably later. And Roger Zelazny, then flashing like a meteor, winning awards. All good enough folk, though later I was to have some fairly formidable differences with some. This was not a matter of competition, for we were really not competing, but of special concerns, such as mine with integrity. I am glad I met them all.

One special item of business came up in that week. Sol Cohen, publisher of *Amazing Stories* and *Fantastic Stories*, came to engage in a dialogue with the group. He had bought the magazines and proposed to draw on their considerable backlog of stories for reprints, thus avoiding the expense of paying for new fiction. The writers objected, because this represented the loss of a significant market that had launched a number of us as pros. We selected four or five spokesmen who engaged Mr. Cohen, trying to get him to see our side and to return the magazines to the publication of original fiction, or at least to pay a decent amount for the reprints. He was courteous but adamant; he had only so much in his budget, and that could be divided one way or another, but the total was fixed. So it came to nothing, and for a time the Science Fiction Writers of America (SFWA) boycotted his publications.

Do I recommend such functions as the Milford Conference for others? Yes, I do; they can represent a fine interaction between writers, and that can be helpful for those who are serious about writing. Having experienced one, I was satisfied; I never participated in another. Some other writers were regular annual attendees. It's all a matter of preference. There are workshops for hopeful writers, too, and while I am cynical about whether they can actually do much to forward the career of an unsold writer, surely they do provide useful advice and encouragement. It is possible to break into print without indulging in any of this; I did. But I think many people need this type of interaction in order to get really into the job of writing.

3.

PENNY

My sales continued to poke along, though I was making as many as twenty submissions in a month, keeping all my work in circulation. Then things took off in the latter part of 1967, when I sold three novels: *Omnivore* to one publisher, *The Ring* (a collaboration with Robert Margroff) to another, and *Sos the Rope* won the *Pyramid/F&SF*/Kent Productions five-thousand-dollar contest. My annual income from writing leapt into the five-thousand-dollar category, where it was to remain for several years. I was definitely on my way!

Meanwhile, we were ready to try for a baby again. My wife was coming up on thirty, so our time was running short if we were going to do it at all. The third miscarriage had finally revealed the cause: she had a septum dividing the uterus, so that the developing fetus was crowded out before its time, bringing on miscarriage. The doctor had tried, after the delivery, to break down that membrane by hand, literally; he said he put his fist in there. He thought he had failed—but later X rays, preparatory for surgery, showed no septum. The job had been done. I'm not sure whether this was the first time such a thing had been accomplished, but it is possible. But, just to be sure, the doctor planned to use the Chirodkar Procedure, or "drawstring" operation: sewing the uterus closed during the pregnancy, so that premature delivery would be impossible.

With all that preparation on my wife's part, it behooved me to do my part, and in due course she was pregnant again. It can be a lot of fun, being with a woman who wants to get pregnant soon. It was a nervous business, considering our three prior losses, but all went well this time, and on October 12, 1967, our first surviving child, Penelope Carolyn Jacob, was born. I was in the middle of typing the novel *The Ring* when I received the news. No, I didn't wait at the hospital; I knew from prior experience that my wife's labors could be delayed indefinitely, and I did have work to do at home. I am like Isaac Asimov in this (and in a surprising number of other respects): I live for my writing, and when in doubt, I will be at the keyboard. This does not mean that other things are not important to me; certainly the birth of the baby was. But when the choice was sitting all night in an anonymous hospital waiting room, or getting work done at home, I chose the work.

Thus Penny came into our lives. Cam and I agree that this was to change our lives more than marriage itself had, eleven years before. We had wanted a family, but we had gotten accustomed to a childless marriage, and adjustments had to be made. I found that I was unable to relax, at any hour of the day or night, without being assured that my daughter was safe. Perhaps the average man simply leaves the matter to his wife; not so with me. Cam went back to work after she recovered, and I took care of Penny. She was very much my child. She had blue eyes and dark hair that later turned blond. I have an explanation for that: I used to bounce her on my knee, singing "Truly Fair": ". . . songs to sing her, trinkets to bring her, flowers for her golden hair." (Only I couldn't remember all of it, and had to hum portions.) So as she grew, her hair turned golden, to match the song. Everything, you see, makes sense, if you take the trouble to work out the rationale. Actually her hair is the same color as mine. You might wonder how this can be, when my hair is dark. Well, when I was a child my mother always thought I was blond, while I always suspected she was colorblind. Now that mystery was penetrated: my hair is the same color as Penny's hair, at the same length. Were mine as long as hers, it would (and probably did, long ago) bleach out to blond. Were she to cut hers boyishly short—absolute, total horrors!—it would be as dark as mine. Penny's hair has never been cut, except for occasional trimmings of ragged ends. She was hyperactive, and so I explained that her energy was because of her long tresses; like the Biblical Samson, she would lose her strength if her hair were ever cut. She was active from the start. When Cam was pregnant, and said something silly to me, I pointed to her belly and said, "Kick her!"—and Penny did, from inside.

At any rate, I fed Penny, I changed her diapers, I put her down for her naps, I took her out to play. She would never truly settle down; the very act of placing her in the crib would bring her screamingly awake. I had to settle into a rocking chair with her on my shoulder while she nodded off; when she was sound enough asleep I might, with luck, be able to put her safely in the crib. When she weighed seven and a half pounds, that was easy enough; I propped her in the crook of my left arm, braced it with my right, and held a book up to read while I rocked. When she weighed fourteen pounds it got wearing, especially when I was up all night with her. My writing efficiency was cut in half; it took me a full year to write one novel, *Macroscope*. Now the book on babies says a parent is a fool to allow a baby to insist on being held all the time. There's a great deal the book doesn't know about a hyperactive baby. For example, it says that you must simply put the baby down to sleep and let it cry; after half an hour it will subside and sleep. Next night it will take less time, until finally sleep comes immediately without fuss.

Well, I tried it. I put Penny down, then retreated to the bedroom. She screamed. Half an hour passed, with me feeling terrible. She still cried. After an hour she was still crying, but I held miserably firm. After one and a half hours I heard a kind of choking. Alarmed, I hurried into her room. Something was wrong. I turned on the light—and saw she had vomited on the bed. The vomit was a reasonably bright red.

I spent an instant totally appalled. Then I remembered: she had had cherry pudding for supper. That accounted for the color. It wasn't blood.

But that finished the book method. My little girl was still crying, and she had had no rest, and neither had I. I picked her up, put her on my shoulder, and settled into the rocking chair. She went right to sleep. After that I viewed the book with considerable skepticism, and when it deviated from common sense and experience, I ignored it. I have never regretted that.

But I did have work to do, and Penny threatened to monopolize my time. I loved her—and I don't think I affront my wife when I say that she became the second female in my life once Penny came on the scene—but something had to be done. For a while I was able to type my first draft by balancing her bassinet on my lap. The sound of the keystrikes lulled her to sleep. But when I paused to consider my next sentence, she would wake and fuss. I *had* to keep typing!

Penny never really learned to crawl; she would wriggle rapidly along the floor. Then she started walking at exactly nine and a half months. It was impossible for me to remain at the typewriter, even before she walked; she was too active. So I converted to pencil, writing my first draft on a sheet of paper on a clipboard. I got one with a container for the paper, so that I could save my sheets as I worked. Once Penny was playing with something on the couch, and I sat there with my left hand on her back so I could keep track of her position without having to use my eyes, and my right hand writing text on the clipboard balanced on my knees. She remained there for over an hour—an extraordinary time for her—and I got something like seven hundred words written. So I adapted, and discovered that pencil was really more versatile than typing, because I could do it anywhere, anytime. Thereafter, for seventeen years, all my first drafts were done in pencil, until finally I leapt to first drafting on the computer. At age seventeen, Penny no longer needed quite the same supervision.

There were problems, of course. Once I turned away from her to adjust the station on the radio. Penny, of course, inherited my taste in pleasant songs and light classical music. When I turned back, she was standing beside the couch. She opened her mouth—and blood welled out. She had taken a fall and cut her lip, in those few seconds. She also had a hyper digestion, and could throw up virtually at will. I learned to ignore this, but remember one meal in which she had two throw-ups, two bad spit-ups, and a bad coughing spell. It was hard to get any food to stay *in* her! Finally I had to do what may seem cruel: start condemning her for vomiting. That did it; gradually it stopped, for she was socially conscious, and it never was a problem thereafter. We never hassled her about toilet functions, and by her second birthday she toilet-trained herself.

She was bright. Cam, who wasn't with her as much as I was, (in fact, our roles were reversed; it was her mother whom Penny greeted coming home at day's end) kept saying that Penny was starting to talk, and knew a number of words. I dismissed this. I remembered her first word: she had picked up a big plastic yellow duck and said, "Duck!" Wonderful! Then she toddled into the kitchen, picked up a cardboard box, and said "Duck!" So much for that. But finally my wife got my attention, and I did what comes naturally to me: I started counting words. I counted only those that Penny spoke intelligibly and knew the meaning of; that is, if I said, "Penny, where's the doll?" she would go and fetch the doll, even if it was in another room. I was shortly amazed.

Penny was then fifteen months old. I counted 220 words. Oh yes, I still have that list today. When she was eighteen months old she had over 500 words. Now according to the (discredited) book, the average child can speak 10 words at age eighteen months. Some extraordinarily bright ones have been clocked as high as 200 words. I was never able to find any record of any child who spoke 500—but every word was double- or triple-checked, and I have the list. Some surprised me, as when I took her out near a hedge and said, "Penny, can you find a hedge?" She clapped her hand to her head. I hadn't known she knew "head." I explained the distinction, and three days later when I retested her, she had both words straight. We showed her off to neighbors, who were similarly amazed. "Is there any word she *doesn't* know?" one asked. But when I reported it to the members of my family, in one of the monthly family letters, open skepticism was expressed. I suppose I can't blame them— but it was true. We had a prodigy on our hands.

Later, we were setting up new bunks for our children, and didn't want Penny to catch on. So we referred to the "B-E-D." "B-E-D!" Penny exclaimed, and dashed in to see it. Another time I sat down with her and opened a book with a picture of a frog. "Croak!" I said. She was disgusted. "That's not a croak, Daddy, that's a frog!" What a little bundle of joy she was.

Pride goeth before a fall. When Penny entered the school system, things began going wrong. After a long struggle, in which like as not a teacher would tell us what we knew was untrue, that Penny could not do this or that, we found that she was not only hyperactive, she was learning disabled. She had problems with dyslexia and emotion and small and large muscle coordination. We put her in special schooling, and that helped, but she never outgrew it entirely. I wrote an article on the "Hop, Skip and Jump School" as I dubbed it, to the school's pleasure, describing the types of therapy they had, building up the confidence and coordination and educational skills of learning-disabled children. They did good work, and I remain grateful; Penny needed this attention.

In 1970 we had our second daughter, Cheryl. I let Cam keep this one; it was after all her turn. Cheryl turned out a lot like her mother, with darker hair and such; she was not learning disabled, and though not as bright initially—she only spoke 360 words at eighteen months—she worked out much better in school, becoming a straight-A student.

So now we had the family we had wanted, and the success in writing, and because I worked at home my job did not separate me from my family, and I had the whole joy of it. We were, as my success increased, in a position to take much better care of our children than we could have before, because we no longer needed to count the pennies (puns on Penny abound), and as they grew up my daughters were to have the pleasure of the notoriety of a well-known father. Still, that image of the monkey's paw lingers. I feel a kind of guilt at having so much joy of family and profession, built upon the ruins of earlier hopes.

4.

CONTRACT

Naturally it couldn't last. As Penny got older we discovered the complications of the L-D syndrome, and her seeming genius became at one point a struggle just to prevent her from failing a grade in school. At the same time, I encountered a major episode of what I term the Swinehood Syndrome. Real pigs are decent animals, on their own terms; it is only when human beings are termed swine that the context becomes negative. My use of it here is mixed, and derives from a line in the 1875 poem "The Symphony" by Sidney Lanier:

> The beasts they hunger, and eat and die;
> And so do we, and the world's a sty;
> Hush, fellow swine: why nuzzle and cry?
> *Swinehood hath no remedy . . .*

I encountered Lanier's work in the course of becoming a teacher; since the state had not prepared me adequately (education courses relate to irrelevant theory, not to subject matter) I took literature courses at the St. Petersburg Junior College in summer. The material was jammed in, and as I recall I received more or less automatic B's, and much of the material passed through my mind and out the other side in the manner of any student. But Lanier caught my attention, and I remembered him, and used him in my major novel *Macroscope*. I suspect he is underrated in American literature, covered passingly as a matter of completism. I have sympathy for the kind whose genius is neglected; the public seems chronically fickle and the critics biased. Lanier was experimenting with new forms of poetry and introducing new concepts, trying to integrate it with music. He understood music; he may have been the finest flautist in the world. "The Symphony" concludes: "Music is Love in search of a word."

My problem began deceptively quietly. I had sold two novels, *Chthon* and *Omnivore*, to a publisher, and submitted a third, the sequel to *Omnivore*, to them for consideration. (I shall henceforward refer to them simply as PUBLISHER, because the name, though hardly secret, now represents what amounts to a completely different company with different policies.) In January 1969, PUBLISHER notified me that *Omnivore* was being picked up by SFBC for publication that July. The book club formerly had republished only hardcover novels; they were expanding to two science fiction books a month and for the first time drawing from original paperbacks. I believe my novel was the first such paperback they did. In March the senior editor herself wrote me that our British agent, Ted Carnell, had sold *Chthon* to MacDonald in England for hardcover publication: £200, and that they would send me my share as soon as the money came in. (The author's share, according to the contract, was fifty percent.) She had explained before that though the contract gave PUBLISHER 10 percent of translation sales, it was their policy to give all of it to the author after a British sale had been made. Since there was also a sale of *Chthon* to a publisher in Holland that same month, this was further good news. Already I had three subsidiary sales on my novels! The foreign ones did not amount to a lot of money, but that SFBC sale should have represented a hefty amount. After all, with more than sixty thousand members . . .

But time passed, and none of that subsidiary money was forthcoming. I inquired, in a very polite and seemingly offhand note, just in case there had been some slipup in the works. That is, June 27, 1969, when submitting *Paleo* (later retitled *Orn*) for her consideration, I said: "I have no information, no copies, and no money from the book club edition of *Omnivore*. Any word on this?" An editor acknowledged the letter, but said that the senior editor was out of the country till July 21. There was no response to my query about the book club edition; indeed, I was never to receive even an author's copy, and had to buy one in a local store.

Well, maybe they were holding the information and payment for the semiannual statement of account, despite the senior editor's note; a rereading of the contract showed me that they had the right to do this. This was awkward, because I now had to pay taxes based on estimated income, and since PUBLISHER hadn't told me what to expect from SFBC, I had to guess. I had been penalized by the IRS for not paying enough estimated tax, when I discovered that a check received in January 1978 in connection with the contest winner *Sos the Rope* had been credited for 1977, forcing me to change my 1977 tax statement at the last moment. I think the IRS was swinish to penalize me for not paying advance tax on income I never even received in that year, but that's another matter. So I judged the likely income from SFBC as well as I could: sixty-five thousand members, maybe fifty thousand would buy my novel, so there would be ten percent royalties on those copies at $1.50 each, or $7500, a half of which was mine. Since the entire PUBLISHER's advance had been only $1500, it was obvious that a good deal of money was owing. But maybe I was too optimistic about the percentage of sales, so I cut my estimate to $3000 total, half of it mine. I paid tax on the extra $1500, though it strained our resources at the time.

Finally, in August, the royalty report arrived. It listed 43,937 copies sold, earning total royalties of $1,166.85. Subtracted from my advance, that left me $333.15 in the hole.

What about the three subsidiary sales, made in January and March? *They weren't even listed.* I realized that I was dealing with something more than simple oversight. Accordingly, on August 14, 1969, I wrote a stiff letter of inquiry, no longer trying to be polite. I am reproducing the entire text of that letter here, dull as it may be for the reader, because of the effect it was to have on my career.

Dear [Senior Editor]:
Item #13 in the [PUBLISHER]/Jacob contract for *Chthon* specifies that I receive 50% of British monies. Item #14 gives me 90% of translation monies. Your letter of March 13 notifies me of such a British sale, and says "As soon as

the first payment comes in, we'll be sending you your share."

I now have in hand your royalty report covering that period, and it lists neither that British payment nor the Dutch payment that Carnell sent you on May 17, and no such monies were enclosed.

Item #17 in that same contract says in part: "The Publisher shall render . . . statements of account as at . . . August 1st of the estimated net sales of the paperbound edition to the public, and sale or lease of any and all other rights in the work to the last day of . . . March preceding, and pay in cash with the statement the amount due the Author . . . (except) when as of any first day of . . . August a sum of less than $10.00 (ten dollars) shall have accrued to the Author the Publisher shall be under no obligation to render a statement or make payment . . ."

Stamped on your statement is "Returns equaled or exceeded sales during this royalty period." Fine—so the total royalty stands at $1,166.85 today. And technically you don't have to issue me a report, since you owe me no money. BUT—the report you did send is in error, because it omits mention of those extra sales.

Item #18 says you can keep the other monies due me until they catch up to your $1500 advance, too. OK—my information is scant because you are not giving me an honest accounting (and that will cost you, please understand), but it shapes up about like this: My share of the British MACDONALD sale, half of half an advance = 50 pounds − 10% agent's commission, × approximate conversion to dollars = $108.00. My share of the Dutch advance of approximately $300 (which, in the absence of other information, I assume was paid entire) − 10% agent, − 10% Publisher = about $240. Total foreign net income of $348 combined with total royalties of $1166.85 add up to $1514.85—fourteen dollars over your advance. By that reckoning you do owe me a statement, and because it exceeds ten dollars, you owe me money too.

Bear in mind that both foreign sales were made within the accounting period—that is, prior to March 31, 1969. There is no reason, either in the contract or as a practical matter, to delay such payments to me, so long as they arrive prior to the actual statement of account. It is the *sales* that count, not the specific dates of payment.

Why did you fail to make such a statement on *Chthon*, and why didn't you pay the money owing?

Now on to *Omnivore*. I own the foreign rights to that, so no problem there. But Item #9 in that contract gives me half the net proceeds of a book club placement. A letter by your managing editor [name deleted] dated January 22, 1969, informed me that *Omnivore* had been selected by the SF BOOK CLUB for July, 1969. Fine—Item #17 requires such notification, and since I did not request immediate payment of my share, makes it payable at the next royalty accounting period.

No such payment has been received, and again, the statement makes no mention of this income, that should have reached you prior to the date of the statement. My presumption, based on the size and nature of the book club involved, is that more than enough money was received to make up the royalties still unaccrued per Item #18, and that I therefore should have been paid the excess. Why was this not the case?

Please be advised that unless I receive satisfactory answers to the questions raised in this letter, I shall make a formal complaint and documentation to SFWA, and shall invoke Item #33 of the *Omnivore* contract: my right to examine your books of account, at your expanse if more than 5% to my disfavor is discovered.

Also, my novel *Paleo* went off to you June 28. If you want it at all, I suggest that you not delay too much longer about making a report.

Sincerely,

Piers Anthony Jacob

That letter, of course, ended what had until then been a quite positive relationship. The senior editor, before, had answered my questions and had even sent me books without charge that I had sought to order. But with me everything was nullified by the reneging on the agreement to pay me my subsidiary income when it arrived, and by the inaccurate royalty report.

The senior editor replied promptly. When, subsequently, I proposed to make my case to SFWA and asked permission to quote from her letter so as to have her position accurately represented, she refused to permit either quotation or paraphrasing, though expressing willingness to have a member of SFWA review the entire matter. More on that anon. The question now, faced with that refusal, that I am sure still stands, is how can I present the publisher's side of this fairly? I think that since that position was the basis for the ensuing situation, I can consider it legitimate to present here. If someone, at this late date, wishes to sue, I shall pursue the matter in court in a manner calculated to discourage further such attempts. The original material would of course be presented in court, showing that I have fairly stated the case.

The fact is, as I learned privately from another source at a later date, when the senior editor received my letter, she had a fit. If she talked to a publisher about me, or an agent, or another writer or an SFWA representative (I had the feedback of all these types on this), she informed them in most emphatic terms what a difficult and unreasonable writer Piers Anthony was to deal with. As a direct result, I lost sales and reputation. Were this matter to come to court at last, I would name specifics; I do have them. But here I will simply say that it was true. All on the basis of that one letter, reproduced above. And everything I said in that letter was true to the best of my knowledge and belief.

Her reply listed the dates and amounts of the Dutch and British payments, showing that they came to less than I had said, mainly because my share of the Dutch payment was $208.18 rather than the $240 I had judged. Apparently a $300 foreign advance shrank somewhat in translation; it has happened on subsequent occasions. The money had arrived in June. Therefore the publisher owed me no money. She evidently thought that sufficient refutation of that point. It was not. The key here is my sentence: "The report you did send is in error, because it omits mention of those extra sales." The contract, which I had quoted, stated that the statement of account was required to cover "the sale or lease of any and all other rights in the work" within the reporting period. Since both foreign sales were made in March, and the reporting period ended the last day of March, these belonged in the report. The senior editor interpreted it to mean that only the date of the actual receipt of the money counted. I would be happy to settle this in court too; my definition of a sale is when the agreement is made and/or the binding contract signed. To assume otherwise is to lead to paradoxical complications.

On the sale of *Omnivore* to the book club she said this: the first payment had not yet arrived. She reminded me of the clause in the contract that said the publisher could pay the proceeds within fourteen days of receipt, and said that "proceeds" did not mean the sale of rights, but the actual money received for such sale. She said she wished I had not jumped to the conclusion that the publisher was attempting to cheat me; hadn't it occurred to me that an honest mistake had been made, despite her promise to send the payment for the British sale of *Chthon* upon receipt. She felt that such a promise (though not honored, as the yielding of the publisher's 10% of translations sales was not honored) did not indicate any intent to rob me. She said that she was old-fashioned about honesty and courtesy.

Uh-huh. I think it is evident how our definitions of those concepts differed. She concluded with a similar fillip: she understood that Gulfport had been ravaged by a hurricane. She hoped I had not been affected by it, but she was holding the return of *Paleo* until she was sure there was a safe address to which to send it.

Note the essence, here: that hurricane had indeed struck the city of Gulfport, Mississippi, wreaking such havoc that it was deemed to be the worst of the century. But she was not responding by admitting any error or forwarding promised money, but by delaying the return of the manuscript. In this manner she notified me that my novel, which they had already begun to copyedit, had been summarily rejected.

Well, that hurricane had taken aim at Gulfport, Florida, where we lived, and then swerved aside and gone on to devastate the other Gulfport across the Gulf of Mexico. We were undamaged. But I think it is clear why I gave no more credence to the senior editor's good wishes than I did to her old-fashioned honesty and courtesy. I sent her a card clarifying that my home address was safe, and saying that I would follow up on my contract differences in due course.

Now let's explore certain other implications of her letter. She had informed me therein that the SFBC payment was not due until ninety days after the date of their publication of the novel. Thus not until October 1969. Thus it would be listed then, and my share would be relayed to me in August 1970.

Payment of the author's share of an advance—more than a year after the book was published? Yes, that was the way they had engineered it. The book club really did pay their "advance" *after* publication, making the term a misnomer. They sent out advance notice and received orders, and generally distributed their books before the actual publication date; then, after the money was in hand, paid the agreed amount to the author. I was not the only writer to be astonished by this revelation. So PUBLISHER really did not owe me any money yet, and would not pay it for another year in any event. And I *still* did not know the actual amount of it. I had paid taxes on money I was not to receive that year. Why hadn't PUBLISHER informed me of any of this before? There seemed to be no positive purpose in that neglect, and indeed I suffered because of it.

Why was the reaction to my letter so extreme? The word was being spread all over the genre that Piers Anthony was a bad person, and I still receive evidences of it today. Yet my points were correct; they should have given me an accurate accounting, including the listing of the two foreign sales and the book club sale. It is true that my letter was not polite; it was a stiff demand for information that had been denied. But such a response?

I have pondered this matter at some length, for I always like to understand the true situation. I conclude that there are two major roots to this reaction. First, some publishers seem to develop the notion that they are employers, and that the writers are employees. An employee does not charge into the boss's office and demand an accounting of his finances—not if he wants to keep his job. So when I did the equivalent, the senior editor did the equivalent of firing me. Of course she should, even at that late date, have apologized for the errors and corrected them. That way she would have saved herself the loss of a writer who was to become best-selling, and a nasty hassle that I think cost her as much credibility as it did me, and for better reason. But she tried to tough it out—and she tried it against the wrong writer. An executive cannot afford to lose her head the way she did.

Second, later indications suggest to me that my threat to make a formal complaint and to invoke my right to examine their books of account struck a very sensitive nerve. I understand that back in the 1950s when this publisher was founded it paid a generous 8% royalties to the authors, and was acclaimed for it. Evidently things had changed, because my contract specified 4%. Had it been at the higher figure, my advance would have earned out, and I would have been owed royalties on the American paperback sales. Why had it changed? Obviously the generosity did not extend to beginning novelists like me—but I think also that the publisher had been losing money at the higher royalty rate, so had cut it down. And I think PUBLISHER was still in a financial bind, so was scratching for extra cash any way it could. That was why it was so grudging in paying me any of the subsidiary monies, and arranged to hang on to them for as much as a year after receiving them. In fact, I believe it went further than that: I do not believe the sales figures. Now most publishers have a "reserve against returns" clause. Since some books seem to be sold, but then drift back from the booksellers unsold, the publisher cannot be sure at first what the sales are, so it reserves some of the payment to the author until the returns are known. This reserve can be something like fifty percent—and later, when the book goes out of print and it is known that money is owing to the author, the publisher can just sort of forget to bring up the subject, and the author never gets it. A well-known science fiction literary agent has said that he suspects that the majority of cases go that way. But my contract specified only a ten percent holdback for returns, so that loophole did not exist. I always suspected that PUBLISHER could be systematically underreporting sales of my books. Ace Books had done something similar, as became evident when SFWA arranged for what amounted to a class-action audit, and had to pay out a lot of money. Perhaps a number of publishers were doing it, so that it became, by their reckoning, "right." But an audit would have laid this open to public view. Then, not only would I have gotten my money, but PUBLISHER's other authors would have dived in and gotten theirs. I, as the only person to threaten effective action, had to be put out of the way.

Meanwhile, I was pondering ways and means. Should I follow up through SFWA, or go directly to a lawyer? The former course might yield a quieter settlement, but the latter might be more effective. I didn't want a lot of trouble, I just wanted my contract to be honored. So I sought advice about both.

I wrote a letter to Damon Knight, of the SFWA Contracts Committee, summarizing the situation and my feelings about it, and asking him what course I should follow. This was not a formal complaint, but a private request for advice. And I went to my local lawyer, presenting my case to him. I told each about the other, as my approach was not secretive.

Would you believe: each condemned me for approaching the other! The lawyer felt that law was the only way to settle such a question, and SFWA—well, that was very interesting. You see, I never received a response from Damon Knight. I received one from Robert Silverberg, former president of SFWA, on SFWA letterhead. He told me that Damon Knight had turned my letter over to him for handling, because he was more conversant with the operations of PUBLISHER and the SF Book Club. He had gone directly to the senior editor and SFBC. He informed me that the SFBC advance was a thousand dollars, a standard figure, and that no publisher indicated potential income on a royalty statement, only cash on hand. (*No* publisher did? Then what of the wording of the contract, that required PUBLISHER to do just that? To say that "everybody is doing it" is no legal justification for wrong.) So he felt that PUBLISHER was justified in its actions. But, he continued, in view of my obvious distress, the senior editor had agreed to waive her contractual rights and send me my five hundred dollars for the book club share as soon as it arrived—provided I dropped the matter there. She was, he explained, more interested in avoiding an incident than in hanging on to my money. He advised me to cool it and accept her offer, since I had no case against her, and would certainly lose if I took legal action. He recommended against my "badmouthing" PUBLISHER in print, as the senior editor might then have to sue, and that would do me serious damage.

He continued that there was no "blackball" among publishers— I had mentioned that my lawyer had warned me about this possibility—but that there was such a thing as a grapevine. He said that word would get around that Piers Anthony had called in a lawyer over a simple misunderstanding of the terms of a contract, and other publishers would get the impression that "Piers Anthony is troublesome, obstreperous, and perhaps dangerous to do business with." He warned me that as I built a reputation for unfounded accusations and such, I would cut myself off from my markets. He concluded that he meant all this in the friendliest possible way but had to tell me that I had dealt hastily and rashly with one of the most fairminded publishers in the world, and possibly done myself a great deal of harm. He said that one word from Damon Knight, or from himself, could have spared me the needless battle with the senior editor.

Note the finesse of this letter. In the guise of friendly advice, Silverberg managed to insult me in several ways by telling me I had no case and had been wrong in pursuing it, and that my private queries to first the publisher, then the lawyer and to Damon Knight constituted hasty and rash action. He had ignored the wording of my contract, and suggested that I should have queried one of the very people I *had* queried: Damon Knight, whose letter he was answering. And he offered me a payment of five hundred dollars to drop my case. To tell a person he has no case, but can receive money for dropping it—what kind of a payoff should that be called? I have never since had any respect for Robert Silverberg's integrity.

And what of SFWA? I had made *a private* query—which had been funneled to the publisher, who then, as we shall see, accused me of libel because of it. Didn't Damon Knight or Robert Silverberg or the senior editor know the distinction between a private request for advice and public charge against a publisher? My confidence had been violated.

Meanwhile, the senior editor responded to a query by my lawyer. She condemned the way I had guessed at figures about which I had only to inquire (I *had* inquired, at first gently, then forcefully) and made unwarranted allegations to the possible damage of the firm's good reputation. She repeated the offer of five hundred dollars, provided that I make no further libelous statements about PUBLISHER to anyone. She said that they would do what they could to protect themselves from my unreasonable attack.

Note how the language has escalated. My original letter and my private query to the SFWA Contracts Committee, which existed for just such matters, were now termed libelous and an attack. I think it is clear that *any* serious inquiry on my part would not have been met favorably; if it could not be ignored, it was opposed. And why was the senior editor so eager to have me drop my case? All I wanted was what was due me: an accurate accounting, that I was sure would vindicate my position. Now I *had* to pursue the case, because my reputation was being savaged.

She also informed the lawyer that a German sale of *Chthon* had now been made, and that I was entitled to ninety percent of the money they received. Note again the reneging on the policy of yielding that ten percent.

I wrote directly to the senior editor and declined her offer. "I did not ask for money not due me according to the contract," I wrote, "and will not accept same as the price of silence on legitimate grievances." I said that I intended to pursue the matter with SFWA. This was where I asked permission to quote from her letter. "Since I mean to make my statement definitive, I will need to make no further comment anywhere after its publication," I said. If she really wanted the matter dropped, here was the way: after a fair airing.

There was one other vital aspect, that both the senior editor and Robert Silverberg had seen fit to ignore. We were debating conformance to the contract—but both my contracts with PUBLISHER were technically invalid. The publisher had been required to publish the books within one year. "If," the contracts said, "the Publisher shall fail to publish the work within the period specified in this Agreement, or otherwise fail to comply with or fulfill the terms and conditions hereof, this Agreement shall terminate and the rights herein granted to the Publisher shall revert to the Author. In such event all payments theretofore made to the Author shall belong to the Author ..." PUBLISHER had not published either novel within the deadline. *Chthon* had been one month late, and *Omnivore* three months late. So, according to the contract, both novels had automatically reverted to me. Technically, both published novels had been pirated; PUBLISHER no longer had the right to publish them. I had been aware of this all along, but had not made an issue because I had after all wanted the books in print and had not been inclined to cheat the publisher on a technicality. But now that the publisher was doing it to me, I felt it was time to pursue this avenue, if only to get PUBLISHER to admit error. Note how the senior editor and Robert Silverberg had condemned me for my supposed ignorance and false accusation, while ignoring this rather tangible evidence of the publisher's error. *The terms under which PUBLISHER was holding my money did not exist.* But this aspect of the case surely would be recognized by a court of law; the wording of the contract and the dates of manuscript acceptance, contract, and publication were all on record. The publisher was in fact throwing up a smoke screen to confuse a case I had to win.

Another thing I wanted to get straight was whether, under the contract, the publisher had any right to offset my share of subsidiary income against the unearned advance. Publishers customarily did not do this; they passed subsidiary payments along to the authors. My contract on *Chthon* listed the advance as being "against royalties," in contrast to, for example, the Ace contract of the time that listed the advance "against monies that may become due the Author." Ace could offset any money that came through the publisher, but it seemed to be that PUB-LISHER could legally do it only on royalty money. Had they meant it to be against subsidiary income too, they should have said so. This business of keeping half the book club money outright, and offsetting the other half against the unearned advance (when their sales figures were suspect) seemed questionable.

But they did have one other clause: "18. Payments: All payments made by the Publisher to the Author under this Agreement shall be chargeable against and recoverable from any or all monies accruing to the Author under this Agreement." I had had trouble understanding the meaning of that, when I signed the contract, but had concluded that it simply was legalese for their right to keep all the royalties until they equaled the amount of the advance. Evidently it was being interpreted as giving them the right to keep all my income from any source related to this novel. So I was ready for a court decision: did the publisher's right to half the book club money make the book club sale part of the original Agreement, in effect making *all* of the book club money theirs? Did their right to ten percent of the Dutch translation payment, which share the senior editor had waived but then reneged on that waiver, mean they could keep one hundred percent of it? I wasn't sure, but thought I had a reasonable case. Only a legal decision could set it straight, now.

At this point the lawyer felt I had gained about as much as I could; he wanted me to settle for the proffered money and drop the case. But I knew that others were now slandering me by accusing me of libeling a publisher. If I dropped the case now, agreeing to be silent, the only parties still talking would be those others. That would make me seem guilty. *That* would have a destructive effect on my career. Also, I believe that I had the right of the case; I could not drop it.

Accordingly I parted company with that lawyer and sought a New York lawyer conversant with contract law. That took a while. Meanwhile, Gordon Dickson, then president of SFWA, offered to have SFWA arbitrate the issue. I agreed, being still willing to settle this out of court if that could be done. As I have said, all I wanted was a correct accounting, and the vindication that should bring me. The senior editor agreed. There would be three arbiters: one selected by the publisher, one by me, and the third by SFWA. I chose Joe L. Hensley, a genre writer who was also a lawyer. Why him? Because I wanted someone who knew both science fiction and the law, and who had objectivity and guts. Hensley had had a story in *Dangerous Visions*, and Harlan Ellison, in his introduction to that story, had described how Hensley had come to Harlan's legal rescue when PFC Ellison had been in trouble in the U.S. Army in 1958. Déjà vu! PFC Jacob had been in trouble in the Army that same year. I wish I had had Hensley on my side then. So in effect Harlan Ellison had recommended him, and that was good enough for me. Hensley agreed to serve, and I showed him the fanzine article I proposed to do on the subject, asking his advice. He gave it: While my facts might be correct, my slant was so totally against the publisher that it could be construed as libelous; he advised me not to have it published, lest I be sued and lose. Okay; I had asked his advice; I took it. I did not publish the article. But I did not give up on my case.

To Gordon Dickson I said that while I would be happy to have the arbitration, I had already had some bad experience with the publisher and an officer of SFWA, so: "I must stipulate that at least a minimal report be published by SFWA for the information of its membership. This should explain that an altercation has occurred between Piers Anthony and [PUBLISHER], consisting in the main part of charges by the first party against the second of discourtesy, unethical behavior, and illegal behavior. Some decision should be announced on each of the three charges, whether it be as simple as 'justified/ unjustified' or 'matter of interpretation.' If a verdict of justified is rendered on any charge, SFWA must then be free to take such steps as it deems necessary to correct the condition. If a verdict of unjustified is brought, a similar freedom must be allowed to reprimand me for conduct prejudicial to the reputa-

tion of the publisher, and if need be I will resign from SFWA."
And I sent a copy of the letter to the senior editor.

Dickson asked for more information, so I sent it in a seven-page letter dated November 2. I pointed out that if my case was valid, SFWA should publicize it to its membership, because other writers were probably being treated similarly. And I itemized my three categories of complaint. Digested down considerably, they are these:

Discourtesy: Failure to inform me of the terms of the book club sale, even when queried, or of details of the foreign sales, though I needed this information for my tax estimate, thus forcing me to guess at figures. Badmouthing of me to others, documented by an agent who had relayed to me a report that I was on a "shit list," and false accusation of libel.

Unethical Behavior: Reneging on the promise to yield the publisher's ten-percent share of translation sales. ". . . such a promise . . . should be honored . . ." I said; readers of this book will understand how important any commitment is to me. Failure to honor the statement that my share of British proceeds would be relayed to me upon receipt. Then: "More generally, I believe it is unethical for [PUBLISHER] to employ a bear-trap, let-the-writer-beware standard contract that forces inequitable terms upon the beginning novelist" such as four percent royalties and trick clauses that enable the publisher to keep most subsidiary monies and hold the rest for as long as a year. The bouncing of *Paleo* simply because of my complaint about their handling of subsidiary rights on the prior novels. "If a writer cannot complain directly to the offending publisher when he has cause without being treated this way, there simply is no justice. To me, this indicates that [PUBLISHER] simply refuses to deal honorably with legitimate grievances against it." The offer to pay me five hundred dollars provided I dropped my case. "I take strong exception to the publisher's assumption that my principles can be purchased in this fashion."

Illegal Behavior: Failure to publish my novels within their contract deadlines. Failure to report subsidiary sales in the royalty reports. I did not charge the publisher with false figures on the royalty report, because only an audit could prove that. I hoped to get that audit, though.

I concluded that I wanted to use the findings of the arbitration as a lever to clean up the contracts, so that I and other writers would be treated more fairly thereafter. "And I want vindication for my personal reputation. I have not, as I see it, been jumping to conclusions, libeling anyone, or even being unreasonable, and it galls me to be condemned for such things. It also hurts my marketability as a novelist. I feel [PUBLISHER] is the one who was arrogant and who jumped to conclusions and who spread libel . . . and I do not see how much of the damage can be undone except by some publication of the truth." And I finished: "The most important function of SFWA, as I see it, is to handle just this sort of thing."

You might have thought that my case could hardly be ignored at this point. But to the best of my knowledge, Gordon Dickson did nothing. There was never any arbitration. When months passed, I followed up on my legal avenue. I got a New York lawyer and presented my case to him—and suddenly in February 1970 I received a payment of eight hundred dollars from PUBLISHER representing the book club and foreign payments on my novels.

A change of heart by the publisher? Not exactly. Apparently the senior editor acted the moment she heard from the lawyer, and realized that my action could not be stifled by bottling it up in SFWA. So she paid. That brought the monetary amount of my complaint down to the level where the lawyer could not make enough as his share of any judgment to make it worthwhile, and the case floundered. So I regard this as another tactic—more effective than the prior ones. Thereafter my foreign payments came directly to me, and some of my book club revenues, and later I got both novels reverted to me, so that there was no longer any question about their status. The furor was over, but I didn't have verification on the accuracy of those royalty reports. Half a loaf.

Yet since those statements of sales of copies and royalties earned had suddenly changed to show that the novels had just earned out, making the subsidiary income now payable, it was evident that the figures could be altered at the publisher's will and convenience. In retrospect I regret I was unable to pursue the case further; I really would like to know what kind of accounting was being done there. You bet they didn't want an audit! Those whose accounts are honest need have no fear of an audit; in fact they would be the first to require one, knowing that it would vindicate the publisher and be at the author's expense.

Disgusted with SFWA's inaction, I dropped my membership

after a decent interval to wrap up my commitments with the organization, and my statement (with the names deleted) was published in the SFWA Bulletin, then edited by Ted Cogswell, the one who had driven an ambulance during the Spanish Civil War. I saw only two comments on it by other members. One was by Richard Delap, who remarked that he thought this was the kind of thing Silverberg was trying to clean up. He didn't know that Silverberg was involved, ironically. The other was by George Scithers, who condemned me for my unprofessional behavior in agreeing to the arbitration; he said I should have taken it to court. (No, I don't know what he was thinking of, since in that statement I had covered my legal pursuit.)

Since that time I have maintained distant and hostile relations with SFWA, an organization I would gladly take to court if given any further cause. Individual members are all right, and I'm sure it represents a pleasant social organization for writers, but as far as I can tell some of the officers tend to run to the same indifference or arrogance typical of those I encountered, and I am not certain whether the good it does is not outweighed by the evil. There have been some instances of abuses just as bad as those I encountered. The full story of SFWA will probably never be known, as the errant officers do not publish the negative side, understandably, and so few members know.

5.

NEIGHBORS

This prolonged hassle occurred while Cam was pregnant with our second child, Cheryl, and represented an additional strain on her. I remain angry about that, too. But now things had been settled with my apparent victory (that is, I had gotten my money and made my case, though I was having trouble selling a new novel) and Cheryl was born into a relatively quiet time.

Because pregnancy was a serious matter with us, we decided that two children were enough, and my wife had a Cesarian-section delivery and a hysterectomy. As we tell Cheryl: We broke the mold after we made her. Cam stayed home now and took over the family operation, while I increased my output. My income had peaked at just under ten thousand dollars in 1969; thereafter, thanks in part to what I considered suspicious rejections and in part to recession, it dropped for several years to the six thousand dollar level. I accumulated a backlist of eight unsold novels. But Avon continued to publish me, and gradually my sales elsewhere picked up. I was surviving. I appreciated the advice of Ted White, to whom I had written because I knew he had been in a lot of trouble, and I wanted to know how serious my problems might become. He replied that publishers were generally unable to organize well enough to keep an author from being published, and that turned out to be the truth. The longer I endured, the better it was for me, as the truth gradually became known. My reputation as both person and writer was improving. Later, the senior editor left the company, for reasons I don't know.

Much of this section is negative; let me lighten it momentarily with the story of how at this time forty-seven degrees Fahrenheit became my favorite temperature. We had moved to a larger house after Penny arrived, one with two stands of bamboo on the premises and a fireplace inside. Naturally I decided to heat the house in winter with the fireplace. The truth is that this is very inefficient, as most of the heat goes up the chimney. But I bought loads of large pine logs that were being taken from other properties, and sawed and split them, and they burned nicely in our fireplace. In fact, sometimes they burned too well. The heart of pine is full of resin, and it burns in the fashion of a blowtorch.

One evening the temperature was forty-seven degrees and going down, so I had the fire going. To cap it off for the night I loaded a final, heavy log. Inadvertently I had put heart-of-pine on. Instead of banking down for a slow burn, it blazed way up. The light of the flames illuminated the whole living room and the staircase too. My wife went into a female tizzy, afraid it would burn the house down. So I did the sensible thing: I poured a cup of water on the wood, to dampen it and slow the fire. It made no difference. So I poured another cup. I think I wound up pouring about fourteen cups of water, and still the thing blazed maniacally. My wife was blazing similarly by this time. "We can't leave it like this!" she exclaimed. But we couldn't remove the burning log either. We would just have to stay up and watch it until the blaze subsided enough to represent no danger to the house.

The children were asleep upstairs, and we did not want to risk waking them by turning on the lights downstairs. We would have to wait by the light of the fire. Terrible as that light seemed in the circumstance, it still wasn't enough to read a book by. Now I hate to sit idle. What could we do in that time? Then I had a notion. It was the kind of notion that seems to occur to men who must spend time in the dark with attractive women. My wife had nothing of the kind in mind, but had to accede to my logic: "Why not?" So we did it by the flickering light of the fire, and ever since then forty-seven degrees Fahrenheit has been my favorite temperature, and I always think of that night when the thermometer passes that point.

We had good and bad neighbors. The good ones were the finest anyone could have, but the bad—well, I learned after the fact that little Cheryl, who was normally the sweetest of children, had been put in a metal trash can and a rock placed on the lid. She hadn't even told us; a neighbor had noted the episode, and quietly reported it. Apparently Cheryl didn't like making a fuss. But when I heard of it, I seethed. She could have been suffocated! The same neighbor's boy who had done that had once pushed Penny so that she fell and got both her legs scraped on both sides: huge red welts and bleeding. His older sisters sometimes yelled insults at my children, apparently just to entertain themselves. Once when a new neighbor moved in, with a girl Cheryl's age, the little girl of this bad neighbor told the new girl to get rid of Cheryl by hitting her. The girl did, and poor Cheryl came back to me in tears, dangling the tin-can toy phone she had made and taken out as an offering to play. I was so angry I could hardly see straight. To have such friendliness met with such viciousness! I got that cleared up, but I remembered. The ogre in me had been alerted.

The girls came in once to tell us that the neighbor's boy was teasing them, saying that he was going to dig up the stake so that our dog would get out and get run over. This dog was a basenji, the so-called barkless dog (but they *can* bark if they want to) and ornery; we had picked him up from a vet when he had been run over, repaired, and unclaimed. He had no sense about cars, and could climb the fence; thus we had had to put an L-shaped topping to keep him in, and drive stakes into the ground where he tried to dig out. To interfere with any of that was deliberate vandalism that could cost the life of our dog; we were not amused. But when we went out to see, there was no one there at the fence.

Fed up, I told the rest of the family to pile into the car and drive off, while I remained at home. Then I quietly circled the block to come at our fence from the other side. Sure enough, the boys were there, the one with his hand on the stake as he dug. I took him to his mother. "I want this stopped," I told her curtly. I had caught him red-handed; I figured that would settle it.

Well, it did, as the fence was not thereafter molested. But the boy started making threats to my children. He was going to beat someone's face in. Then, when I had the dogs out on a walk, the boys attacked. I returned to find both my daughters dirty and crying. They had been set upon by three boys, tackled, and their heads rubbed in the dirt. It was to take my wife three days to get the sand washed out of their hair.

I swerved toward the neighbor's house, the dogs still on their leashes. "Keep your boy away from my girls!" I bawled at the house. The man came out. "I want to talk to you!" I said. I must have looked like an ogre indeed. More than that; violence was very close. But the man took a good look at me, turned about, and went back in his house. I think it was the smartest thing he could have done. I proposed, frankly, to do to him exactly what his son had done to my daughters. I figured that would finally get through to him. He probably hadn't been paying attention to what his boy was doing; he preferred to believe that others were inventing stories. They weren't. I suspect that if you check into the situation of the average juvenile delinquent, you will find disinterested parents.

I returned to my house and called the police. When they arrived I showed them my daughters, identified the culprits, and said, "If you can't protect my family your way, I'm going to protect it my way." They understood. They talked to the other family. That boy never touched my girls again, and it's just as well. When I was a child, I was little and got beaten up; as a father I was determined to protect my children from anything similar. Those who refused to learn the easy way, did learn the hard way. I relate this not with any special pride; it is just the way I am. There really is some ogre blood in me. But my daughters, protected, have grown up sweeter than I am.

Another case concerned an obnoxious dog. We kept our two dogs confined to the yard on the leash; others were not as scrupulous. A loose beagle harassed mine, following us about and baying so that mine were too distracted to get their business done. I spoke briefly to the owner, reminding him that there was a leash law. Apparently that infuriated him, though I had been businesslike in my approach. He ignored the law, and his dog continued to run loose and bother us. Finally I put in a complaint, and then took him to court to require him to obey the law. The judge gave him a nominal fine and told him not to break that law again. But he still did not confine his dog, so I brought him to court again. This timed he committed perjury, saying that his dog was never loose, and that it was some other beagle that was bothering me. So when his dog still ran loose, I picked it up and took it to the pound. He recovered his pet, but that finally got through to him; he could no longer get away with it by lying to the judge. He couldn't know where I would take his dog if it ran loose again. We had a confrontation. I had my lawyer send him a letter advising him that we had now proved he had lied in court about his dog, so the next charge would be perjury. Thereafter he kept his dog under control, but would scream insults as he drove past our house.

A third case was slightly more distant. Penny was a very shy child—a remarkable contrast to her later manner—and could not be out of sight of at least one of her parents for more than a moment without getting alarmed. When she was a baby I had been unable even to go to the bathroom alone, unless she were asleep. I had to sit in the room when she went to the Sunday school programs, so she could see me. The second year I was able to sit in the hall outside; periodically she would open the door, peek out, see me, smile, and return inside, reassured. I never betrayed her in this, remembering how I had felt when left among strangers as a child. I was always where I told her I would be. But at age four we wanted her to get some experience in nursery school. We picked the best closest one, which happened to be associated with a Jewish synagogue. We enrolled her for half time, fearing that full time would be too much for her. This was against policy there, but they were understanding folk and permitted it. We explained to Penny what it was, and that she should try it and if she did not like it we would withdraw her. She knew we would keep our word— how important that is, for any child!—so she agreed.

She tried it—and liked it so well after the first day that she wanted to go full time. So she did, and we never regretted it. It was a very good school, which evidently knew how to reassure children. I would take Penny there on our tandem bicycle, and pick her up at noon. (Later we set up a tandem for three, so I could take both girls; that opened the eyes of bystanders!) It got baking hot on the pavement, so I would arrive about fifteen minutes early and wait in the shade of a tree, then go up and take her. The others used their cars, and would line up with their motors running so as to keep their air conditioning on, even during the period of the gasoline scarcity.

One day I was chatting with a man in one of the cars, amicably enough. Then the children were released, so I went around to the side and took Penny and went home. One would not have thought that that was the trigger to a crisis, but it was.

Next thing I knew, I received word that a man was roundly condemning me for breaking into line and holding up others while I took my child out of turn. Yep—the man was doing it, apparently because I got my child before he got his. He talked to everyone except me, raising a storm.

Well, no person who knows me would expect to do that without facing the music very soon. I approached the man and inquired. He told me that everyone was angry at me for breaking into the line as I did. Oh? I went to the next car and asked, "Is this true?" "No," the women said. Then she reconsidered, and said, "But you know, fair is fair." Apparently they wanted me to take my child last, even though I was generally the first or second on the scene, because I did not wait out in the sun. The fact was, I was not breaking into line, and did not delay anyone else; I simply took my child without interfering with the cars at all, just as those within walking distance did. They had two or three teachers handing the children to the cars, and the main delay was getting the cars through.

The man insisted that he would make a complaint to the management. "Fine," I agreed. "I'll ask for an appointment." But somehow he didn't do it; he just kept talking about me. So I approached him again, and he wouldn't talk to me; it's amazing how many people shy off when they see the ogre coming. He had started this, and I intended to finish it. I told him that I was asking to see the rabbi. Then I went to the office and asked for an appointment.

Well, later the rabbi phoned me. I asked him if he had talked to the other man. He said he had. "Well, then you know the situation," I said. "What is your decision?" The rabbi seemed taken aback; I wasn't even arguing my case. Of course I wasn't; I knew that the rabbi could see the merits of it himself. He told me that, to avoid the appearance of breaking into line, I should pick my child up at a side door thereafter. I agreed.

Later I learned that the man had not made any appointment. He had simply barged in and caught the rabbi wherever he was. The rabbi, evidently struck by the contrast between the accuser and the accused, gave him no satisfaction. As a result, the man withdrew his boy from the school, and we never saw either again. *He* had been the one breaking into lines, not me. This is a useful lesson for life: when one person makes an accusation, check to be sure he himself is not the guilty one. Sometimes it is those whose case is weak who make the most clamor.

I also learned that his boy had been a bully, and was starting to push Penny around. Had I known that before, I would have been considerably less polite than I had been. Perhaps it is just as well I had not known, because as it was, I came off as a reasonably decent person.

Two years later we sent Cheryl to the same school, and all was well. As I said, it was a good school. About the only fault I see in it was when they took the children for swimming lessons, and the instructors were taking the children out to deep water and dunking them. This was a terrifying thing to a child who could not swim; it was like being threatened with drowning. When Penny became reluctant to go, I went to one of the sessions and saw it happen, and she was so upset she vomited right in the water. Had it not been in other respects such a good school, and had the instructors not been part of the city program, rather than associated with the school itself, I would have terminated our relationship then. As it was I took Penny home, apologized to her, explained that I had not known what they were doing, and assured her that I would see that it never happened again. She knew I meant it. We bought a twelve-foot-diameter surface pool, and showed her that the eighteen-to-twenty-four-inch depth of water it held made it impossible for her to get in over her head. Then we let her play in it, never forced, and one of us was always there watching. Neighborhood children were permitted to join at Penny's invitation, but no dunking or even splashing was allowed. And Penny taught herself to swim, and lost the fear of water that the city course had so carefully instilled. As far as I know, Penny has no trauma about swimming, thanks to our decisive action.

When Cheryl was three, I tried to discourage her from taking the swimming course, telling her why. But she decided to risk it—and was treated similarly. So she was scared of the water, but the experience was not as traumatic for her because she had been prepared. What those city swimming instructors think they are doing I don't know; I had thought the sink-or-swim mode of instruction had gone out generations ago. The worst thing about is that they speak gently and reassuringly to the children, promising that they will *not* turn them loose in deep water; then they shove them down under and let go. The child thus receives the kind of lesson they use to train guard dogs to be vicious, trusting no one. I urge any parents to attend any swimming instruction given to their children, so they can prevent this kind of abuse. Do not accept assurances that things have changed; instructors evidently don't consider this sort of thing to be abuse.

Thus, then, I list some neighbors as among the swine. All they ever needed to do was obey the law and treat others decently, but some folk have no respect for that sort of thing, any more than some publishers do. There seems to be no remedy but force—which is one reason why I am not a pacifist. Never quarrel with an ogre unless you're pretty sure of your turf.

Yet I must say that things were not universally sweet between me and my children. Two episodes pain me particularly. One was at Christmas, when wrappings and toys and things got piled everywhere so that we could hardly get about. I gave my daughters fifteen minutes to pick up anything they wanted to keep; the rest would be thrown out. They worked for five minutes, then lost interest and watched TV. When the deadline came, I started in, cleaning up everything remaining on the floor. In the midst of the wrappings was a present I had given Penny: a chess set. I picked it up. "Hey that's mine!" she protested. "Then why didn't you pick it up?" I demanded. She was silent; the stipulation had been clear. I put it in the bag I was using to clean up. No, we didn't throw it out; it was my intent to hold it for long enough to make a point, then let her have it back. But I might as well have destroyed it; thereafter she showed no further interest in chess, knowing that I would have to teach it to her. She had wanted to learn, before. What had I accomplished by my strict enforcement of the rule? Something very like what my father had accomplished when he enforced his no-noise edict. I wish it had never happened.

Another related to Cheryl. In the mythology of our family, Penny was my daughter, and Cheryl was Cam's daughter, and indeed the alignment was evident, physically and socially. But there has been some crossover. Cheryl's mind is more like mine; she loves puzzles and games, and when she locks on to something, she doesn't quit until she masters it. We joke that Penny would scream if I ever even touched Cheryl, and to prove it I will touch Cheryl on the arm with one finger, and Penny, across the room, will cry "Eeeeek!" But we are all one family, and we all know it. Cheryl and I once amused a nursery-school teacher: We were walking from place to place, trying to get to the center of the fog, which somehow always was thin where we stood, and thick elsewhere. Once Cheryl was angry with her mother, and packed up her things and set out on foot, running away; everything was done openly, in orderly fashion, for that is Cheryl's way—and mine. I intercepted her, persuaded her to come to the study with me, where I talked to her and encouraged her to reconsider. She did; I needed no artifice to show that I cared. The loss of either child would devastate me, and I feel no shame in letting them and the world know it.

On this occasion Cheryl was with me when I was checking the rain gauge. I held it up to the light to see the level better, than put it back, for neither the day nor the rain was yet finished. "Don't empty it," I told Cheryl, and she agreed. Then as I started away, she took the gauge, checked it, and emptied it. I exploded. "Why did you do that?" I demanded. She couldn't answer. Back at the house Cam wanted to know what the problem was, and I exploded again. "She agreed not to empty the gauge, then she did!" I said. "I can't explain it," Cheryl said. Of course this never happened again—but the memory hurts me. When I pondered it privately, as I do anything that seems significant, I realized that Cheryl, like me, tends to follow the forms in set ways, automatically. On one level she had understood that the gauge was not to be emptied; on another, she had proceeded through the emptying routine. Sometimes the left hand really doesn't know what the right hand is doing. Perhaps this makes no sense to most people, but it does happen to me, and I can understand how it happened to Cheryl. Our minds are not simple one-event things; contrary currents can pass each other without interacting. I had yelled at her for being like me. I wish that this, too, had never happened; I should have understood immediately, instead of after hurting my daughter.

6.

DOCTOR

In 1972, after ten years of the mysterious malady that had gotten me labeled as a mental case, my local doctor sent me to a specialist in Tampa. I had pointed out that my entire situation had changed since the original diagnosis, so that I now had two fine children and a successful career as a writer, so that if my ailment were the result of psychological stress, it should have abated. Instead it had remained constant.

The specialist was in Tampa, across the bay. I went and had a full physical, complete with skull X ray and five-hour blood-sugar test. That did it: diabetes. Now I had the proof that I had been right all along, and that my malady was physical, not mental. Of course now I get ridered for diabetes, but I regard it as an improvement.

The doctor explained that he was interested in writing a book about kidney disease; would I collaborate? Intrigued, I agreed. Thereafter I learned more about kidney disease and treatment, including dialysis and transplantation, than I had thought existed. We published a collaborative article in a newspaper and worked on the book. I interviewed many patients, and developed a real feeling for their situation; it cost about twenty-five thousand dollars a year to be maintained on dialysis, and the quality of life was not up to the standard enjoyed by healthy folk. The first local transplants were performed during this period, and I have the inside detail. Even now, years later, I'm sure I could address an audience and talk indefinitely on kidney disease, albeit as a layman.

But the doctor was a busy man. I was dependent on him for information, yet often he never got around to correcting my text. The project dragged out for some six years, as I tried one approach and then another. I found a publisher—and then the doctor had a change of heart and stepped out of the project. I informed the publisher, and dropped it with regret. I had expended an enormous amount of time and energy—but it was not a total loss, as I do appreciate the knowledge I gained about this aspect of medicine. I am sorry the book was never published. Years later I drew on what I had learned for use in my fifth Space Tyrant novel, transposing today's medical technology to the twenty-seventh century.

No, I don't blame the doctor. I think he did not properly understand the nature of writing and publishing, and that I did not properly relate to his concept of the project. It is quite possible that publication of the material we had would have embarrassed him, as some of it was intimate and fascinating. Things do go wrong in hospitals, and private remarks can be salty. What use to have an interesting book in print, if it prejudices a doctor's career?

One interesting sidelight is that the doctor's secretary was the daughter of Theodore Sturgeon. Sturgeon was one of the finest writers in the genre. She was willing to work with me on the project, but for reasons that do not reflect on her capacity I declined. Over the years I have become turned off on collaborations, having found that I can work far, far more efficiently alone. And a sidelight to the sidelight: I had met Sturgeon's daughter. In 1982 he met mine, for I had Cheryl with me when I met him in Kansas. She was just twelve years old then, mature for her age, an attractive girl: the very picture of dawning womanhood. When I shared a panel with Sturgeon, he spent the whole hour looking at Cheryl in the audience, somewhat to her discomfiture. Sturgeon was the genre's apostle of love; I can readily understand what he saw in Cheryl.

7.

MINOR SWINE

I was never a proper part of science fiction fandom, but maintained some ties with it. Some fans are good people, but some are obnoxious and arrogant. In general I kept them at arm's length. First, when I received copies of fanzines, I would send polite notes explaining that I was not into this sort of thing, and please to drop me from their mailing lists, But sometimes one would run my note as a letter of comment, perhaps criticizing it. Sometimes they would run part of a comment, so that if I said something positive and something negative, only the negative would appear, making me look negative. Once a fan criticized me as being a hypocrite, because I used a pseudonym but had my books copyrighted in my own name. (No, *you* figure the logic in that comment; I cannot.) Another lambasted me in print for being someone who thought he owned fandom after being in it for only two weeks, while he was an old pro after two years. (He had not been in long enough to know of my participation years before his time.) There is no arrogance like that of an ignorant fan. I tried to keep my address out of circulation, so as to cut down on this sort of thing.

But the fanzines kept coming in. Finally I tried stronger medicine: I wrote a comment on three of them simultaneously. I told them I had no time or interest for this. Then, to soften the blow, I took pains to comment on each, politely and to the point, including even some published fan fiction. I hoped they would get my message and leave me alone.

Ha. One of them printed a part of my letter, making it seem that I had not offered any positive comment, and then published several negative comments about me. I sent him a brief disgusted card—which he printed out of context and with typos that made it incomprehensible. A fan who liked me sent in a comment; this was cut up so as to become nonsense. Another fan, Roberto Fuentes, wrote a generally positive letter with one negative comment about me; only the negative comment was run. Even a pro, Wilson Tucker, wrote in to condemn me. I had remarked that my total earnings from writing amounted then to about seventeen thousand dollars. I have never been shy about figures. Tucker said that he had made that much on a single contract, and he wondered how I managed to live on so little.

Well, now. If that was the way they wanted it . . . I wrote to a friendly fanzine (because there was no point in writing to the attacking one, that had no fairness in publishing letters) and challenged Wilson Tucker to demonstrate that he was a better writer than I was. I offered to have an impartial jury compare his novels to mine, and suggested that he have a story published in the volume Harlan Ellison was then assembling, *Again, Dangerous Visions*. Since I already had a story therein, the readers could read both and judge. (Never quarrel with an ogre . . .)

The fans got together and published an entire fanzine whose only purpose was to lambast me. They sent copies everywhere— except to me. Wilson Tucker, according to an article published in *Locus*, recommended doing just that to "Fuggheads"—which term seemed to apply to any person who disagreed with him. But of course a friendly fan relayed a copy to me. Tucker said that he couldn't put a story in *A,DV* because Harlan Ellison was mad at him for prior comments he had made about Ellison. (Tucker seemed to be good at that sort of thing.) I wrote a long rebuttal, published in a friendly fanzine, and also this statement published in what was perhaps the leading fanzine of the day, *Science Fiction Review*:

> In reply to my urging that he publish a good new SF story in *Again, Dangerous Visions* (so as not to let the volume go entirely to pot by being filled with the crud of neo writers like me,) Bob Tucker says he would not have a fair chance with Harlan Ellison . . .

Since it is important to me that Tucker be in that volume, I am forced to rear back on my hind limbs and tackle the bull by the balls:

Harlan Ellison—are you there? I challenge you, by the authority vested in me as one of the youngest and turkiest of the young turks, to publish the excellent SF story Bob Tucker offers you for *Again, Dangerous Visions* and to pay him at least 3¢ per word against hard and paper royalties, and not to tamper with one single word in it. (You may say what you please in your introduction, however.) Kindly signify your abject acceptance of these rigorous terms by so stating publicly in this fanzine.

OK, Bob, you're on your own now. Submit your story. (I always like to give the tired old timers a helping hand in coping with today's more demanding market.)

Of course the "rigorous terms" were exactly those that Harlan normally extended to contributors to the volume. The thing was a pretty pointed spoof calculated to embarrass Tucker. It took about three months for that statement to be published. Meanwhile, another fan had read the Anthony-condemnation fanzine. That fan had invited me to contribute to his own fanzine, and when I politely declined, he simply republished the entire condemnation issue, giving it considerably broader circulation. Harlan Ellison read this reprint, saw Tucker's comment about him—and got on the phone to demand a contribution from Tucker. And Tucker, in the end, was unable to oblige with anything suitable. I had made my point. I also made it by reviewing a new novel of his, and calling out the fatal flaw in it. I don't believe Tucker ever messed with me thereafter; if he did, he was careful to see that I never learned of it.

But Harlan Ellison was annoyed by my reference to *him*, mistaking its nature and thrust. He thought *he* was being criticized. So when *Again, Dangerous Visions* was published, he quoted that statement in the introduction (I copied it from there for this volume, trusting him to have gotten it right) and said:

"Well, Piers did it again.

"Foot in mouth, he did a no-no." And continued to say that long before I got into it, he had been in touch with Tucker to solicit material.

Harlan was in error. His solicitation to Tucker was a direct result of my challenge; he had not been cognizant of the background there. It was an honest mistake on Harlan's part; I just wish he had checked with me before telling the world. He had taken a fanzine statement and moved it into a professional context, without checking, and that was unfortunate. Nevertheless, I think my statement stands up well enough.

I had a juvenile novel published in hardcover, *Race Against Time*, and it was reviewed in *Locus* by Dave Hartwell, who claimed that its conclusion was racist because the white boy married the white girl, and the black boy married the black girl, and the yellow boy married the yellow girl despite having had some interest in those of the other colors. Now that novel was not racist; it showed that the cultures of the three couples were in the end the deciding factors in their relationships. Readers are welcome to verify this in that novel for themselves; it has been reprinted in paperback. I never took any guff from reviewers, and I did not this time. My comment, published in Frank Lunney's "Beabohema," was approximately this: "Some ass in *Locus* is making me out to be a racist. He should come to the south and see what real racism is." I, you see, had seen things like hooded Ku Klux Klansmen meeting openly, and I regard racism as an abomination. To suggest that any person who does not marry a person of different color may be a racist, and to condemn my novel on that ground—that was fighting language.

That started a ten-year problem. Hartwell became an editor, but never published any book of mine.

I think a person who does a negative review should then listen to the author's rebuttal. Certainly he should not take a fanzine quarrel too seriously. Hartwell developed a fine line of books in his Timescape series, but in the end it was cancelled by the publisher.

There was a science fiction magazine called *Vertex*. It was an attractive publication, edited by Donald J. Pfeil. The June 1974 issue published the collaborative Anthony-Fuentes story "Ki." The editor sent author's copies, and my direct dealing with him was amicable.

Then I learned of the case of another writer, who had been wronged by this editor. Now I have little tolerance for wrongdoing, but it was not my business; the other writer needed to protest his own case, and didn't do so. But when I was discussing why I sold material to Ted White at *Amazing*, having been challenged on that, I said that while there were some problems there, the editor was doing his best, and had not treated writers in the manner some other publications, like *Vertex*, had. Don

Pfeil challenged this; if I had anything against *Vertex* let me say it openly, or shut up.

He should have known better. I obliged in detail, telling how the other writer had submitted his story, waited a reasonable time without response, and finally requested it back. Then Pfeil had written angrily that the story had been set in type already, and he never bought a story from that writer again. (Note the similarity to my experience with PUBLISHER: a reasonable request brings an unreasonable response.) He had never bothered to notify the writer of the acceptance of the story, or to get a contract signed for it, or to pay anything; he had simply set it in type without notice. Yet he was so furious at the writer's request, that instead of apologizing for the oversight and sending the contract, which would have made everything all right, he chose to reject the story. I spelled all of this out in print. Pfeil claimed that this was standard operating procedure for his publisher, but of course it could not have been; lawsuits would have put that publisher out of business.

That was all to my exposé; I had documented my case. Not that long thereafter *Vertex* folded and Pfeil lost his position. As far as I know, I had nothing to do with that. But my revelation of Pfeil's way of doing business could not have had any favorable effect on the reputation of the magazine, and I suspect it was the turning point for it. Certainly Pfeil practiced a swinish mode of editing, and the genre is well rid of it.

Another case was that of Lin Carter. Back when I was compiling my review index, I had learned of his review fanzine *Spectrum*. I sent in money for a subscription, with a note asking his permission for me to index the *Spectrum* reviews along with those in the prozines. He never replied, and he sent only two of the four issues I paid for. Since the money involved was small, I wrote this off as another arrogance of fandom. But later, in another fanzine, Lin Carter stated that he always answered his fan mail. I wrote to that fanzine that he must have turned over a large new leaf, because he hadn't done anything like that in my case. No reply. Then that fanzine published a "review" of my novel *Sos the Rope* by Lin Carter, roundly castigating it—for a number of things that weren't even in the novel. It seemed that the castigation was the point; Carter's intent had predated his reading of the novel. Evidently word of my private comment had reached him.

They never seem to learn. I did a column-length commentary in a different fanzine that exposed the whole thing, including the errors in Carter's "review." He was unable to refute me, and offered to send me the missing issues of my subscription. I declined; by this time my review index, torpedoed by other circumstances, was history. I had made my point. Carter never challenged me again; indeed, though known as an expert on fantasy, he tersely states that he doesn't read Anthony. He had learned.

A number of cases have been denatured in this section and others because of the publisher's fear of legal action by those named. All uses of the word "bl—ckl—st" have been expunged. Thus it may seem that I exaggerate when I say I've had about as much trouble in Parnassus as any writer—but I believe it is true. There have been some very bad feelings, and bad stories were spread about me, such as the "ogre" one that is responsible for the title of this book. I achieved success despite this, but have not forgotten. I have always been ready to make these charges public, thereby exposing their nature, but I was at one point advised by a lawyer that I could be sued for libel *and lose* despite proving the truth of what I wrote, because this would damage the reputation of those I named. This seems to mean that it is safer to do wrong than to protest it, in the eyes of the law. If so, I think American law needs an education in the fundamentals of fair play. It is wrong to deny the rights of the victims in the interest of protecting the rights of the wrongdoers. But it is true that even a victory against a "nuisance suit" of no validity would be more expensive to defend than a payoff would be. The ogre would rather fight it out, but some concession has to be made to the party who is putting up the money to publish this volume. Thus this book has been "vetted" —reviewed to eliminate anything that might provoke legal action. More's the pity.

Here, then, is passing anonymous mention of some of what isn't here. There is the story of the prominent figure in a certain writer's organization who arranged to have the definition of the calendar year changed so as to give his book more time to win an award—thereby messing up *my* novel, which got shifted to the wrong year. Yes, I protested, about that and similar abuses, thereby getting myself branded as a troublemaker. Even today my work is not considered for certain genre awards or listed in certain articles about fantasy, or given favorable reviews in certain quarters. Indeed I am found well outside the top ten or fifteen in some listings of the best fantasy authors. One panelist at a convention, when pressed about this, stated: "If Piers Anthony ever writes a good novel, I am sure we will know of it."

There was the prominent genre author who criticized my novel *Hasan* as an attempt to cash in on the fantasy fad. I responded by suggesting that in that case his most noted novel could be judged as an attempt to cash in on the juvenile fad. He later reported this as my scream of outrage against his objective critique. Uh-huh. There was the noted genre critic who submitted an appallingly bad story to a critique group; no one spoke candidly until it was my turn, but I called it out without mincing words. He never forgave me, and his friends spread the word that I was uppity, but no one refuted my comment. I feel that critics should be able to take their own medicine, especially when it is deserved.

There was the editor whom I termed "a blacklist looking for an object to focus on." And the writer who stated that he made eight to ten times as much as I did in a year, and took this as a reason to disparage my personality. He may have been embarrassed when I later demonstrated the manner my novel outperformed his on bestseller lists, when both were published in the same month. On and on; I never suffered fools or rascals gladly, and it shows.

And so I am an ogre. This is the legacy of the no-holds-barred realm of professional and amateur interaction, of fierce rivalries within the genre, and of the misshapen self-promoted "elite" that resents the success of an outsider, particularly an outspoken one. The ogre has little use for any of it, and open contempt for much of it, and that perhaps is my greatest crime. Swine are swine, regardless of their credentials.

PART FIVE

The Moving Finger

1.

JUDO

One of the fans whose letter was cut to only the negative aspect about Anthony, during that fanzine feud, was Roberto Fuentes. I had written directly to him, to correct a misimpression, and as an afterthought inquired whether he was Spanish, as I had once been in Spain. He replied that he was Cuban. That began a considerable correspondence, and in the end we collaborated on a science fiction novel, *Dead Morn*. It was a time-travel adventure set in Cuba after WWIII. It never found a publisher, though it was a good novel.

Roberto visited me, with his wife Graciela and son Robertico. He was interested in judo; in fact he had been the judo champion of Cuba, before the Castro takeover. He took Penny and me to see a judo class in Tampa run by Ed Maley, a fifth-dan black belt. As I watched, my imagination percolated, and I began to work out a story. We collaborated on it and marketed it, but it bounced. So we did other stories, and finally merged them into a novel, *Kiai!*, and marketed that. It also bounced. But then the TV program *Kung Fu* came on, and suddenly there was a martial arts craze, and two publishers that had rejected our novel asked for it back again. We sold it to the first who asked: Berkley. That began the series of six martial arts novels, generally conceded to be the best of that genre, because Roberto knew his martial arts and I know my writing. The sixth novel was rejected when Dave Hartwell assumed power at Berkley, ending the series.

After doing several of those novels, I decided it was time for me to learn something about the subject, so my daughter Penny and I signed up for classes at the local judo club. Penny did not stay with it, though later Cheryl did. Cheryl was in four matches with another little girl; she lost the first three, won the fourth—and the other girl quit the class. Uh-huh. I was in the class three years, rising to the rank of yonkyu, or green belt, about in the middle of the student grades. My advice to people considering such activity is don't start it when you're forty. I was injured a number of times, and it was rough going up against healthy teenagers. I lost my first match to a fourteen-year-old, tied the second, and won the third; those were all I was in.

I can't say I was an apt student of judo. Intellectually I had no trouble, but my understanding did not translate readily to action. I discovered that mental comprehension was not the same as physical comprehension; a throw I could visualize perfectly became clumsy when I tried to perform it. There were others who were the opposite. When I tested for my green belt, I suffered stage fright and balked several times when attempting throws. I can talk to an audience of hundreds and be at ease; I really don't get stage fright. But when trying to perform physically before an audience of no more than twenty people, I froze. I found that a useful if awkward lesson.

I'm glad I had that training. It stopped when I moved to the forest and was too far away to commute, but I was in trouble anyway. I was having knee problems, and my knees finally were damaged to the point where I was unable to squat or to flex them fully. I think this was partly the stress of certain actions in judo, and partly the squat-jump exercises I was doing to build up my legs. I learned the hard way that knees do not heal; my loss of function was permanent, unless I wanted surgery. I preferred simply to ease up and take better care of my knees. I am able to run, and if there is any twinge of pain, I ease up. But the training itself taught me how to defend myself. If a man charged me with a knife, I would know what to do. I might do it clumsily, being out of training, and break his arm or his head, but that's a risk I'm willing to take. The techniques of judo can be devastatingly effective; that martial art is no fake. Some other martial arts do have fakery, though, such as karate. The serious karateka can kill with a blow, but would not do it; the dilettantes may only hurt themselves or others. If it should be necessary to subdue a drunkard without hurting him, judo or aikido will do it; karate would be problematical.

There was one episode that bothered me, however. A black belt (that's instructor grade) visited from elsewhere in the state, and informed our club that it was required to pay a portion of its earnings from tournaments to that parent organization. Our club was independent, in that respect, and preferred to remain so. But the man said that if we did not, we would not receive any further black belt promotions. Now the judo ranks are supposed to be determined by merit, not money; this was not the way judo should operate. In fact, in judo, the spectators are admitted without charge, while the contestants have to pay entry fees; nobody does it for money. The money is used to run the tournament: trophies, rental of the hall, and such. I queried privately and learned that indeed the national organization did not operate this way. If we would put in a complaint, the national organization would set things straight. I relayed this news to the officers of the club. They considered, and concluded that a complaint could generate a great deal of mischief, and leave the club worse off than before. I was disgusted, but that was it. And I do understand; after all, look what my complaint about my publisher did for me in Parnassus. That, unfortunately, is the way of the world; right does not necessarily make might, and all too often it is the most expedient course to keep your complaints, however justified, to yourself. I don't practice that course myself—but few would care to suffer the mischief I have as the result of my militancy. Still, it was too bad that judo, one of the cleanest of sports in the world, should suffer this kind of corruption. At any rate, our club declined to make the payments, and took its chances with the promotions.

2.

Ps & Cs TREES

We never wasted money, and my income from writing was rising. My acquisition of an agent was helping, and my conversion to marketing by summary rather than by whole novel was to triple my income within two years. Editors seem to like to bounce complete manuscripts, knowing that there is no way other than publication that the writer can recover his investment; when they know that won't work, because a bounced summary represents relatively little investment, they are more likely to buy. (Editors might have a different opinion about this.) At any rate, it was so for me. I never bothered to write a book that I couldn't sell from the summary. Thus in 1975 I earned about twenty-two thousand dollars. We were ready to find a better place to live, where we would have better control over the neighborhood.

We started looking. We checked the geography and decided that the closest country region and our farthest feasible moving distance coincided around the area of Citrus County, Florida, about eighty miles north by road. We made several trips to check out properties. One morning we got stuck in sugar sand for an hour and a half, and got out only when a local property owner described a route that didn't require us to try to drive uphill through the stuff. That afternoon we looked at another property, and the more we considered it, the better we liked it, and in the end we bought it.

We dubbed it Ps & Cs Trees—the P's for Piers and Penny, the C's for Cam and Cheryl—and made plans to put up a cabin. It was forest land, adjacent to the Withlacoochee State Forest, so that it could never be built up into a city. We have had a policy of buying all available adjacent land that we can afford, so as to guarantee it will not get built up, and increasing income has facilitated this. Thus the land remains forest, and is not likely to change.

The cabin was a challenge. A lumber company would put it up in one day, but we had to prepare the foundations. That meant we had to haul water up eighty miles to mix the concrete, and we didn't have enough. One day it rained, and the rain helped wet the mix, so that we got by. We came up weekends, as Cam still worked, and did what we could. Then the lumber company put up the cabin, which was a twelve-by-twenty-four-foot red cedar gambrel-roofed structure. Then we had to put on the roofing. When we drove up to see it, we discovered that they had set it up backwards: our south entrance was to the north. We had given the instructions clearly enough, but they had not paid attention. Yet the door seemed to work as well on the north side.

That roofing job was a horror. In my youth heights didn't bother me, but with the increasing problem with my knees came increasing wariness of both depths and heights: anything that might put me in a knee-bending bind. Our ladder was too short, so I had to struggle to get to the roof. As I worked, a wind came up, which was scary, and then a storm. I flattened myself across the top beam and hung on as the rain pelted down, but the wind whipped a roll of felt off and it fell to the ground. My wife came out, alarmed; she had heard the thunk of its landing and feared it was me. Fortunately it wasn't, but I could not even see the ladder from above, and could not afford to guess, because the rain had made the surface too slippery to allow me to crawl safely down. Cam had to direct me, and I aligned myself above the ladder, and as my hands slipped I had to trust that my feet would find it. They did, with her corrections, and I stopped my slide. I got safely down—but thereafter I was afraid to go back up on that roof, and could not finish the job. Once when we stayed overnight, it rained; Penny and I were in the loft, with my waterproof poncho protecting us, but the drip washed across it and on down to Cam and Cheryl, who were sleeping below.

On another date the man from the lumber company delivered more material and stayed to help us complete the roof. He had a larger, longer ladder, and that made the difference; I was able to go up there and work. But I don't remember the experience with any particular fondness, and remain wary of roofs.

For two years we saved our money again, having depleted our savings by buying the property, until we felt we could afford to build. We made arrangements with a local contractor, who undertook to put up a house of our design for seventeen thousand dollars. It was to be unfinished, in the sense that we would take care of the interior paneling and such ourselves; such matters greatly affect costs. We signed the contract and made the first payment, and he started work. The job was supposed to be complete by June 1977, so we could move in during the summer and enter the children in the local school system in the fall. But somehow the work never seemed to progress unless we were right there watching—which was hard to do just on weekends. Also, everything was wrong. The contractor used the wrong materials and made rooms and windows the wrong sizes. We required him to make corrections, and the workmen grumbled about how we were making more work for them by changing our minds. Uh-huh.

When June came, the house was not complete. Also, it was shaping up into a kind of disaster. We had solar water heating, and planned to have a vertical water tank in the attic, so that the hot could separate from the cold. The plumbing was atrocious; it all had to be redone subsequently, to eliminate the leaks. The contractor did not honor the specifications, and made the attic too low to be used for a vertical tank or for storage. That put us in a space bind, for we had a lot of things to store. Our siding was supposed to be cedar; he made it Douglas fir, which would not be proof from termites. Our roof was supposed to be terne, a kind of metal that would last without needing periodic replacement. The contractor gave us a long story about the problems he had getting it, but without telling us he actually put on galvanized. I clipped a piece and had it tested to verify that; when I did, I sued him. He never did finish the house; we had to hire other contractors to do much of it, and to redo much of what he had done, and we did a lot ourselves. But we got an eight-thousand-dollar judgment against him. He was broke; we didn't get any money, but we did put him out of business. So the house cost us much more than it was supposed to, and some things never could be fixed, but at least it became liveable. Seldom did a dream house have a more problematical reality.

Actually, it was not complete in the fall, when we *had* to complete our move, because we had the children registered in the Citrus County schools. We moved into the cabin and camped. We brought rocks to make an outdoor fireplace so we could cook. One evening it rained, so Cheryl stood with an umbrella shielding the fire so we could finish. She got soaked, but the fire survived. It was hot, in late August and early September, and the cabin hung on to its heat. At 9:00 P.M. as we tried to get to sleep—no electricity, so there wasn't much to do after dark—it was still ninety-one degrees Fahrenheit in the loft. There we were in our sleeping bags. But we survived.

After two weeks the house was close enough so that the inspector granted us a temporary permit, and we were able to turn on the electricity and move in. But the soffiting wasn't in place yet, and the windows fit so loosely that there was space around them, and the bugs entered freely. It was love-bug season; the bugs were so called because they mated on the wing, and flow indefinitely in pairs. Love bugs are harmless, but they were all over. When we got up in the morning we had to clear their crushed remains from our sheets; they had joined us in bed. We had to fish them out of our soup. I believe it was the worst love-bug season in years, and we seemed to get them all. Worse, in their fashion, were the assassin bugs: called bloodsucking cone-noses, or Mexican bedbugs, they moved into our bed and caused welts that were much worse than mosquito bites. My wife became allergic, and her arms would swell up, and she had to get medical attention. Some always got in, no matter how tight we tried to make the house. In later years wrens took up residence on our property—we encouraged them—and that abated the cone-nose problem.

Meanwhile, we were trying to get our old house in Gulfport fixed up for sale—and the contractor for that was just as big a scoundrel. The evidence of the leavings was that he spent the money on liquor and had parties there, while the work did not get done. The amount involved was in the hundreds of dollars, rather than the thousands, so we didn't go to the trouble of suing; we just took our losses. But for the time we owned two houses, and were beset by additional expenses on both, and my wife left her job—wouldn't you know it, my income that year dropped to eleven thousand dollars. We were in a bind.

Again, we survived. We managed to sell the old house, and my income rose again, and we were all right. In fact, that squeeze of 1978 was our last. Later my annual writing income passed the hundred-thousand-dollar mark, and financial problems were behind us. Most important, we were established in the forest where we had wanted to be, and the hassles of moving were over. In fact, all our significant problems were over; from that point till the present, our lives have been increasingly comfortable.

We kept buying land, until we owned forty acres around us. I made a running path that circled our property and bordered the state forest, for my exercise. I did my pull-ups every morning on a rafter in the study. After three years, we had a line run to the study so I could have light and a fan. Civilization was coming to the forest at last.

3.

NOVELS

I have tried to group things by subject within the broad chronology, but some subjects stretch across decades. Each novel is a case history in itself, and when I was fifty years old my fiftieth book was published: *Politician*, which novel I completed in May 1984, shortly before my fiftieth birthday. So there is too much to cover in any detail here, though a complete bibliography of my fiction will appear in an appendix. Instead I will summarize the more interesting cases prior to my serious entry into fantasy.

The Unstilled World—This was my college thesis novel, completed in 1956 and rejected by *Astounding Science Fiction*. I set out to explore and expose many of the common theses of the genre, such as time travel, telepathy, nuclear holocaust, restoration of culture, robots, and technological religion. The story was of a young army deserter, James Ambler, who gets sent to the future, only it was via suspended animation, thus showing how a form of time travel could exist. In a more advanced scientific world he encounters an attractive young woman, who then accompanies him on further trips forward. Her name is Maple, and it was our intent to name our first daughter after her, Maple Irene Jacob. But our first was a boy, and he was dead, and by the time we had a daughter we could keep it was a decade later and our tastes had changed. Still, I do have Irene as a character elsewhere, and I'm sure Maple will appear in due course in some other guise.

A decade later, when I wanted to enter a five-thousand-dollar novel-award contest (I never seemed to learn about contests!), I dug up *Unstilled World* and considered it for revamping. I concluded that the novel was, in general, a loss; my writing ability had improved over the years, and most of this was not salvageable. But the longest chapter, "Battle," about thirty thousand words in itself, was like a short novel. I tried to expand that. Again, I saw it wouldn't work; the thing was too clumsy. But the framework and some of the characters were good, so I simply started writing a new novel on the old foundation. I did this when I had to spend time at my wife's office at the newspaper, because she was working until midnight on computer projects and I didn't like her having to walk a block or so alone downtown at that hour. But I knew nothing of computers, so I just settled into a vacant office and started writing my revamp. It moved phenomenally well. Since I was then hung up on a section of the novel *Omnivore*, I simply continued on the project that was moving, and in about ten days I wrote forty thousand words, just about the whole first draft of the novel *Sos the Rope*. This was a revelation: When one project wasn't moving, try a different one. It was the material, not me, that was blocked. Ever since, I have had more than one project available, of different types, so as to be able to switch off. Today I seem to be able to move well on anything I start, but then it was not necessarily so, and I recommend this to early writers as a prime treatment for that dread malady, writer's block. I suspect the problem of block is mostly in the will, when a person really isn't as interested in writing as he thinks he is, and block becomes an excuse for not doing what he didn't want to do anyway. Some women are the same way with sex and headaches. But where the will is present, and the text won't move, this can be an effective remedy. Certainly it was so for me.

Later I typed *Sos* in second draft, and it expanded forty percent. Then I typed it in submission draft, and it expanded again similarly. So I had a sixty-two-thousand-word novel, and I entered it in the contest, and it won, beating out a novel by Barry Malzberg, who was gracious. The contest, as it turned out after I sent in my entry, was flawed, having some unconscionable terms; I considered withdrawing my entry, but figured I was unlikely to win anyway so didn't need to make an issue. Norman Spinrad pointed out some of these flaws, and his points made sense to me. Then, when I won, it was a bit late to change my mind, though I considered it. Spinrad, too, was gracious. We used the money to pay off our mortgage. That was one of my first big breaks as a writer, and it does date, in its fashion, back to my first novel of 1956. Today *Sos* is in print as part of the one-volume trilogy *Battle Circle*. I considered writing two more novels in that series, but publishers weren't interested, so I never did.

Chthon—I had the notion for this novel back in college, but felt I lacked the ability to complete it properly, which I believe was an accurate judgment. But in the army I continued to ponder it, and worked it out in my mind, and wrote portions of it. Then in 1965, seven years after I started writing it, I completed it, and it became my first novel sale. All that you know; what you don't know is its nature.

I regarded myself as a story writer, and my most comfortable length was the novelette. *Unstilled World* was actually a collection of episodes set in different times, each an adventure to itself. My structure there was influenced by that of Clifford Simak's *City*, my favorite novel in early years, which had first been published as stories or novelettes in magazine form, then collected as the novel. That was certainly one way to do it, but I knew I needed to be able to do a unified, one-piece novel before I could call myself a true novelist. I struggled to achieve this with *Chthon*, but found it horrendously difficult. My narrative kept forming itself into short individual episodes. So I made of this liability an asset, by unifying them in a complex framework. In fact, I believe that *Chthon* is the most intricately structured novel the genre has produced, and this should have been its primary claim to fame.

It is structured like a doubled hexagon, with six major parts, each split into paired sections: one describing the novel's present, the other describing a different time. The dates are indicated by the "section" symbol, §, and the "present" is §400. That is, 400 years after the emergence of man to space. The first three parts cover §381, §398, and §399, and the last three parts cover §401, §402, and §403. Thus the novel starts and finishes in the present, §400, with three major flashbacks and three major flashforwards in between. As far as I know, no other science fiction novelist has used the flashforward technique as systematically as I have here; that was the first great innovation I made. All of this is plainly shown in the table of contents, with every part dated, and the system of dating is described in the prologue.

More significant, the story of the present is the same as that of the past/future. Each subsection is numbered, with the present having Arabic numerals—1,2,3—and the equivalent other time narrative having written numbers—One, Two, Three. Every one of them matches up with its equivalent. Thus, 1 describes the protagonist Aton Five's introduction to the nether prison world of Chthon, where he encounters a woman who offers him love but tries to kill him instead. In the parallel One, the seven-year-old Aton encounters a lovely woman in a glade in a forest, who kisses him and tells him he will never find another woman as beautiful as she. Through this parallel the hint is delivered: It is death to love this woman. So it continues in careful parallel, sometimes literal, sometimes figurative but always there. I worked harder on this than on any other aspect of the novel; every set of numbers matches. Thus we have two complete versions of the same story, with the flashes signaling the meaning of the present sequences. Just to be sure the readers understood, I mentioned it in the Author's Note of the original edition, though the current edition does not have that.

So what was the reader response? Oblivious. As far as I know, no one understood the true nature of *Chthon* or fathomed its structure. Certainly the publisher didn't, and no fan commented to me, and no reviewer remarked on it. The novel made a fair run for both the Nebula and Hugo awards, coming in approximately third in each (there was a tie for third place in one), apparently on the basis of the least of its qualities: the overt plot line. Writers like Roger Zelazny and Samuel Delany got awards because of their sophistication as writers, which sophistication I do not question, but I was regarded from the outset as an entertainment writer. In this and other novels, what I was doing was too complex and subtle not only for others to understand, but for them even to realize that it existed. However, Zelazny and Larry Niven wrote to praise my work, and Harlan Ellison told everyone to read *Chthon*. I suspect that, as a general rule, the better a writer is, the more generous he tends to be about the work of others. Thus my work has been condemned by the likes of Lin Carter, and praised by the likes of Theodore Sturgeon.

This novel also has the dubious privilege of being my first pirated book: a Spanish edition was published, with no contract or payment to me. The publisher went out of business, so there is no recourse. I suspect that my name was forged on a contract by another party, but he's in South America and can't be reached.

Hasan—This was the fourth novel I completed, after *Unstilled World, Chthon,* and *Pretender.* My father read to me when I was young, and it is a tradition I carried on, reading to my daughter Penny. (Cam read to Cheryl.) One of the things he introduced me to in that manner was *The Arabian Nights*—the tales of a thousand nights and a night. Today few people seem to be conversant with these fabulous stories, and that's too bad. So I sought a way to bring them to the attention of contemporary readers. I obtained three translations of the *Nights*, one of them running to sixteen volumes, and read as much of them as I could, seeking the ideal tale to adapt. I decided on "Hasan and the Bird Maiden," a phenomenal story that I had in all three versions. It described how the young, innocent Hasan of the city of Bassorah (Basra, today) was lured by the promise of the secret to convert gold from copper, into slavery and likely death. But in a far land he escaped, and encountered the Bird Maiden, whom he loved and lost, and sought to recover. In the end he did locate her, and rescued her after horrendous adventures. I rendered this into contemporary language, and researched to make sense of some incongruities and to flesh out the details of the cultures, and I made it as compelling as I could. When Hasan saw a tornado, he took it to be one of the jinn—and later it turned out that *was* how the jinn operated.

But I also operated on another level. I recognized in this tale a historic basis. The pattern of some genuine exploration was there, masked by the magic explanations provided by those who did not understand or did not believe the truth. What was the truth? I researched to discover it—and believe I succeeded. Hasan traveled to Ceylon—now called Sri Lanka, but which I called Serendip. Delany challenged this, saying I was putting an obvious Western term in what should have been an oriental myth. I advised him of the story of the Three Princes of Serendip, who always found what they weren't looking for; in the eighteenth century Horace Walpole used this story to coin the word "serendipity." Serendip was the original name for Ceylon. When I corrected Delany on this, he dropped the correspondence. The descriptions in the tale of Hasan align with this interpretation. Hasan later traveled through India to

Tibet, where a wise man sent him along to China (Cathay), then down the coast to Indo-China, Malay, and finally Sumatra. I researched the geography and cultures all along the way, showing at the end how a volcanic explosion accounted for the destruction of the pursuing army as Hasan escaped with the Bird Maiden. I had not only rendered a tale of magic into contemporary language, I had shown its factual basis. I don't believe that is often done.

So how did *Hasan* fare on the market? I couldn't even find a publisher for it! Larry Ashmead at Doubleday heard of the project and asked to see it, but rejected it on the basis of a sample as inadequate. Isaac Asimov swears by Ashmead as an editor, but Ashmead was never able to see value in my work when it was offered. Ballantine rejected it as not fitting within its ambience; apparently what that publisher wanted at the time was what Lin Carter provided. Later, under the del Reys, that publisher's fantasy program developed genuine power—more of which anon. I kept trying it, through 1967 and 1968: Ace, Lancer, Avon, Fawcett, McGraw-Hill, Harper & Row, Viking, *F&SF* (sample chapters), Dell. Hardcovers, paperbacks, magazines—all rejects. Avon responded in a fast three weeks, while Lancer took almost five months and only returned the manuscript after two queries.

Seeing that I was making no headway the conventional way, I tried an unconventional approach. I wrote to the fan reviewer, Richard Delap, and asked whether he would be willing to review my novel unpublished. Flattered, he agreed, and I sent him the carbon. He did publish his review, in a fanzine, and the review was favorable. Delap found fault with several of my published novels, but *Hasan* he really liked, and I don't think this was because of the circumstance. It was just his kind of novel. Meanwhile, Walker was in the process of rejecting it, giving a progress report in two months but returning it in four. That made twelve bounces.

Came a letter from Ted White. Now my relations with White had been mixed, and I feared something I had said somewhere was setting him off. That sort of thing happens to ogres; can't think why. But no, he had seen the review and wanted to see the novel. The top copy wasn't back from Walker yet, so I sent him the carbon May 10, 1969. May 29 came his phone call: He was buying it for *Fantastic Stories*. He could only pay a penny a word, and by his estimate that eighty-seven-thousand-word novel was only seventy thousand words long, so that meant seven hundred dollars. No, he wasn't trying to cheat me; Ted White was on a tight budget and honestly didn't know how to calculate wordage. When he ran the novel, in two installments, its full length manifested, and squeezed out part of his own editorial. I was so glad to get the sale, after a dozen rejections, that I wasn't about to quibble about wordage. The novel was well received by the readers, and I remember the entire matter with pleasure. My persistence and innovative marketing, combined with Richard Delap's willingness to give fair coverage to an unpublished manuscript, and Ted White's acumen in seeking material combined to put this novel in print and make a special kind of history, and I don't believe that any of us ever regretted this. I don't think any other novel has been sold that way, before or since. Though I have my differences with Ted White, I regard him as a better writer than credited, and an excellent editor. I speak as one who has had some terrible editing on occasion.

Meanwhile I continued to try the book market, and picked up rejections from Pocket Books' new Trident imprint and Macmillan. Then I had word from my collaborator on two other novels, Robert Margroff, that he had been to a convention and met the editor at Berkley, who was eager for material. So I sent *Hasan* there—and in just seventeen days had an acceptance. Berkley paid an advance of fifteen hundred dollars against six percent royalties. That money, coming as it did at the time I had assumed the expense of moving to a larger house to accommodate our expanding family, in late 1969, was a godsend; it eased a financial bind. So now I had fourteen rejections and two sales. Then Berkley changed editors, and the new editor, in the manner of that kind, wouldn't publish what the old one had bought. *Hasan* was written off—that is, they simply never published it. I kept the money, but had no book publication.

Enter fandom again. A fan, Robert Reginald, wrote to ask me for biographical and bibliographical information, as he was compiling a book about genre authors. I obliged, not expecting much; these projects come and go and few amount to anything spectacular. But this one *was* spectacular; in 1970 he published *Stella Nova* under the imprint Unicorn & Son and it was a phenomenal production, with information on several hundred genre writers. Later he set up his own publishing house, Borgo

Press, devoted mainly to a series of critical booklets on genre authors. He expressed interest in *Hasan*, which he had read in the magazine version. So I signed a contract with him, and the novel had its third sale, and was published in a nice small-press edition in 1977.

An editor at Dell read that edition and bought it for mass-market publication. That publisher had rejected it, a decade before, but the change of editors can blow fair as well as foul. Fourth sale. It was published in December 1979. Its success was not spectacular, and it was allowed to go out of print. Then in 1984 Tor picked up most of my out-of-print novels, *Hasan* included, for republication under its imprint. Fifth sale. Which I think concludes the most remarkable of my marketing histories: fourteen bounces, five sales, and the first sale the result of a fanzine review of the unsold manuscript. The lesson here, I believe, is never to give up hope.

Macroscope—This was the eighth novel I completed, and the most important of my early years. At 190,000 words it was no lightweight, and I did a massive amount of research into every kind of science for it. It took me a year, because it was the first novel I did after my daughter Penny was born, and that cut my writing efficiency in half. Here I treated astrology as a science, though I do not believe in it myself. I worked out a way to travel on the galactic scale by generating temporary black holes; in order to survive such a trip, human beings had to be melted and then gasified, then reconstituted, a somewhat grisly process that is an eye-opener for some readers. I had some conjectures whose accuracy remains to be ascertained, such as the presence of a moon of a moon—that is, an ice moonlet—orbiting Neptune's moon Triton. I do that sort of thing. But the story of this novel does not lie in its writing, but in its marketing. I knew I had a good novel, and I didn't like waiting one to five months for reports from publishers. There was a recession due that I thought could affect the publishing industry—a true assessment, as events proved—so I wanted to get this placed promptly. So I tried multiple marketing. I sent it out simultaneously to six publishers, and when a copy was bounced early I sent it out again, so that I had seven submissions in all. I picked up five rejections and two offers, and I accepted the better offer. Thus I made my first sale to Avon Books, who was to be my main science fiction publisher for the remainder of the period covered by this narrative. Few authors have the nerve to try this kind of marketing, as it can aggravate publishers, but it paid off for me.

The novel was published in 1969, and was to be distributed free to the membership of SFWA for consideration for the Nebula award for best science fiction novel of the year. But Avon fouled up and sent their novels to the membership late, so that they arrived after the deadline for nominations. Members who, knowing the distribution was coming, waited for the free copy instead of buying it on their own, were thus unable to nominate it, and it missed the ballot. I knew that it was a strong contender and quite possibly a winner—but how could it compete if it wasn't on the ballot? So I wrote to Gordon Dickson, President of SFWA, and asked that write-ins be permitted. He refused. Because of complications of another nature, Tom Disch had withdrawn what was thought to be the leading contender for the award, *Camp Concentration*, so the ballot was minus two heavyweights. The best novel remaining on the ballot was *The Left Hand of Darkness*, by Ursula Le Guin, and that won, I think, by default. Le Guin's career took off, while Disch and Anthony languished. *Macroscope* did make the Hugo ballot, but by then the pattern had been set, and the Le Guin had the edge and won, while mine came in third. When the annual anthology of Nebula award stories was published, there was a discussion of the novels that had been contenders—and *Macroscope* was there, though it had not even been on the ballot. Did SFWA know that wrong had been done? *Macroscope* has remained continuously in print, and last time I checked several years ago had passed a quarter million copies in American sales. My light fantasy sells twice as much, of course, but it's still a good showing. How any publisher could have bounced it, considering either quality or sales appeal, I don't know. The average editor, as I believe I have said, seems to be an idiot.

Orn—This is the one that PUBLISHER bounced when I demanded a correct accounting on prior novels. It is the sequel to *Omnivore*, and concerns dinosaurs. In fact, here I set out to write the definitive dinosaur novel, and I haven't seen anything else to match it. John Taine's *Before the Dawn* was one of the books I read when researching for it; Taine was an excellent writer, but much has been learned about dinosaurs since his day. I made listings of all the creatures of the late Cretaceous and fitted in as many as I could, together with my conjectures on how they actually lived and operated. In an essay at the end

I presented my theory of the extinction of the dinosaurs, showing that it was related to the breakup and drifting of the continents. As far as I know (but of course I cannot know all) I am the only one to make this connection, and I believe it was the most plausible of all the explanations until the comet/iridium theory of a decade or more later. Even that does not conflict; it could have been a combination of the two. So I remain pleased with this novel, and feel it shows some of what I can do with hard science, though I am not known as a hard science writer.

Prostho Plus—The twelfth novel I wrote. It started in my dentist's office, when I had sixteen gold onlays (not inlays; these are like caps only more of the tooth is saved) done. I researched on dentistry and did a story, and then others, and got some of them published, then collected them into a novel and got that published too. I use this as an example for the unlikely sources of notions: If you can make thousands of dollars from the work done on your own teeth, how much more likely is all the rest of the world to provide notions?

3.97 Erect—In 1969 the erotic science fiction market was going strong, so I rose to the challenge and wrote my own. It concerns a man with a small penis—three point nine seven inches long when erect—that nevertheless has a remarkable property: its smegma cured venereal disease. A luscious female doctor steals the penis by amputating it for her research. He has to go to her equally luscious sister for a prosthetic, but really wants his natural one back. It was small, but he liked it. And on into space, and a mountain made of ice cream, and the most fantastic (literally) sexual exploits. I enjoyed working on it, and feel it is a remarkable example of its type. But while I was writing it, the major market for it abruptly shut down, and it was simply too hot for other markets. By the time it found a publisher, most of two decades later, the appeal of my fantasy to young readers was so great that I did not dare publish this under my own name. So it appears with a new title and name, not "Anthony."

Steppe—This is a direct translation of history to science fiction. I have always been fascinated by history, though it was sometimes a poor course for me in school. They didn't teach true history in school, they taught rote memory of names and dates. Using that technique, it is possible to make even the subject of sex become dull and incomprehensible—as indeed they have discovered. So here I set out to render true history into a form that retained its original fascination. This is the story of the peoples of the great steppe region of Asia: the Huns, and the Turks and the Mongols, and their formidable empires. In the novel, there is a galactic-scaled game in which history is replayed, with citizens assuming the parts of the key historical characters. Naturally our protagonist manages to assume the role of Jenghis Qan (Genghis Khan) and become high scorer. I was very pleased with this novel, and planned on several sequels covering other aspects of history similarly—but for a dozen years, from 1972 to 1984, it remained unsold in America. It did sell in England in 1975, however, and picked up a German translation. I suppose if I had had it as a conventional sword-and-science hackpiece I would have had less trouble placing it; editors seem to shy away from anything meaningful. I can write exciting adventure as well as anyone; it's that second level of significance that can torpedo me with editors.

OX—Third novel in the *Omnivore* trilogy, which trilogy was later to be titled *Of Man and Manta*. The first concerned advanced fungus life, the second dinosaurs, and this one inanimate intelligence. For about six years it was in stasis because I couldn't figure out a satisfactory mode for nonliving mind; this was before the days of the computer revolution, remember. Then I spied the game of Life in *Scientific American* magazine, and there was my answer; I based my inanimate intellect on that, postulating a three-dimensional pattern entity. Again, I don't think anyone else had done this; others just have computers coming alive, or humanoid robots taking over. Not that I object; I love stories like Harlan Ellison's "I Have No Mouth and I Must Scream" (there was a femmezine—female edited fanzine—convention report taking off on that, "I Have No Mouth and I Must Giggle") and Jack Williamson's *The Humanoids*. But I have an original mind that just won't leave well enough alone.

But What of Earth?—a new genre publisher Laser Books, edited by Roger Elwood, wanted novels that would appeal to a mundane audience, so I wrote this one very close to the present. The theory was that population controls the level of civilization, so that if world population abruptly declined, human culture would regress. I had it decline by massive emigration to other planets, and today's normal society regressed toward tribalism. My main problems were the short deadline for delivery of two months, and the length, set at fifty-five thousand words, when I normally write longer. I learned later that that was the *minimum* length; I wish I had known! But I got through and delivered the manuscript. The editor told me there were some minor changes to be made, and that he would have another writer, Robert Coulson, retype it with the changes at the publisher's expense. But when it was published, it was listed as a collaboration with Coulson, and it was completely rewritten and, I believe, degraded, and Coulson had been promised half the royalties from it. This was a massive contract violation. I complained, and the rights to the novel were reverted to me, the editor was let go, and the line shut down. Perhaps this was not cause and effect, but it did save the publisher a lawsuit that I think would have finished it anyway. A decade later I made arrangements to have the novel republished in its original form. I believe this sets my personal record for inept editing; whether it is a world record I can't say, but surely it is a contender.

Cluster—This was the first novel in what was to become a five novel series, one of my more popular ones. This is related to the framework for *But What of Earth?* and to that for *Tarot*, so there are nine loosely linked boots spread across three publishers. The theory, again, is that population affects civilization, with a higher level of civilization required to maintain larger populations, much as a large animal requires a more complicated system than a small one. Also, the limitation of light velocity made galactic empires become more primitive at their edges, because of the time it took for advanced technology to reach the fringes. So in this framework all levels of human society could be found, from the paleolithic to the supertechnological. I had fun with that; it allowed me to give play to the range of my imagination.

Tarot—The culmination of the Cluster framework, though it takes place in the time of *But What of Earth?*. The protagonist, Brother Paul of the Holy Order of Vision, is sent to the planet of Tarot to determine whether the presence manifesting there is or is not God. He gets caught up in a phenomenal series of animations that lead him eventually to hell. The full novel is a quarter million words long, and I regard it as the most important one of my career. It covers a considerable range of religious subjects, such as the commercialization of Jesus by those who have no real interest in the real nature of his doctrine, and I have said that anyone who reads it without suffering some discomfort probably doesn't understand it. I have some pretty caustic opinions, for example, about those who evidently consider a baby to be God's punishment for the sin of sexual expression, or who claim that injustice should be suffered in this world for the sake of a reward in the next one. I don't like abortion because I don't like to kill the most truly innocent creature there is, a baby, but I don't trust the motives of others who oppose abortion. Questions like these are explored in the novel, sometimes very pointedly.

But the marketing—disaster! I wrote it on a contract for Avon, but when I delivered it the editor had changed (that almost always means trouble) and such extensive revision was required that I simply took the novel back and wrote them a different one to satisfy the contract. We then showed the novel to three other publishers before finding a taker; it was simply too much, in size and concept and language, for some to accommodate. Jove offered $15,000 if they could break it up into three volumes. Since it was a unified novel, we declined, and sold it to them for $11,500 on condition that it be published in one volume. Jove then decided that the novel still had to be broken up, and I reluctantly agreed, since I did want to get it published. The three volumes would be published in one year, with renewed promotion for each, so that it would be clear that it was one novel in three parts, not a trilogy. I have a signed agreement to that effect: it would never be called a trilogy. Then Jove's science fiction line was shut down, and bought out by the Berkley complex—which had rejected my novel before. Crowded by the new novels, the two later volumes were put into the following year, destroying any chance of the novel being considered a single item. It had, perforce, become three. And the novel that should have thoroughly established my credentials as a writer of major serious fiction became lost in the fragments. Oh, it has sold well enough, and in the first years earned a good income from all sources, but my reputation remained that of an entertainment writer.

I'm happy to say that Tarot is now finally available in a single-volume trade paperback from Ace.

Thus my career in novels—until Xanth.

4.

XANTH

On March 3, 1976 I received a mailing: a kind of brochure from Ballantine Books showing examples of the covers of books they had published and describing the directions they were going. Judy-Lynn del Rey was now in charge of their SF/fantasy program. We entered into a dialogue, and I wrote to Judy-Lynn: ". . . let me state the one requirement I now make of all publishers: that the contract be honored. That's all. You'd be amazed (then again, maybe you *wouldn't*) how many publishers shy away from any such commitment . . ." You see, I had queried the publishers with whom I did business, asking them to sign an agreement that they would honor the terms of their contracts. Would you believe, not one one them would. That pretty much speaks for itself. But Judy-Lynn didn't blink, and I must say that Ballantine under the new auspices turned out to be absolutely straight on contractual matters.

But there was another problem. I had been selling my science fiction to Avon, who had been treating me quite decently. Ogres remember their friends as well as their enemies. I would not simply start selling my new work to Ballantine when Avon had the option—that is, the right to see Anthony science fiction first. I make it a point to honor both the letter and the spirit of any deal I make, which meant that though there might be technical ways to void the Avon option I would not do it.

I had a bright idea. Suppose I split the option into science fiction on the one hand, and fantasy on the other? The two were like sister subgenres, lumped together on the stands, but the difference between them was like that between fact and fancy. Science fiction requires a scientific or pseudoscientific rationale, while fantasy is just plain magic. Could I sell science fiction to Avon and fantasy to Ballantine? I checked with Avon, and that publisher was as generous as ever and agreed, provided that if Ballantine did not want my fantasy, Avon would get the next look. So I told Judy-Lynn I would try fantasy, though I wasn't sure how well it was selling.

She replied that they believed they could do well enough with fantasy, and she shunted me across to her fantasy editor, who happened to be her husband, Lester del Rey. Now this situation was of course nepotism, but there is a place for it. Nepotism is wrong when a person puts relatives on the payroll merely to fatten the family coffers. But when a person has a relative who is well qualified for the position, so could have been hired on merit, it would be wrong to exclude him merely because he is related. As it happened, Lester del Rey had perhaps the best qualifications in the genre. He was a writer and novelist of established stature, and he had been a magazine editor more than once, demonstrating unusual competence. In fact, I had admired his editing in the golden fifties, and felt that had I been a selling writer then, I could have worked well with him. I jumped at the chance to work with him now.

So we commenced negotiations. Did he want to look at my prior fantasy novel, *Hasan*? No, he preferred something new. I tried another notion or three on him, but these were not quite right. He encouraged me to send in only a summary, no sample chapter required, since I was an established pro whose basic ability was not in question. This facilitated things. And then I came up with the notion of Xanth.

Remember, this was when we were setting up Ps & Cs Trees, our retreat in the forest of central Florida. The forest and countryside came readily to mind when I sought a setting for fantasy adventure. There were the huge spreading live oak trees, with their trailing tentacles of Spanish moss, and the prickly cacti, and the roads and trails disappearing intriguingly into the state forest. I've always loved paths; I want to know where every one in the world goes. Blackberry bushes abounded. Once when my daughters and I were exploring a trail (they inherit some endearing traits from me, such as the love of puzzles and trails) Cheryl, last in file, cried, "Oh! It got me!" I froze, having a vision of a rattlesnake or something. There are four types of poisonous snake in America, and all four are in this region. Then she added: "With its thorn." It was a blackberry vine, reaching out to grab her in the way they do. And there was that railroad cut, resembling a huge forgotten chasm.

Xanth formed. Instead of live oaks, there were tangle trees, whose tentacles not only dangled, they grabbed. The cacti could literally shoot their needles. Paths were magic, sometimes being one way: existing only in one direction. And there was a huge forgotten chasm in the center. I had in fact transformed the entire state of Florida into the Land of Xanth. At first I think this was unconscious, but in due course I caught on to what I was doing, and intensified it. But I didn't tell the publisher, for fear this would make my magic land seem too mundane. I was long accustomed to editors and readers failing to grasp the other levels of my writing; they could survive, as usual, without that appreciation.

The name "Xanth" was from my "Names" book. I use these books not for the usual purpose of naming babies (though when we finally did have babies we could keep, I cheated and used the books for that) but for naming characters in my fiction. I am fascinated with unusual words and odd spellings, and Xanthe appealed. I used it in a short story that never sold, so then I used it again as the name of my magic land, dropping the terminal *e*. It means blond, or yellow-haired, like my daughter Penny. It was an incidental use; neither the publisher nor I realized just how successful Xanth was going to be. But I remain satisfied with the name.

So I worked up a summary of the novel *A Spell for Chameleon* and sent it to Lester, and he accepted it in June 1976, suggesting some revisions. His points were well taken, and I agreed. I completed it by November, and Lester asked for some further revisions, and it was published September 1977. Perhaps the novel would have been successful without the revisions, but I don't think so; Lester did know what he was doing. Before it saw print, however, Lester asked for more fantasy from me, and I pondered and found that I had no better framework than Xanth, so wrote a sequel, *The Source of Magic*. *Spell* did well, and was reprinted. Then one day I got a call from Judy-Lynn: *Spell* had won the British Fantasy Award. Now in America there seems to have been a general understanding that Piers Anthony was an obnoxious character who should not be encouraged to compete for awards, the legacy of my prior situation and my quarrels with arrogant fans, but evidently the word had not reached England. So I had an award after all, and I am sure it helped my career in fantasy. But the leading American news fanzine, *Locus*, which had its own recommendations and balloting for best SF and fantasy novels each year, would not give me any favorable review since the Hartwell business, would not recommend my novels, and failed to list the British Fantasy Awards that year, though they were listed every other year, before and since. When I challenged this directly to *Locus*'s publisher, Charles Brown, whom I knew personally from my 1966 visit to New York, he expressed his belief it was coincidence. Thereafter the *Locus* policy toward Anthony began to ease, but when my books are recommended there is always a disclaimer that this is not necessarily the preference of the *Locus* staff. *Locus* is an excellent magazine, but not as good as it should be. Fandom hasn't changed.

I wrote a third Xanth novel, *Castle Roogna*, and it also was well received. Now that I was firmly into fantasy, I found that I liked it. It was easier to write than science fiction, and a lot of fun, and it sold well. I did not regard it as any great literature, but I do not sneer at entertainment fiction. I like to do all kinds.

The fifth Xanth novel, *Ogre, Ogre*, made the New York *Times* best-seller list. As far as I know, that is the first time that an original paperback science fiction or fantasy novel—that is, one with no prior publishing history—has done that. *Locus* did not run the news. Then when the following Xanth novel, *Night-Mare*, did it again, I received a call from Charles Brown. He thought that was the first novel to do it, and was surprised when I advised him of *Ogre*'s success. Since *Locus* had been listing other genre novels that made the NYT list, I had assumed that *Locus* was merely practicing its normal policy of ignoring Anthony successes, but it seems that this time it really was an oversight. Thereafter its coverage of Anthony improved another notch.

Xanth became the series for which I was primarily known. My income from it dwarfed that from other novels or series, and my mail increased. The novels refused to die; they just kept selling more copies. Other writers get reissues after their novels go out of print, picking up the new market that develops from normal turnover after a few years. Xanth never goes out of print. Thus my fame as an entertainment writer increased. Ah, well; I am, as the saying goes, crying all the way to the bank. But I did not forget my desire to write meaningful fiction.

5.

OTHER PROJECTS

Lester del Rey and I agreed that three novels was enough for Xanth, back before the readers started making their will known, so I tried a different fantasy trilogy, *The Apprentice Adept*. I knew that some readers liked science fiction, and some liked fantasy, and some didn't like to have any of one in the other. So I set out to give them something really aggravating: novels carefully crafted to be precisely half and half. (I checked with Avon, because this did constitute the writing of science fiction for another house; once again Avon was understanding.) The science fiction portion had computers, robots, androids, cities, and terminal pollution in a thoroughly scientific society. The fantasy portion had whole herds of unicorns, packs of were-wolves, flocks of vampires, trolls, dragons, elves, and enchantments in a thoroughly magic society. Yet they were but aspects of the same geography and population, with things and people existing in both, separated by a kind of curtain. The first novel reflected the forbidden nature of this project, via a pun: *Split Infinity*. It sounds like split infinitive, a thing the grammarians claim is not to properly be done. Only this is the opposite: The infinities of science and fantasy are merged, also not to properly be done. Apart from that naughtiness, I wrote the best fiction of either type I could.

So what happened? Del Rey (now the genre arm of Ballantine, possessing its own hardcover facility) put both their fantasy basilisk and their science fiction bedspring on the volumes, cooperating with the impertinence. But there was no outcry. I don't believe I received one single complaint about the merging of genres. The series was accepted by the readers, and received good reports everywhere except at *Locus*. And of course *Locus*, who had listed an Anne McCaffrey novel whose nature was fudged under both the science fiction and fantasy categories for their awards, did not do so for mine, listing it simply as fantasy though as good a case could be made, by no accident, for calling it science fiction. According to *Locus*, there wasn't much fantasy in it, and not enough science to make up for the lack of fantasy. Par for that course. The concluding volume of that trilogy made the paperback New York *Times* best-seller list, joining Xanth there.

When I was working on the last of the Cluster-series novels, I got ill. For a month I had daily fever that nothing seemed to abate. I wound up in the hospital before it was diagnosed: cat scratch disease. That is not a serious illness, just a mysterious one that simply has to run its course. But the mystery of its persistence naturally evoked my morbid streak, and I pondered my career seriously. I concluded that it was time for me to ease off on the entertainment writing and start getting into new challenges, and into social commentary. You see, I don't see my life as merely a matter of feeding my own face ever more comfortably; I want to use whatever abilities I have to make of my life an instrument to accomplish some good in the world. My position as a writer had been pretty well established; now it was time to start using my talent for a more constructive purpose. The illness merely helped focus my mind on it, by reminding me of my own mortality. So I planned to slow down on the writing of science fiction while I put my effort into new things.

Well, I tried. But I discovered that I was pretty well typecast as a genre entertainment writer, and that was all that editors wanted of me. I tried marketing horror and WW II fiction, with no takers. I had tried historical fiction before, with the same blank wall; eventually I had converted that to science fiction, and then it found a publisher. That was the collaborative novel *Pretender*. My interest in history had not abated, but I could not justify spending a lot of time on it if the result would never see print. I had, after all, a living to earn.

Meanwhile, I filled in with the easy stuff, fantasy. It required no great organizational effort or deep emotional commitment to turn out a fantasy novel; the stuff was fun and easy, and I had a ready market for it. Del Rey would issue a contract for one of my fantasies almost on receiving word of the projected title. Of course I did the best I could on each novel; I always do that, and Del Rey understood that. I kept hoping to break through with a more significant project. But while I was failing to do that, and dashing off fantasy in the interim, that fantasy was forging its way to the top, to the mundane best-seller lists. I became one of the handful of best-selling genre authors of all time—on the basis of this offhand work. The ironies of my career had hitherto been mostly negative; this one was positive. It should also be noted, however, that this success was not mine alone; Del Rey had correctly read the potential market for fantasy when other publishers had not, and Del Rey had developed a promotional mechanism that gave any novel a jet-assisted takeoff. Of course this could not do much for poor novels, but when good, entertaining novels got this treatment, such as those by Stephen Donaldson and David Eddings as well as Anthony, things really moved. One of the mysteries I have not fathomed is why other competent writers who can do excellent fantasy, such as Poul Anderson and Fritz Leiber, never chose to get on this bandwagon. Gordon Dickson did one, *The Dragon and the George,* and failed to follow up. Larry Niven did *The Magic Goes Away* for another publisher with phenomenal success, but never pursued this strongly.

I pondered, and achieved a realization. If I could only sell genre work, why not include the serious themes and social commentary within it? Why not simply stretch the boundaries of the genre, to include the meaning I desired? At worst, no one would know the difference, which was the normal course for my work anyway. At best, I could achieve everything I wanted to. And so my career assumed a significant new course, without sacrificing the old course.

I set up two major new series. One was science fiction, the other fantasy—but both were really the same in their secret essence. That is a common mechanism in my work, starting with the paired parts of *Chthon* and continuing through the paired science fiction and fantasy frames of the Adept series. Like male and female, opposites, yet unifying for the whole.

The science fiction project was *Bio of a Space Tyrant*. Each volume was to cover one portion of the life of a refugee boy who survived and eventually became the leading figure of the human culture of the day. The setting was contemporary Earth— transposed about six centuries into the future, with the continents and nations becoming the planets and moons of the Solar system. Thus America became the planet Jupiter, and Asia the planet Saturn, and the one was an English-speaking democracy and the other was a Russian-speaking communist dictatorship. The rest of the world matched the rest of the system. Instead of ships crossing the ocean, they crossed interplanetary space. This was a hard-science framework, based on one major assumption: that it is possible to deflect gravitons the same way as it is possible to deflect photons. Just as a magnifying glass can focus or diffuse a beam of light, so could a gravity lens focus or diffuse the force of gravity. That made interplanetary travel cheap, and the colonization of other planets feasible, for gravity was no longer a barrier. Apart from assorted standard science fiction gadgets, all the science in this series is hard; that is, the things could operate exactly as I describe, granted the initial assumption.

But the essence of it lies in the social commentary. There is much in today's world that is bad; it is my hope to help expose it and encourage my readers to think about it and push for its correction. Ranting at the evils of the world does not accomplish much; I suspect that the true hearts of people can be reached more readily via the sugar-coating of entertainment. So the first volume, *Refugee,* reanimates the plight of two contemporary groups: The Vietnamese boat people, and the Haitian refugees. Both have been fleeing oppression and poverty by going to sea in small craft; neither has been well received at their destination. I translated those merged stories in all their savagery to my framework, crafting a truly savage story. But it is only the story of unfortunate refugees of our own day. I want people to be aware of this. Other novels in the series focus on other aspects of contemporary society, and on possible solutions. Thus this is a half-million-word essay on social conditions, spiced considerably by blood and sex. Naturally the critics completely missed the point, dismissing this as simple space opera. (One reviewer in England caught the point, but described the series as "simpleminded allegory" that was "bathetic.") It is space opera, but it is not simple or meaningless; those qualities lie only in the minds of the beholders. The third novel in the series, *Politician*, was the fiftieth book I had published, while I was fifty, completing my listing for this period.

The fantasy series is *Incarnations of Immortality*. The setting is contemporary, with science and magic mixed. Certain fundamental human concepts, such as Death, Time, and Fate, are personified by living people, and the nature of each one's duties are explored. The symbolism is obvious, and each novel is buttressed by a long Author's Note that helps make the point. This obvious presentation has gotten through to most reviewers, and the series is being quite favorably received, and the first volume made the best-seller lists. There is a rough parallel between the volumes of the two series, with death being much of the life of those in *Refugee* and Death being the main character of *On a Pale Horse*. The second volume of each series changes character, the one taking the protagonist from adolescence to midlife in military service, the other following Time and his struggle with Evil. In the third SF volume the protagonist uses the political process to rise to the most powerful position of the system, while in the third fantasy volume Fate herself opposes Evil's political machinations. The same basic social commentary in each, in quite different guises—and I hope that the social awareness of my readers is sharpened thereby. If not, at least they are being entertained.

6.

SUCCESS

So the decade from age forty to age fifty was one of enormously increasing commercial success, and perhaps some literary success too. There have been consequences. I became aware of taxes and investments, as I found myself passing beyond the 50% bracket in income tax. (Then a revision cut the limit back to 50% tax; still, that's a lot.) It had never bothered me how much the rich man got soaked; now it did. Why should my increased efficiency of production and appeal to my market require me to pay a greater percentage of my earnings to the government, that was not doing any more for me in return? Thus my trend has been toward financial conservatism, though I remain liberal in other respects. Thus I struggle to keep my money out of the hands of the government, but also make significant donations to causes and projects I deem worthy.

My correspondence became voluminous. Early in my career I received few fan letters; one letter a week was maximum. But with best-seller status came the mail, increasing to one letter a day, and then to two, on the average. In 1985, technically beyond the scope of this volume, it rose to three per day, and for some months, four or more. Because I do answer my mail, I found my time increasingly crowded. I had to digest my answers down to cards whenever possible; even so, one quarter of my working time went for my mail. Because of the value of my time, it would be cheaper, literally, for me to stamp the writers' return addresses on fifty-dollar bills, in lieu of the personal answers I write. Yet each fan letter represents a living, feeling, hoping human being, more often than not a child (the youngest fan to write to me was eight years old; many are in the ten-to-twelve range), and I feel has to be answered. My later computerization helped me to handle this problem; I can now answer many letters with cards that I type and print a score at a time, and I have worked up "boilerplate" essays to answer the most frequent questions in detail, without having to retype material constantly. These essays represent a kind of minicourse in writing for the amateur, as well as covering my background in summary. See Appendix F.

My opinion of reviewers and critics was never high, and has lowered as I have experienced more of their attention. Persons of genuine accomplishment and perception do commentary for outfits like the New York *Times*, but that publication treats science fiction and fantasy as if they are chimaeras. *Publishers Weekly* does a fair job overall, though seems obliged to make cute, cutting jabs, and careless reading is evident. Elsewhere, reviewers seem to believe that they can judge a book by its cover: If the cover is hard, the book merits their attention, if soft, it doesn't. Unfortunately, the first impression most people have of any book *is* its cover, and the blurbs on it, which are notorious for their distortion. So I wish that reviewers and critics—I am defining a reviewer as a person who reads, summarizes, and gives a brief opinion on a book, and the latter as one who does analysis in greater depth—would do a better job, so that readers had a better reference before paying their money for a book that may disappoint them, or passing up one they might have preferred to read. But reviewers and critics don't do an adequate job, so the most reliable remaining guide is the name of the author. Thus we get books selling by names, and that's not ideal, but it seems to be the best of a bad lot of choices.

The typical genre reviewer seems to be some hopeful writer who hasn't made the grade, and therefore casts his jaundiced eye on the work that *has* made the grade. It seems to be to his interest to persuade the reader that the book in question is not as good as the one that he, the reviewer, could have written. Thus what I call the "warts-on-Miss-Universe" syndrome: If all you see is warts, you are apt to miss the point. The greater the commercial success of the book, the more jaundiced the perspective. Thus reviewers may praise work that has little chance of commercial success, and condemn books in direct proportion to their success. So when a writer emerges from the obscurity of small sales to the limelight of best-sellerdom, the reviews can become quite negative. Apart from being annoying, this is also a disservice to the reader, who is not interested in the frustrations of the reviewer so much as in the merit of the books. No wonder reviews carry little weight in the marketplace! It has been said (I wish I could remember the source!) that it is time that reviewers stopped condemning the readership for the tastes it has, and started learning why it has the tastes it has. A reviewer or critic who does not relate to the tastes of the readership for which he writes is wasting everyone's time.

Awards are an intensification of this problem. Typically they are voted by a small segment of the readership, whose tastes can be biased toward the esoteric. Thus, sometimes, the best guide to a book to avoid is an award winner. For example, there is the novel *Riddly Walker* by Russell Hoban, which won the annual SFRA award. The average reader cannot get past the first page. The author of that book ignored what I deem to be the most fundamental rule of narrative writing: clarity. If the text cannot be understood, then all else is lost. This is unfortunate in this case, because as nearly as I can tell, Mr. Hoban does have a good story to tell. But other awards may simply be compromises, with the outstanding entries bypassed in favor of something the judges can agree on. Some awards appear to be corrupt. There is also such a plethora of awards that it's hard to keep track of them. Thus the coinage of awards has been debased, and their meaning is only a fraction of what it should have been. Should they be abolished? Perhaps; but since there is much interest in them, I suspect they should be left for those who believe in them. I think I would favor a rating system, somewhat like that of the motion pictures, with a brief coding describing the type and quality of each novel. But ultimately, the readers are the judges of merit. That is the way it should be.

Another complication of success is the demand for interviews and appearances. Interviews can run afoul of what I call the Penis Syndrome. In the book *How to Teach Your Child About Sex Without Making a Complete Fool of Yourself*, which is a marvelous humorous discussion of just that, it is shown how a mother can explain all about the birds and the bees to her little boy, mentioning in passing that the name for the male organ of intromission is called the penis. The boy fixes on that one word, then goes out to regale the neighborhood with it. Well, interviewees learn to be very careful what they say to interviewers, because otherwise some offhand remark can be publicized in lieu of the serious commentary, making that interviewee seem biased or conceited or crude or an idiot. I got torpedoed that way by Charles Platt for the *Dream Makers II* volume. He got lost on the way to meet me, and was running late, so I did my best to facilitate things by hurrying it up—and got described as a wild-eyed, fast-talking character. When I mentioned that we were buying up the forestland around us so that it could never be developed, that translated not into my love of forests but into a condemnation of my neighbors. Since Platt showed me the advance copy of his article, I was able to undo some of the damage, but the experience taught me to be more cynical about such things. So as I get better known, my inclination to be interviewed diminishes. Which is not to say that I maintain bad relations with Charles Platt; we still get along well enough, and have interacted in other projects. He's a clever and innovative writer, probably doomed to nonentity.

Much the same goes for personal attendance at assorted functions. I have accepted invitations, and shown up, only to discover that the organization of the program was such that there was little purpose in my attendance, and my time was, by my definition, inefficiently spent. I was invited to attend one convention, and declined, and was then told that if I didn't attend, they might have to disband the convention. I don't like that sort of pressure, and did not go. The mere time it takes me to attend a convention is worth thousands of dollars in my working time; quite possibly the cost to me is greater than the gain to that convention, in monetary terms. It has to be worth it on some other basis—and that's not necessarily the case. So I don't visit many conventions, and am unlikely to change my attitude. I don't like to travel anyway, and do like to stay home and write. The truest success, for me, is the comprehension and appreciation of what I write by my readers: one mind speaking to another.

And there are autographs. Again, I would rather have my words understood, than to have the physical signature of my name honored. But fans always want autographs, so I oblige with the best grace I can muster, trying to allow time to chat briefly with each person so that there is at least that little bit of personal interaction. Similarly each letter I answer is individual and personal, and that is the way I prefer it. Autographing blank sheets has little meaning for me.

Meanwhile, I have had the pleasure of seeing my two daughters growing up, of teaching them the things they need to know to survive in life, like driving and handling a checking account, and knowing that they are well equipped. Both are pretty girls and bright and motivated. Penny plans to go into teaching, working with learning disabled children. Cheryl is interested in archaeology and getting some real experience in; there will be more about that at such time as I do an update on this volume. All too soon I know they will be marrying and moving away, and that will be good because it means they are safely into adulthood, but sad because they take up a huge place in my life, and there will be a void without them.

I have had my bad moments, too. In 1980 I had a mysterious malady that put me in the hospital and turned out to be cat-scratch disease. In 1982 I had a six-hour siege with a kidney stone. These are described in some detail in the Author's Notes following *Viscous Circle* and the Incarnations series, and could be considered updates on this volume.

But overall, I feel that success is a wonderful gift, and I have had more than I ever really expected, and I am trying to be worthy of it. Not every person can handle success. For example, the singer Elvis Presley was younger than I was; his enormous success led him to practices that killed him. I expect to turn the remaining portion of my life increasingly to socially beneficial effort, so that, as I said in the Author's Note in *On a Pale Horse*, when I must at last lay it down, I will not be ashamed.

7.

COMPUTER

For seventeen years I wrote my first drafts in pencil, finding it handy and versatile, and typed the second and then the submission drafts on my manual typewriter. But my last typewriter, an office Olympia with a long carriage, set up in Dvorak with some customizing of my own, was getting battered after ten years and ten million words. I discovered that they weren't making them anymore. I didn't like being locked to a defunct system; that typewriter might last for many more years, being an excellent machine, but eventually I would have to change. I checked out the electrics, and found that the best for my purpose, the daisy-wheel models, did not have Dvorak; it would cost me seventeen thousand dollars to have a custom Dvorak wheel made. The element machines did have Dvorak, but not with my custom variants, and the total number of characters was too limited for my purpose. I never liked the notion of having an electric motor punch the keys for me when I could do that perfectly well myself; this is another aspect of my wipe-my-own-nose syndrome. In addition, the reliability of electric typewriters falls below my standards. When I asked for a machine that would go five years without service or repair, I was told that no such typewriter existed. But that's what my manual machines did.

So I decided that if I had to go electric, I might as well go all the way. But here again my special keyboard was a problem.

We had an Atari 800 computer that my daughters used for endless games—it was a fine kind of baby-sitter!—and we could use it for word processing. But the company claimed that it could not provide me with my keyboard. Apple Computer could—but I know from both published and private experience that Apple was monstrously arrogant about consumer relations, and I did not want to do business there. IBM could do it—but I had discovered the power of IBM when searching for a typewriter; it was ubiquitous, and tended to be overpriced. I preferred to do business with a smaller company, though I kept IBM in mind as a backup resource.

I looked at an IBM clone, The Leading Edge. Their system appealed, in both price and performance, but their keyboard seemed fragile to me; I didn't like the feel of it. The same store had a Televideo system whose feel was great, and I was about ready to buy that. But when I checked, I learned that the service reputation of that company was abysmal. That ended that. (I understand that Televideo has worked hard to improve their service, but I am wary of lapses. As for Leading Edge, I believe it would have been a satisfactory investment; we would have returned to that, had our other options not worked out.) So we kept looking, and made appointments to see both Digital Equipment Company (DEC) and Wang. Digital had a nice system, but the salesman could not guarantee our keyboard; he would have to check into it. Wang not only had a nice system, it had Dvorak. That very nearly clinched the sale. But, cautious, we took home their literature and analysed it, and their case began to fall apart. They were not selling us the system they had demonstrated for us, but another, older one, that had the Dvorak as an option—yet they were charging an additional thousand dollars for the conversion. The Wang word processing software was supposed to be so simple that any normal person could understand it and use it within half an hour—but they were scheduling and charging us for some forty hours of instruction. And the hardware was limited to a maximum of 90°F for an operating environment, when our summer days routinely go well above that, and my study can break 100°. "But all computers have the same limit!" the salesman assured us. That was not a satisfactory answer; we were not going to put air conditioning in our forest residence just for the sake of a computer. There were other matters, and the end result was that the system was not what had been represented to us; it could not function in our environment.

Meanwhile, the DEC salesman was following up, trying to work out a software program that would provide me with my keyboard. We learned separately of SmartKey, a program that could do just that, by making every key of the keyboard completely programmable. We told the man, and he followed up, and learned that SmartKey was just coming out with a program for the DEC Rainbow. He got a copy, tried it, and it worked. That was the deciding factor; we bought a Rainbow system. We had already ascertained that it could be operated at temperatures up to 120°, which was fine for our purpose.

There were headaches, of course, as I got into computer word processing. The first time I tried it, I typed in the proper coding, and the machine did not respond. When my wife checked, she advised me that I was supposed to hit the RETURN button after every command. No one had told me that; they just assumed I would know. How does a person who has never used a computer before know a detail like that? At other times the machine went astray for no reason I could ascertain; they say the computer has no will of its own, but obviously it does, and it knows how much it can get away with with a beginner.

On the third day I was trying to do a letter, while my wife supervised so as to be sure I remembered to hit RETURN and such, and the power blinked. That wiped out my text, five minutes into it. Annoyed, I started in again—and shortly before the end, forty-five minutes along, the power blinked again, wiping out my text again. "I can't operate this way!" I cried, furious. I shut down the computer and retired to the house to read a book. The storm that had caused the power blinks got worse, and a lightning strike caused a power surge that blew out our lights, our good color TV set, part of our Atari system, and parts of our electric stove, which fired sparks at Cheryl. Evidently it traveled on up to the study and damaged the two all-band radios there though they were not turned on. Obviously its real target was the ten thousand dollar computer system—and that was the one thing it missed. But if I had had it on at the time . . .

That experience caused me to ponder precautionary measures. We ordered an Uninterruptible Power Supply (UPS) box that would keep the computer running for ten minutes or more despite power failures, and we put power-surge protectors on our key outlets. When we duplicated our computer system, we got another UPS box too. Those boxes have saved my text many times, and I recommend them for any writer who uses a computer and values his text. We also cast about for a better word processing system. I started with Select 86, which cost four hundred dollars and wasn't worth it; the thing was clumsy and annoying to use. In order to save my text partway through, I had to exit the program, then call it up again, a cumbersome procedure that caused me to delay saving— sometimes at the cost of my entire text, as with the power blinks. Also, when I underlined, it showed it on the screen by a caret, ˆ, before and after the underlined section. Sometimes I forgot to un-caret it, or my finger hit the caret key by accident, and I discovered this when I printed my material and found six pages of it underlined. So I wanted two things: an easy save, and underlining shown *on the screen*. As it happens, few systems have the capacity to underline on the screen, but the Rainbow is one of them; it was ridiculous not to have it.

A man from DEC recommended the PTP-100 text processor. This was like a word processor, only it didn't have all the refinements and obscure capabilities that a full word-processing program is supposed to have. It was a simplified program, easy to learn and to use. And it had an easy save and onscreen underlining. So we ordered it—and when I tried it, it was love at first sight. In the course of the first month I had more or less grasped the use of Select 86; in the course of three days I had done the same with PTP. The cursor control was vastly superior, and I could do just about anything I wanted to do without having to struggle with the program. For example, if I saw a typo, three lines up, I could just move the cursor there and type the correction over it. With Select 86 I had had to go into a different mode, which was like making a federal case for peanuts. When I wanted to delete something, I could touch the REMOVE key once to delete one character, or hold it down to delete several characters, or hit SHIFT-REMOVE to delete the entire line, or hold those buttons down to delete several lines, or hit DO-SHIFT-REMOVE to delete the entire remaining text instantly. Or I could touch DO, and type a number such as 5, and then hit my SHIFT-REMOVE and it would delete just five lines. Or I could touch the button labeled SELECT, then move the cursor anywhere, and it would highlight the text covered; then when I touched REMOVE it would remove only the highlighted text. In short, I could delete anything I wanted, readily and accurately. If I made a mistake and deleted the wrong thing, I could touch CANCEL and it would be restored intact.

Other common functions operated similarly, being as it were squared by SHIFT and cubed by DO. As far as I know (though my knowledge is far from comprehensive), no other word processing program was as simple yet versatile as this. In addition there were the macros: buttons that could readily be programmed to do complicated tasks with one touch. PTP was in due course upgraded to have twenty-two macros, so that I could set up everything I desired; one button to save my material and return the cursor to the line I started from, another to run the full print routine, another to fashion an arrow pointing down the left margin that required twenty-two button pushes otherwise. So I had come to PTP for the save and underline, but I kept it for many other features I discovered when using it. I suspect that it is the best program for a writer who is being introduced to the computer to use, because of its common-sense operation; everything in it makes sense, in contrast to what is found elsewhere. The top-rated and top-selling programs, like Wordstar and Word Perfect, didn't have the "oops" feature, so that one mistake was disaster, and were complicated to learn. I feel that I came at computing much as I came at writing: late and partly by chance. But I wound up with a system and program that, also like my writing, was about as good as anything else you could find at the time. Of course times change, and I was later to get into more sophisticated programs.

And so, less than two months before my fiftieth birthday, I had made that major change in my career. The computer was to speed up my fiction writing by about forty percent, and was well worth its cost. My output did not actually increase, because of the ballooning fan mail and other calls on my time, but I fear it would have decreased without the computer. If they started making good manual typewriters again, I would not voluntarily change back. Not only did we duplicate the entire system, we got a third for my daughter Penny to take to college; PTP is good for youngsters too, and the Rainbow is a nice system. Each member of our family has his/her own User Numbers, which blank out everything in the computer except that coding; it is as though the whole computer is devoted only to that person, and no other files exist. So my daughters set up their own margins and keyboards (they use the conventional one) and macro buttons, which operate only for them, while mine operate only for me. We are now very much a computer family.

8.

ANALOGIES

I operate under the assumption that man is not placed on earth merely to feed his face and replicate his kind. A life that accomplishes no more than that seems inadequate to me. Thus I ask myself, what am *I* accomplishing that might in some way benefit the cosmos? I don't find an easy answer. I have been trying, through my writing, to entertain others, and to express what I feel are beneficial concepts in such a way as to influence others to consider them, but I can't be sure that the concepts *are* beneficial, or that anyone else is influenced. So doubt is one of the hallmarks of my existence; I don't really know if I am accomplishing anything worthwhile. But I hope I am. Certainly it is no bad thing to entertain; certainly man does not live by bread alone.

I have mentioned here and there that I don't operate quite the average way. Of course every person is different, each unique in his own fashion. But from the reactions of others, in and out of the profession of writing, I can tell that I am not coming across in quite the standard fashion. The computer analogy is useful here, because it helps clarify the importance of wiring. A particular button does not cause the same action on different types of computers. With programming, it can be made to perform similarly, but the hidden wiring remains different. Human education and culture establish a set of standard responses that help people to communicate and get along, but underneath they may be more different than is apparent. I visualize the human brain as being wired in a number of conventional ways, while some brains, as in the case of the dyslexics, are wired in unconventional ways, and have difficulty aligning with the standard mode. What button do you push to obtain a particular response, when that computer has no such response in its system?

I think that seeing the trouble my daughter had with dyslexia and related complications helped me to understand the problem I had had in school. Dyslexia isn't just a matter of culture or training; it seems to relate to the hard-wiring of the brain, and the training is necessary not merely to teach such a child to read and relate, but to get around the barrier that exists. Penny never read straight from the page; she picked up the printed symbols, whirled them about in her head, and paraphrased them for the teacher. This was a far more complicated procedure than the teacher understood. Penny was actually doing an ongoing translation. I don't remember the specifics now, but I can recreate an example, exaggerated for clarity. THE BOY PETTED THE DOG might come out THIS CHILD STROKED HIS PET. I suspect that a person translating from one language to another would perform a similar feat. Penny had a vocabulary beyond anything her teachers would have believed, but the imprecision of translation made her seem clumsy. Thus she was placed simultaneously in advanced and retarded classes, by teachers who hardly understood her nature. But when I understood it, I was able to take action to facilitate her progress through school. One of my favorite sayings—again I do not know the author—is that a child is someone who passes through your life, and disappears into an adult.

Similarly, I believe I must have struggled with translation in early school—but when I finally achieved it, the power of my brain manifested, and I moved at a rate few others could match. Today I am not just a writer, I am a good writer, as versatile as any—after trying for eight years before making my first sale. When I oriented clearly on my market, I brought my skill of adaptation and comprehension with me. I fancy the average person as a sports car, while I fancy myself as a locomotive. When the race begins, the car takes off, leaving the locomotive far behind. It is not lack of power that makes the train slow, but the much greater mass it is moving. Once that mass *is* moving, the locomotive closes the difference, and achieves a sustained velocity that the car can not match. In my case, the mass is not physical, but the problem of adapting to a somewhat alien system.

Another analogy: In Florida we are visited by hurricanes. These are devastating storms, their radii of destruction varying directly with the velocity of the winds and inversely with their distance from the target. One terrible one, back around 1960, was Hurricane Donna, with winds as high as 180 miles per hour. It missed our area and wreaked its havoc elsewhere, but I remember the long watch as it approached, seeming to aim directly for us. In my mind I align it with a popular song about a girl of the same name; thus the words become "But I loved my hurricane; Donna was her name." More recently a storm with top winds of 125 miles per hour passed by, but it was small as these things go and we hardly felt it. Then one with top winds of 90 mph passed, and it was farther away. I dismissed it out of hand; lower winds and greater distance eliminated it as hazard. "But it's a larger storm," the weatherman warned. Well, for three days those gale-force winds of the periphery of that storm battered us, and I learned a lesson. Size does make a difference. It can be a mistake to judge solely by top winds and distance; judge by the total mass. Likewise with people: The height of the IQ and the relevance of the training may make one person seem more effective than another, but it is better to judge by the total capacity. Thus I have prevailed where those who seem to have had better qualifications have failed. My qualifications do not necessarily show up well on tests, but in the final test of the reality of the marketplace they do manifest. This may of course be one of the problems with critics: They are judging merit by somewhat artificial criteria, so can miss the reality.

Reality, of course, has always been my problem. The worlds of fantasy can be appealing to those whose mundane reality is indifferent or negative, and perhaps it is not surprising that I became apt in fantasy. But I spent a long time seeking some firm anchorage in reality: something to relate to, a point of contact that all people with all perspectives could agree was valid. I believe I found that with the concept of integrity. Integrity as I see it is the quest for the truth. The truth is What Is; the truth is Reality. Anchored to that, a person may find all else manageable. Honor is a related concept, broader, embracing integrity and decency. Just as the classic small boy's definition of faith is believing what you know ain't so, honor is doing what you believe is right even if it makes no sense to others. I remember when I considered changing from one literary agent to another. Another writer was amazed when I went first to the agent I had, to tell him of my intent. (My agent, Lurton

Blassingame, was so generous about the matter that I did not regret changing my mind instead of my agent.) Similarly a classmate was appalled when I discovered an error in my favor on a test paper, and took it to the instructor, who reduced my grade from 100 to 94. Or when I discover monetary errors in my favor, and promptly return the money. Apparently this is not the way it is done by others. But honor means far more to me than a grade or money, and this was true when my grades were poor and money scant, as well as in my more comfortable present situation.

I have always liked the concept of the analog computer. Most of what we see are the digital computers, which resemble thousands of on-off switches. The analog computer resembles the turning of wheels. Thus if you want to add decimal numbers, Digital is great, while Analog may seem imprecise. But if you want to work with pi, Digital can't even print out the number, while Analog can handle it readily. Sometimes I feel like an analog in a world of digitals; the problem is relating. I like the type of watch that has both analog and digital presentations: each has its validity. The analog is the old-fashioned hour-, minute-, and second-hand style, while the digital is the new-fashioned line-of-digits style.

I see that analog/digital analogy in many respects. The Digital mind tends to think in terms of on/off, while the Analog mind has gradations between the two. Digital has a hot water tap and a cold water tap, so that you must burn or freeze; Analog has a dial that mixes the water at the temperature you want it. Digital sees things as white or black, while Analog sees shades of gray. Digital says, "Either you are for me or against me," while Analog tries for accommodation. (Reviewers have dismissed my tendency to conclude my stories with accommodation as "typical Anthony" as if it is a fault.) Digital demands a yes/no answer, while Analog offers maybe. Digital speaks of right or wrong, good or bad, salvation or damnation; Analog recognizes compromise. Digital says Us or Them; Analog perceives a larger unity. There can even be a man/woman analogy: the man is Digital, with his straight-line thrust, while the woman is Analog, with her accommodation. (I have a lot of sympathy for the female situation, but have been branded a sexist writer.) The male/female symbols may relate: the male has an upthrusting phallic arrow, the female a descending pubic matrix. But there are elements of each within each, for we are one species despite differing outlooks. Those who deal with electrical on/

off switches should bear in mind that it is a *circuit* that such a switch activates.

Obviously I prefer Analog. Some may now call me Piers Analog, or Piers Analogy. But because this is my preference, I do not condemn Digital; I see value in each. I use a Digital computer, and like it. But it is my inclination to try always to consider the total picture rather than merely the salient or measurable aspects. One riddle I have posed to female writers, sometimes startling them, links the male/female relationship to that of the writer/reader. It is said that the man desires the woman, while the woman desires the desire of the man. Can it also be said that the reader desires the writer, while the writer desires the desire of the reader? If so, is there a parallel between the position of the woman and that of the writer? I like to think that this riddle provides me some perspective on the female view, and I keep it in mind as I write female-protagonist fiction. Understanding is important in all the aspects of our existence, from the personal to the practical.

So my daughters and computers are helping me to understand, and I hope that my effort of understanding can help others in my situation understand too. I spend much of my writing time working out the rationale of my fiction; similarly I try to work out the rationale of my life, without quite being sure there is one. My daughter Penny wants to help the learning disabled; so do I, but on another level. So that my life will prove to be worthwhile.

My career continues, as I expand into new types of writing while maintaining the old types. As it is said in *The Rubaiyat* of Omar Khayyam:

> The Moving Finger writes; and, having writ,
> Moves on: nor all your Piety nor Wit
>   Shall lure it back to cancel half a Line,
> Nor all your Tears wash out a Word of it.

And so I leave my readers with that thought: that what has happened has happened, and cannot be undone, and this is the record of what has happened to me. I am the Ogre, with some deliberately provocative thoughts here. I have writ what I have writ, and I recommend to my various critics the vision of that Moving Finger.

APPENDIXES

A

THE SPANISH CIVIL WAR

by Norma Jacob

My adventures in the Spanish Civil War began early in 1936, when the Friends Service Council of London received from an English Friend living in Catalonia letters urging that they explore the possibility of starting a Quaker center in Madrid, similar to the ones in Paris and other European capitals. They agreed rather reluctantly that my husband, Alfred Jacob, should go out for a few weeks to see how things looked, and his report persuaded them that it was worth a try. Meeting for Sufferings, the body of London Yearly Meeting, took action on this on July 6, 1936; they told us, with perfect truth, that we were much too young and inexperienced for such an assignment, but they hadn't much choice since we were the only two Spanish-speaking Quakers in the British Isles. We were busily packing up, getting ready to leave for Madrid with our two young children, when the Civil War broke out on July 18. This of course meant that the first plan must be abandoned, at least for a time.

It did seem that there might be work for Quakers to do, even if it wasn't just what had been planned, and so Alfred went off in September, accompanied by a much older and weightier Friend, John Harvey. It amuses me now to recall that this highly respectable Quaker drove into Spain with the spare tire on his car stuffed with foreign money. This was our first encounter with Catch-22, which always operates in wartime. Money was contraband and might not be carried across frontiers, yet it was impossible to do anything without it. This was just the beginning of our subsequent career as lawbreakers.

When Alfred arrived in Barcelona, it was apparent that he would not be able to get to Madrid, and so he looked around for help in getting something started in Catalonia. He went to the YMCA and had the amazing good fortune to meet with Domingo Ricart. Domingo and his wife Margarita were the heart and soul of the whole later Barcelona operation. A book could and should be written about them.

The first relief action that Domingo and Alfred were able to get started was giving hot drinks of Cadbury's cocoa to refugee children from Madrid. They arrived, usually in the middle of the night, from a long journey and they were cold, hungry and scared. The main railroad station was constantly bombed, but never hit. It was a happy coincidence that this first Quaker operation in Spain got under way on Christmas Day, 1936.

From now on, this will be an account of my own small adventures rather than of the whole Friends' relief operation. It had already been expanded enormously by the time I first went out to Barcelona in the early spring, to gather material for a fund-raising campaign. I flew in from Toulouse, my first flight, very beautiful over the snow-capped Pyrenees at dawn. As we were driving into the city from the airport, the air-raid alarms sounded; remember, air-raids were something with which Europeans had had no experience, at least none since 1918. The bus stopped and everybody went down into a subway station, not very far below the ground. A whole group of school children with their teachers was in the same shelter. I thought for a minute or two about the effect of a bomb coming through the roof, then I returned to ground level and never took refuge underground again.

While I was in Barcelona, anarchists took over the city. It really is impossible to ask anybody to imagine a modern city the size of Philadelphia being run by people who seriously believed that any manifestation of government was sinful, even a traffic light. They did, however, make an exception for the police, as people always seem to do. On my way back to London I was arrested at the frontier station and brought back to Barcelona under armed guard. I managed to get word to Alfred and Domingo and they came to police headquarters; we all sat up in comfortable armchairs and waited to see what would happen. I now feel that I wasn't as scared as I should have been; probably at the back of my mind was still the feeling that nothing really bad ever happens to the holder of a British passport. Besides, I hadn't yet learned that in times of serious disturbance the rule often is, shoot first and inquire afterwards. In the morning the chief of police called me in and said it was a case of mistaken identity and I could go; they even paid my train fare to the border. My chief memory of the night is of a succession of young men coming in and being issued revolvers from a huge open safe.

My next visit to Spain was in the summer; I brought the children with me and we all went to Puigcerdá, a town in a beautiful green valley high up in the Pyrenees, not far from Andorra. The international boundary ran through the valley and we lived in a house right beside it; the garden ran down to a stream about the width of the Brandywine at Chadds Ford, on the other side of which was the small French town of Bourg Madame. Spanish and French soldiers had posts on the bridge, but local residents whom they knew went back and forth quite freely.

I have many memories of that summer, but two are especially vivid. One is of standing on a small stone bridge over a narrow stream in that beautiful valley and seeing the water running white with milk. The valley was one of Spain's major dairying areas and it had a condensed milk factory, which was closed down because they couldn't buy sugar in wartime. The grass kept growing, the thousands of cows kept producing milk, and there was nothing to do with it except throw it away. Two things were done pretty quickly about that. The Quakers sent in several tons of sugar so that the factory was able to get back into partial operation, and children were sent up from the city to live in the large houses of the wealthy people who had run away at the outbreak of war. When I saw the milk in the stream, I knew that a hundred miles away children in Barcelona were dying for lack of it. There was no way to ship it out in liquid form because there were no tank cars. The railway on the Spanish side was a light mountain line built chiefly to take skiers up to the ski lodges in peacetime. When the children arrived, the job of our unit was to distribute food to them in ten-ton Bedford trucks sent out from England. Puigcerdá was at that time under anarchist control, as Barcelona had been earlier, and this created many problems for us. Anarchists are extremely puritanical and heartily disapprove of women wearing pants, which of course we had to do for our work on the trucks, and we never quite knew when they might decide to shoot us in order to encourage the others. They also disapproved strongly of women sitting down for a cool drink at one of the open-air cafés in the main square, and this the members of our unit regretfully agreed not to do. Domingo has reminded me that he once had to come up from Barcelona to defuse a dangerous situation which had arisen when a young woman from Australia (with the Foster Parents plan, not with our unit) decided to defy this rule and take a drink in public.

There was often shooting at night, apparently anarchists settling disputes between themselves, and my other most vivid memory is of one night when the racket was appalling. We got the children out of bed and all lay down on the floor, hoping no stray bullets would come through the closed wooden shutters. In the morning we discovered that the previous day had been Bastille Day, July 14, and the noise was caused by the good people of Bourg Madame letting off fireworks.

Late in the summer there were several cases of scarlet fever among the refugee children, and we decided that it would be safer for our own children to go back to England. Here we came up against Catch-22 again; French money was needed in France, in order to avoid being arrested for vagrancy, but one could neither possess it in Spain nor carry it across the border. I made several casual shopping trips over the bridge to Bourg Madame and managed to accumulate a nest-egg in large, new, crisp French bills. Since I knew I should be searched before being allowed to leave, I pinned the money to the front of my younger child's diaper (she was walking but not yet talking, which turned out to be fortunate). As the policewoman at the railroad station was searching me, the child clutched at her stomach and began to cry; the sharp corners of the new money were pricking her. "Poor little thing!" said the policewoman. "She has a stomachache!" I picked up the child and hurried to the train, which however didn't move; we sat for a considerable time before it finally started up and went the few hundred yards into France. Here we discovered that the Paris express had left. This was arranged so that travelers would have to pay for a night in the station hotel. This made me angry. I put our suitcases in the left-luggage office, got a cab, and the children and I drove back to Bourg Madame.

When we arrived there, I walked to the middle of the bridge with the two young children and explained to the guards what had happened. They saw no reason why the children should not spend the night in their own beds in the house by the bridge, so I shouted and Alfred came out. He was of course very much surprised since he had thought us already halfway to Paris. I handed over the children and turned back to find a bed for the night for myself; having been checked out of Spain and into France, I wasn't prepared to go through all that again twice more within a few hours. However it just happened that this was the day before the arrival in Bourg Madame of the Tour de France, the great sporting event where bicycles race all around the country's outer limits. It was impossible to find a bed in Bourg Madame that night. At last I gave up and walked back to the bridge and said to the guards, "If you don't let me go back to my own bed in that house there, I'll just have to sleep under the bridge." They couldn't think of anything else to do so they passed me through. Next morning the children and I crossed the bridge again—no passport, no police search, no nothing—and took another cab back to the railroad station on the French side. This time we got safely to Paris and then back to London.

I was back in Barcelona, without the children, in 1938 and have a number of memories of that time, some pleasant and some less so. We lived at that time in a huge mansion which accommodated our entire unit, then consisting of twelve foreigners, with a native staff of twice that size who came in by the day. In the garden we could pick oranges, tangerines, lemons, olives, and figs. I never particularly liked tea with lemon except when the lemon had just been picked from the tree. The oranges were bitter and grown for marmalade, which of course we couldn't make because we had no sugar. I remember one evening when a large open truck arrived from Valencia loaded with sweet oranges, and driven by the cousin of Rodolfo Olgiati, the Italian Swiss who organized the Service Civile Internationale. We backed the truck up to the second-story windows and rolled out ten tons of oranges by hand onto the office floor. Another happy memory is of the American magazine (*Esquire*, I think) which somehow came into our hands. It contained a quiz by which one was supposed to be able to assess one's own personality. The questions themselves were almost incomprehensible to everyone except Alfred, the only native American in the bunch. He explained them to the English, the English translated them for the Spanish-speaking staff, and they translated them once more for the Catalan-speaking staff. The results were hilarious to say the least.

Another amusing story is of the Christmas dinner to which Alfred and I were invited by an English couple, wealthy business people who had lived well in Barcelona for many years. The table was set with linen, silver, and crystal and in the middle, on a silver platter, was one opened can of sardines. This represented the main course. I think there were a few bits of bread too and probably some broccoli. There always seemed to be broccoli, or perhaps I only remember it that way because I have never liked it. Food was so short that we ourselves lived on the absolute minimum to keep us able to function. From our own stores we drew supplies of oatmeal and cocoa, which were the staples of the canteen distributions. At that time we were feeding just about every child under ten in Catalonia. One hundred-pound sack of oatmeal we had to eat was full of mouse droppings, which we patiently picked out by hand.

The most distressing part of the job was turning away hungry people who came to the house asking for food. We had a huge cellar full of food but we had to send them all away; it was rigidly restricted to young children and older people with ulcers. The job of sending them away was rotated among the staff people, English, Spanish, and Catalan. I don't think one lasted more than two weeks. They would come into the office and say, "I simply cannot do this anymore." People fainting from hunger in our tiny waiting room was not unknown. One day a truck came in from Marseilles bringing all sorts of extravagant goodies sent by our families in England for our Christmas dinner. It arrived just after I myself had had to turn down a request for help from the blind beggar's union of Barcelona. That pile of ridiculous luxury food in the middle of our floor was another thing I'll never forget. But I suppose that is where we got the can of sardines. There was also a pound of coffee which we put aside for the day when the bomb fell in our street, but it never did, though on fine Sunday mornings we could run up to the roof when the alarm was given and try to spot the parts of the city which were being bombed. Sunday morning was an especially favored time for the young Italian airmen taking off from Majorca. Barcelona had three fighter planes and a few antiaircraft guns; I never saw them hit anything, but it was impossible not to hope that they would.

I remember how cold it was that winter—unusually so for a Mediterranean city. The roses in our garden looked ridiculous with tiny pointed caps of snow. Our huge mansion had high ceilings and tiled floors. I don't believe it had any heating plant, but in any case there would have been no fuel. To heat the whole place there were two tiny electric hot plates, which we propped up on their side in the office. When there was an air raid (there were several every day) somebody pulled the main switch in the powerhouse and every light in the city flickered and went out. To this day, if a light flickers I have an impulse to hit the floor. And ever since that time, if the lights do go out for any reason, I always know exactly where to put my hands on candles and matches.

We worked seven days a week, for as many hours as we could keep awake. This went on until the London office sent out a young doctor to join us. He laid down a new law: On Sunday, the office would be entirely closed and everybody would go out to the beach. We obeyed this order and thereafter had one wonderful day each week, racing up and down the beach, screaming and throwing each other in the ocean—to the stupefaction of the dignified Catalans watching us.

We had a vague impression that the war was going badly, but it was impossible to get any accurate information and in January 1939 we actually left for a brief vacation in France. Immediately we crossed the border and saw a French newspaper, we realized that Barcelona was about to fall to Franco's army. Alfred hurried back while I, on orders from London, stayed in Perpignan. It was completely obvious that an enormous movement of refugees over the frontier was about to happen and I went from one French government office to another trying to find someone who would start preparations to take care of all these people. Nobody seemed to be interested. At this point I became aware that I was about to collapse myself, and it seemed unhelpful to do it in the middle of such a large-scale human tragedy: I returned to London and let my parents nurse me back to something resembling health. I was terribly underweight, exhausted and suffering from the aftereffects of every crushing defeat of something in which one has profoundly believed. Nothing in the world seems to have been quite the same since.

The end of the Spanish story did not come for some time, however; the thousands who had fled before the Franco advance were hustled by the French into camps, bare spaces of sand surrounded with barbed wire for the men, and improvised lodgings for the women and children. It was miserable accommodation but probably not much worse than in Spain, except that in France they were surrounded by a hostile population in the small towns where they occupied disused large buildings of various kinds.

I returned to France after some months at home, sent by the Friends to visit these camps. There were several of us from the Barcelona unit, traveling with official credentials from the French government, which didn't always make things easy for us. I remember vividly one occasion when two of us were visiting a small town in south central France (we traveled sometimes alone, sometimes in pairs). Here the camp was supervised by the mayor of the town, who also owned the only hotel. He kept us waiting for several hours so we had lunch in the hotel before holding a very unsatisfactory interview with the mayor. As we were driving on to our next camp, we heard police sirens behind us. I said to my companion, "You paid for the lunch, didn't you?" She replied, "No, I thought you did!" The police finally accepted this explanation but it was a disagreeable moment.

Another unpleasant moment is of discovering that the car I was driving (alone this time) was out of gas, at the top of a mountain pass. I coasted downhill for several miles before finding a filling station. But there are good memories too. The view at the top of that mountain pass was spectacular, snow-covered peaks rising out of the mist. And there was something extraordinary about driving into a camp, in a car with the Quaker star on the panels, and seeing the people come running. "The Quakers are here, the Quakers are here!" For them we represented the only friendly and helpful people they ever saw in their desperate situation. We spent many hours making lists of things needed, like sandals (I don't know how many thousands of feet we measured, to get an idea of sizes and numbers required), and combs and other necessities for the women; also paper and pencils so that the children could continue with schooling of some kind.

It was in the early summer that we went back to Barcelona, this time taking the children with us. Everybody in London thought we were crazy. However, to us it seemed absolutely clear that war in the whole of Europe was about to begin (this was in June 1939). We had already seen enough of what war did to children to feel that our own must be spared that. This time we had a much smaller house on a street nearer to the center of the city. Domingo and Margarita Ricart shared the house with us and we had a woman, Señora Borrás, who cooked on a tiny charcoal stove in the traditional manner. We still seemed to eat an awful lot of broccoli, but our own supplies kept coming in since we were still in charge of a small distribution. The Franco authorities had taken over the large-scale operation, literally overnight. Those whom we fed now were mostly people out of favor with the new authorities, who were denied ration cards.

With our much smaller unit there was extra room in the house, and we had a lodger, supposedly a Swiss. I say "supposedly" because in the light of later events we came to suspect that he was in fact a German, an advance man for Hitler in some way.

We now served only as agents for the transmission of the huge quantities of food still required, which the new authorities took over and distributed through their own institutions. From our own much more limited supplies we maintained a small number of individuals and families whom we knew to be in trouble because of the denial of ration cards. We still had one large car and a truck, the survivors of the eighteen vehicles of all kinds which were in the basement of the big house on Angli when Barcelona fell. It may be appropriate to mention here what I didn't know at the time. Most of the vehicles were involved in the mass exodus to France and either broke down or were abandoned because there was no way of getting them through. The rest were confiscated by the military. In Barcelona itself, the general in charge of the occupying troops threatened to hang Alfred in the main square of the city as a punishment for feeding "red" children. Actually, as later transpired, a number of people on our list during the war period were right-wing sympathizers who had been meeting difficulties of various kinds. What we never knew until after the occupation was that our wonderful secretary, Mercedes, was a Franco sympathizer and had twice been taken out and stood up against a wall to be shot by anarchists who for one reason or other changed their minds. Mercedes stays in my memory as the perfect secretary. She could do everything and knew everything. Just once I teased her gently because she wasn't able to come up instantly with some obscure piece of information. To my horror she burst into tears and ran out of the room. She was still with us in the postwar period and we sadly watched her idealistic view of the new Franco regime and what it would bring as it gradually became eroded by hard reality.

In addition to our list of families needing food we had, of course, ourselves and our children. We used to drive out into the country in search of extra food, mostly eggs and fresh vegetables. Not one of our trips ever returned without something hidden in some part of the vehicle, for instance a big sack of potatoes in the cavity behind the backseat. Because of the Quaker star on the panels we were never searched, though bringing food into the city was strictly against the law (the new authorities used it as a means of control). I used to wonder what would happen to the international reputation of the Society of Friends if ever a search did take place.

There was a shortage of everything, including cooking pots. I can't be sure now when it was that Alfred and I set out on a two-day tour of inspection in a car which had the peculiarity of getting stuck in reverse gear. The signal for this was difficulty in engaging second gear, and the first time it happened, it took two weeks for a replacement part to arrive from England. On this occasion Alfred registered the fact that the trouble with the gears was about to happen again and we told ourselves to be careful not to put the gear in reverse before we got home. On the way through one of the small towns on the Costa Brava we passed a shop which appeared to be selling cooking pots. Not being able to reverse, Alfred drove around the block, pulled up outside the shop on a small hill—and automatically put the gear into reverse to assist the brakes. There was nothing to do but keep going until we found a garage. We drove two miles up Spain's major highway in reverse, wondering on which side of the road we should be. Most fortunately, in the next small village we found a garage where the man in charge forged a new piece while we waited. I vividly recall the peasant women working in their fields who straightened up to gape at us as we went by.

Our thirteen months under Franco involved no major events, though many minor ones brought home to us how things had changed. One day riding on one of the familiar yellow street cars, I was approached by a man who wanted to sell me some kind of lapel button celebrating the new regime. When I refused, a sort of chill of fear went through the crowded car. I began to become aware that care was needed in a city where we had always felt perfectly safe (except for air raids) and free. At the movies a picture of Franco and Primo de Rivera would be thrown on the screen and everybody was expected to stand and give a fascist salute. Since many people quietly left before the end of the picture to avoid this, the operators took to stopping the film in the middle without warning and flashing the picture on the screen to take everybody unawares. One day I had kicked off a tight pair of pumps and when the lights went on and everybody had to stand I was desperately searching for my shoes under the adjoining seats, expecting at every moment a policeman's hand on my shoulder. One was also expected to salute the flag when one encountered it on the street. We had a friend, a distant relative of the former prime minister (luckily with a name as common as "Smith") who found this so painful that she stayed indoors for months. My dislike of flag observances dates from this time; I saw clearly how a flag could be used as an instrument of tyranny. I also learned that if one was compelled to make empty gestures of this kind over a long period, one came in time to find them less painful. Those who at first were forced to turn out and shout "Long live the glorious national revolution!" insensibly began to tolerate and even perhaps at last partly to share the sentiment. This had been observed in other times and places but it was new to me.

A relatively pleasant part of this stay was our taking over the management of a small hotel in Tossa. The English proprietors had gone to France with a group of children and could not get permission to return. We were not particularly good as hotel-keepers, but it was a nice place to spend a weekend, except that nightingales sang in the eucalyptus trees until one had an urge to throw things at them to get them to shut up.

There are also some very painful memories of that time—worst of all, perhaps, of the day when our four-year-old's tonsils were removed. This operation is, or was, usually done in Spain without anesthesia, but I was determined that this should not happen and went to the Protestant hospital which handled most medical emergencies for the foreign population. I talked to the head nurse and got a firm promise that the child would be put to sleep, and that's what I felt safe in telling her before we went to the hospital on the appointed day. To my horror, the two of us had no sooner entered the operation room when she was snatched by the doctor and her tonsils hacked out. I have a hideous mental picture of myself with the screaming child in my arms, screaming myself at the doctor who was waving his bloodstained tools and yelling that he thought it best to do things that way because the anesthetics available in the postwar period were not entirely reliable. (To make things worse, there was a very violent thunderstorm during the night which the two of us subsequently spent in the hospital.)

Life under Franco grew more and more unpleasant and by the summer of 1940 I was fairly well convinced that if the dictator didn't yet know that there was a fundamental incompatibility between Quakerism and his theory of society, we were wasting our time. But we still had a job assignment—representing, now, the American as well as British Friends—and there were all those people dependent on us for the food that kept them alive. The question was solved simply in late June or early July. Alfred went on an inspection tour (this we were still allowed to do) and suddenly dropped out of sight. That is to say, he failed to report back to the office and Mercedes and I could not reach him by phone at any of the hotels where he was supposed to be staying as he traveled around Spain. We became extremely anxious. One day the mailman delivered a very grubby picture postcard, mailed in Zaragoza. He had been arrested there and had no way of letting us know until a prisoner who was being released managed to smuggle out the postcard. (He later described the prison as well run, mostly by former noncommissioned officers in the government's army.) I at once sent the children to Tossa with an American woman who was a friend of ours, and took the train to Zaragoza. At the prison I learned that he was no longer there but had been transferred to Madrid. Another train journey, this time at night, and a very cold trip because my fellow-travelers insisted on having all the carriage windows open. This of course runs counter to two myths—that it's the Anglo-Saxons who always want the windows open, and that Spain is a hot country. On the contrary, on the high central plateau it can be very cold at night, even in July.

In Madrid I went to stay with an American Quaker, Florence Conrad, who had a very nice apartment. At that time a British passport was ceasing to provide automatic protection, as it had in the past, but Americans were still not being bothered very much. We went to the British embassy to ask for help, presenting the grubby postcard as our only evidence of what had happened.

The ambassador did his best to help, and someone from the embassy accompanied us to the head of the prison service in Madrid. All we got from him at first was an abrupt assertion that "we have no such man in any of our prisons." By great good fortune, however, we received invaluable help from a very weighty American Quaker, Howard Kershner, who was able to threaten the withholding of huge amounts of money and food, which Spain still needed very badly in the postwar period of reconstruction. Finally, grudgingly, the official revealed that a prisoner named Alfred Jacob was indeed being held in the prison underneath the Puerta del Sol (the Piccadilly Circus or Times Square of Madrid).

This prison was a former stable; it had one high-up window looking out on the sidewalk where the feet and legs of passersby could be seen. Alfred at first had stood under this window to read the book he happened to have with him, though a long-term prisoner sadly said to him, "You're new here—soon you won't bother with that." All the prisoners slept on the cold flagstone floor; he was luckier than some because he had a raincoat to lie on. Sanitation facilities consisted of a drain in the middle of the stone floor in one room. Except for the streetwalkers who were rounded up every night and released next morning, almost all the prisoners were men. There was just one woman among them, a Hungarian who had been in a Spanish port waiting for a ship to Italy on the day when Italy entered the war. There was, as we had foreseen, war in Europe by the summer of 1940 though as yet not very much had happened. The ship didn't sail, the Hungarian woman's transit visa expired, and she was in prison. I have often wondered since what happened to her. In the two big stable compartments which made up the prison there was one piece of furniture, a short wooden bench, and the men by common consent assigned this to her so she didn't have to sleep on the cold, damp floor. But her condition was still miserable. We went shopping after Alfred's release and came back with armloads of blankets, food and other simple comforts for the prisoners who were still inside. A nineteenth-century painting of Dante's Inferno comes as close as anything to picturing that awful place.

The condition of Alfred's release was that he, and we, must

leave the country as fast as possible and meanwhile he must remain in Madrid and report to the police twice a day. The reason for his arrest was never stated (dictatorships don't have to explain) and we had of course many guesses. We thought about our Swiss lodger, about a belated realization that we stood for what to them were dangerous ideas, but the most likely explanation seemed that he was arrested because he was found near the frontier with two dangerous things: a list of people we had been asked to help, and a large sum of money provided by the British authorities. In the middle of the summer of 1940 Hitler was advancing rapidly over the whole of France and frantic arrangements were being made to ship four hundred British people who were living in the south of France back to Lisbon for repatriation. The plan was that they should cross Spain in a sealed train; this would take several days and food had to be provided. I had already spent several days in Barcelona going to government offices to get permission to buy huge quantities of staples—bread, eggs (to be hard-boiled), milk for the babies, and large crocks to be filled with drinking water. Alfred's trip to the frontier on the Spanish side was to meet the train, if we could guess where it was coming in, and buy some fresh food there and otherwise offer what help was possible. In fact, the trainload of people never arrived and I don't know exactly what became of the four hundred.

I returned to Barcelona to get our office closed down as fast as possible, and almost immediately I became ill with what looked exactly like mumps. The children luckily were still in Tossa with our American friend. I was in the hospital with my face grotesquely swollen when the doctor from the U.S. embassy came to give me a certificate of health; he solemnly signed this, sitting beside the bed. Without this we could never have got our American visas, nor would we have got them if it had been known at that time that our younger child had TB. There was another snag: We could not get tickets for the ship (money and other documentation provided by Alfred's American parents) without a Portuguese transit visa, and the Portuguese would not give the visa until we had our tickets. Again, bread on the waters; a young Spaniard whom we had been able to help was employed by Thomas Cooke in Madrid. He cut a corner and supplied the tickets, which allowed us to get permission to go to Lisbon to board the ship. Meanwhile I had recovered sufficiently to get out of the hospital and go to the local

U.S. consulate for necessary travel documents. I still have the picture taken then for my visa documents which makes me look exactly the way I felt—about to keel over at any moment.

At last we were as ready as we were ever going to be. The children and I took the train once more to Madrid, picked up Alfred at the home of the wonderful Florence Conrad, and embarked on another train for Lisbon. At the border crossing point there was a very long platform, one in each country, and at the Portuguese end they served white bread and real coffee, something entirely outside our experience for over a year. In Lisbon, more coffee—all the streets smelled of it—and familiar English groceries like breakfast foods in the store windows. We stayed in a hotel infested with bedbugs but that was a minor inconvenience. After four days, we went to the harbor and got on board the American Export Lines' *Excalibur*. This turned out to be the last ship crossing the Atlantic with refugees; it was designed for two hundred passengers and was carrying four hundred, but the steamship company did its best to make the voyage comfortable as we steamed across the Atlantic, with the Stars and Stripes painted all over the sides and every light burning at night. This caused us to wonder whether mines— the major peril—could read. Our departure was delayed for several hours because of the nonarrival of the Duke and Duchess of Windsor, who were on their way to take up the governorship of the Bahamas; there are accounts of this episode in lives of the Windsors. At last we sailed; halfway out of the huge harbor we turned and came back, perhaps because the Duchess had left something on the dock. But at last we were away, free and clear, gradually getting used once more to the ordinary amenities of peacetime living.

B

RECLAIMING AN ABANDONED FARM

by Alfred Jacob (circa 1941)

WHY RECLAIM AN ABANDONED FARM?

In Windham County, which covers the Eastern half of the Southern tip of Vermont, the highest mountain is Stratton Mountain, 3,859 feet high. Next in order are Haystack Mountain, Rice Hill, and Glebe Mountain, and the fifth is the highest point in Jamaica Township, known to Jamaicans as Bondville Hill, to Bondvillians as Jamaica Hill, to lumbermen as McGowans Hill, and to others as West Hill. It lies midway between Stratton Mountain and Shatterack Mountain, and between North Branch Brook and West River. On this hill, according to an 1869 map, there were twenty-eight farms less than seventy years ago. Old Mr. Stark, who does occasional plowing, was born in a house just below the old school No. 4; Mr. Crowninshield was born and lived twenty-five years just below that; yet hardly any trace of these buildings is left. Last to inhabit this once-prosperous hill was old Mr. King (" 'E was a worker 'e was") whose ten children gradually drifted away and he sold out in the early twenties. His house is the only one left standing on the hill, and for these odd twenty years has been used mostly as a shack for

244

hunters, except for two years' occupation by Mr. Gordon Roberts while lumbering in these parts.

The main road from Jamaica to Bondville used to run along the side of this hill. Now only half of it is passable. Its four middle miles are uninhabited and not worth maintaining. There was a road which joined the Bondville Road and led to Pikes Falls, along which were the Starks, Sabin, Sturgess, Sage, and Knight farms. Now there is hardly evidence that there was a road beyond King's Farm. The curious explorer will find spaces full of young growth, which once were fields; apple blossoms on rows of trees in the midst of woods; excavations which once were cellars; heaps of stones which once were chimneys; stone walls through the forest, and some of the heavier timbers, rotted and moss-covered, which once framed barns. The forest, rudely pushed back by enterprising settlers, has turned against their descendents and laid claim to its own.

The tourist in England, eager to see the Roman roads, is dismayed to find only green fields where once there was a Roman *stratum*. He asks himself: How can it be that a well-built road should fall into disuse and disappear? Or that a Roman villa should have been covered with earth and vegetation? Yet on West Hill, in Southern Vermont, not two hundred miles from the world's greatest metropolis, roads are falling into disuse and prosperous estates are given over to moss and weeds. Can it be that in these green foothills of the Green Mountain Range we see the beginning of the same disintegration which defeated all-powerful Rome? How can we account for decay where once there was prosperity? If it was possible to live and rear families here seventy years ago, how much more so now with better equipment, more easily available knowledge, more reliable seed, and cheaper materials! How rich are the possibilities of an area accessible to large urban centers like Boston, Worcester, Springfield, Pittsfield, Troy, and Albany; even conceding the production of grain to the West, there must always be a market for dairy products, vegetables, fruits, and eggs.

Yet the facts have been otherwise. The numbers of cattle, horses, hogs, sheep, and chickens have declined since 1910. In 1935 there were only six percent as many sheep as in 1830. The acreage in hay, corn, wheat, buckwheat, barley, oats, apples and potatoes has declined since 1879, in some cases as much as 97 percent. The total number of farms has decreased. The rural population has decreased. Modern methods and improvements have done no service to Vermont, nor to Windham County.

It is said that the trouble was that all the boys went off to the Civil War and never came back. Yet peak production was reached in the years between 1879 and 1910. It is strange that the decline in Vermont's prosperity should coincide with the introduction of modern conveniences—the telephone, motor car and electricity. Yet it may well be that improved transportation and communication, in making Eastern markets accessible to Western large-scale producers, have cut out Vermont from the possibility of future prosperity, just as in the world community, whole nations have had their prosperity cut off. What is the solution for the population of such a state or nation?

It cannot compete with cheaper producers, yet it must go on living. It can emigrate, or could as long as cheap land was available in the West, but that is no longer so. Is the only solution for Vermont, and for all states and nations in like plight, to lay itself down and give up the struggle, liquidate, and disappear? Or can it be that sufficient adaptability will solve the problem, for instance by converting everything into dairy farming?

Whatever else happens it is likely that the trend of boys to leave the farm will continue. They are being drawn away now by the high wages in the war industries. Farm life, with its day-and-night responsibilities, its heavy investment in property, its risks, its exacting requirements, its low and uncertain returns, cannot compete in attractiveness with a regular eight-hour day, no worries after hours, regular wages, no need to plan or organize, and the money with which to enjoy the gentle frivolities of urban life.

Yet is there not a danger here too, in the trend towards a more irresponsible way of life, a more immediate security, a more specialized existence, a more limited range of interests? It is no good blaming boys for leaving the farm. If they leave, either there is something wrong with civilization or with the nature of farm life. It may well be that civilization itself is at fault, in that it awakens the desire for manufactured articles without providing the means to acquire them; sells fifty-one percent of sales and distributive expense with every forty-nine percent of consumable goods; urges the confusion of luxury with necessity in order to reap a profit out of the bewilderment of the average man; offers generous terms and only a small down payment to the farmer of small cash income who is tempted by the shiny white of the automatic refrigerator as compared to the damp and slippery springhouse, encouraging him to squander a whole year's cash income on a magnified toy appropriate to city apartment houses but superfluous on a farm.

The world's problem is too complex for our understanding; but it is possible to begin to understand it by putting ourselves within its sphere, bumping up against it in our own lives, not any longer as the sheltered protégés of a benign civilization offering us comfort, ease, freedom from worry, thought, plan, or responsibility (except that of finding a job); but from the other side, as farmers in a state where civilization has coincided with disintegration, where improved methods have reduced the number of farms, the total acreage in cultivation, the total livestock, and the yearly income. There is, of course, need to reflect on the problem, and debate it, but perhaps more need to live with it and experience it. Yet one does not live with a problem, but with people who share a common problem. It is therefore in order to achieve gradually better understanding of people within the reality of ordinary existence that the effort to reclaim an abandoned farm is in a measure justified.

HOW TO RECLAIM AN ABANDONED FARM

A farm, in our time, is widely interpreted to be a remote place where you do without things. This is the civilized, or city, point of view. It does not occur to the urban dweller that a city or suburb is also a place where you do without things. Society has adopted the city point of view in large part, and considers city things worthwhile and the country things merely rustic. The intending redeemer of an abandoned farm should begin by making up his own mind as to what is worthwhile, not having it made up for him by the accident of time and place. Shakespeare did not write by electric light; Bach did not drive a motor car; Martin Luther did not enjoy hot and cold running water; and it is not reported that their work was hindered by lack of these things. It is not likely that, from any criterion of absolute value, such conveniences occupy first rank. For the traveler who has toiled up a mile of turnpike amid three miles of township road, leaving the last neighbor two miles in distance and eight hundred feet in altitude below him, the first requisite is shelter; the next, fire. The fact of water in the spring is more positive to him than the presence of piped running water is negative. A warm blanket is luxury enough—no need for electric bed warmers. A cellar door stout enough to hold against the nocturnal gnawings of the assiduous porcupine is the best soporific. Only in dreams does he come to the bedside and poking his black monkey face unpleasantly close say: "What are you doing in this place I have owned this twenty years?"

On an abandoned New England farm, whose timbers were pegged together perhaps during Jefferson's presidency, there is a fairly immediate consciousness of the early settlers of this country, many of them God-fearing people, purposely seeking to establish a better way of life than that of the society they had abandoned. The difficulties they bravely met are clearly envisaged by one who, living in their earlier abodes, profits by their enduring industry. They have removed his most burdensome tasks. He does not have to clear of trees and stumps as many acres as he needs to cultivate. He does not need to heave out stones and boulders, risking his precious plough on those hidden from view. He does not have to hew timbers in all weathers with homely tools to make himself a shelter. He does not live in darkness for lack of glass, or in cold for lack of cement for foundations and chimney stack. He does not contend with the red-skinned aborigine. Few bears and wildcats are left to dispute with him. He does not need to improvise a bucket before he can fetch water. In a hundred ways his work has been made easy by those who have gone before. In the true sense, he is not doing without things. He is enjoying many blessings for which he would wish to thank the sturdy Green Mountain folk of earlier centuries.

Approached in this spirit, the task is seen as well begun before it is even under weigh. Provided with essentials—shelter, clothing, and enough food to go on with—only two things are needful: to plant food for self and family; and to avoid precipitous expenditure based on imperfect knowledge or inexact planning. Hurry there must be on some things, for there is a right time for sowing and for reaping; but there must be leisure for others, and the bulk of the necessary farm equipment will have to be acquired slowly, judiciously, after a good deal of knowledge of the terrain has been acquired. Meanwhile, good neighbors will lend, and borrow in their turn.

Materials for construction must be acquired in the same reflective way. On an abandoned place, lengths of pipe have a way of appearing behind stonewalls when weeds and brush are cut; a heap of stones scorned for months may one day be seen to be useful for concrete; a sack of white stuff half spread over the pantry floor like mouldy flour may turn out to be plaster. The abandoned shacks of the lumbercamp down the hill, apparently given over entirely to porcupines, may still contain a stove or two, and the boards may be used for repairs. The bits of old, tarred roofing blown off by the wind can be burned to start the fire, but may be more useful in patching up small leaks in the roof. The heap of sawdust left by the lumbercamp may be used instead of sand for cement; and old sacks of cement may still be lying around, not entirely caked. And so in a hundred ways a leisurely, reflective approach, opening the mind to the possibilities of each object, may result in a saving both of time and expense.

An abandoned farm is ideal for one who loves makeshifts. One of my earliest recollections of England is that on a visit to Christopher Rowntree at York, his sister called to him to come and play tennis, and he called back: "No, I'm awfully sorry, but I can't play—I haven't got my white flannels with me." I felt at the time that he might have made shift and played a tolerable game in trousers of another color just for once. And so it is. Have you no fence stretcher? Nail the fence to a short pole, tie this to the farm truck, and you will get as good a stretch as you want. Have you no bran for the poison bait? Just sift some of your home-milled flour, and you have your bran in a jiffy. Have you no wire to clean out the sink drain? Just undo one of the clothes hangers the cleaners dispense gratis and you have a yard of wire. Have you no wheelbarrow? Surely there is an old wheel lying around, large or small, and with a bolt, or short length of pipe, or piece of iron for axle, and two poles you soon have one.

There must be no hankering after duplication of city objects. The important thing is to answer a need, not to acquire a known brand and quality. You like butter on your bread? The need is for fat—a universal accompaniment to starch. Peanut butter contains plenty of fat—no need to add butter to it. Or in making your bread incorporate some form of fat in it, instead of spreading it on afterwards. You want cereals? No Post Toasties for the farm redeemer, but coarse ground wheat, corn, or oats are very acceptable, flavored with molasses. You want to wash dishes? No trick stunt soaps, free tea cups with each box, every twelfth box free. Washing soda will clear almost everything, and a small addition of plain yellow soap will do the rest. You feel the need of fresh fruits and vegetables? Tomato juice in No. 3 tins will meet both needs over extended periods—not in the conventional way, but quite adequately. Soaked (not stewed) raisins and prunes will help. For his meals the manual laborer doesn't want five-course meals of eight foodstuffs. Let there be one prepared dish, a soup, a stew, a legume, something fried, something boiled; and for the rest let him rely on bread, peanut butter, cheese, and other hardy perennials.

There must be an acceptance of manual labor. Your civilized man will no sooner begin to pump water than he will think to himself: "Couldn't we rig up a machine to do this?" and left to himself would spend more time in a year rigging and repairing his machine than in pumping the water. No sooner will he begin to saw wood than the same thought will occur to him; and likewise when he turns over his first shovelful of soil. Now, not all machines are obnoxious; but there is much to be said for simple acceptance of manual tasks. They give time for reflection which will eventually result in the simplification of the task, and perhaps its eventual abolition. Thought is like water; it finds its way eventually through any material obstacle however hard. One day a spring higher up may be discovered, from which water in a wooden trough can be run down to the house. One day you may repair your neighbor's tractor and he may lend it to you for your harrowing. But it is not wise to delay manual tasks until their magical solution, like Dr. Cody's illustration of the laborer and the scythe that cut as if by magic. One need not sit on the fence and murmur "Hush, it might start." Let the bread be kneaded by hand—it gets less burdensome in time, and in good company. Let the flour be ground by hand—a hand mill is a machine after all, compared to rubbing between two stones, as is done in many parts of the earth. Let the wood be sawn by hand—our forefathers have done it for many generations; and when we can devise a better way, we shall devise it, and we shall benefit by our own handicraft.

Finally, there must be teamwork. The modern family is too small to manage a farm, let alone reclaim one. There must either be several families working in unanimity, or one family with open hospitality to willing workers. Private property is applicable to farming only within limits. It may be well to own all the equipment necessary for efficient working, unless the ownership and utilization are shared among a group large enough to make the ownership economic. The picture of ten small farmers, each struggling with payments on a reaper-binder for his ten acres of grain, when one would serve all ten at one tenth of the cost to each, is the picture of one tendency in modern farming. The ten could solve this and other problems by working as a team; indeed, such cooperation is the price of continued existence. Life seems to impose on us a rude alternative: either cooperate willingly; or cooperate by compulsion; or disappear. If the redemption of abandoned properties is a project with reference to the future, it must be based on teamwork; on a coordination of autonomous elements, with a proper balance between individualism and collectivism.

IS IT WORTHWHILE?

There is a new world to be discovered, right in our midst. God has many more affairs in hand than simply human ones. Indeed, the mysteries of human motives are to some extent accountable to human beings, but can one in a lifetime learn the intricate interrelation of dependence, defense, and resource which reigns in nature at every level?

Why did the cutworm cut off the first six cabbage plants and not the remainder of the row? Why do the birds feed on the worms which are beneficial to the soil? Whence did the porcupine develop the idea of wearing armor so that no animal could attack it? How is it that earth is regarded as unclean, yet water which has seeped through earth is clean? Whence is the blight that attacks apples, and what would they do except for man's care? Is there compensation all through nature—is there a natural remedy for every natural ill? Or will certain trees be annihilated by certain insects or diseases? Why is the color of nature green, rather than blue or yellow? Why do trees so seldom have perfect form, when presumably they could all have it? Why do they compete with each other and crowd each other out? Why does nature sow so much more than she expects to reap?

It may be that all such queries are tokens of blindness, and that further inquiry is more desirable than further reflection. Dr. Pfeiffer has pointed out that the weeds which thrive in poor soils are rich in the minerals deficient in those soils; and that plants have certain affinities for each other and grow best in each other's proximities. Richard Gregg has shown that certain plants will repel the insects attracted by other plants. Can it be that there is much more to learn of the equilibrium of nature and how to use it as a lever to our purpose, than we have dreamed of? There is something exciting in the formulation of theories, the daily watch on the processes of growth, and the variation or rejection of theories in consequence of observation.

There is other excitement on an abandoned farm. The weather itself, classified by city dwellers simply as nice or nasty without further thought, is the chief organizer of days for the country dweller. The farmer lives with one eye on the sky. It is the weather which determines the time of ploughing, the time of sugaring, the time of fence repairs. He cannot tell one day what he will have to do on the morrow. The weather will tell him. There are complicated adjustments to be made at planting time, and at the harvest, for there are conflicts of necessity which must be resolved, since only one thing can be done at a time. The farmer must make decisions, and abide by the consequences. His livelihood depends on his wisdom.

To the northeast there is the silhouette of Mt. Shatterack and a little to the left of it, the shadows of three ranges in graded degrees of mist, the last one sometimes merging with the sky. In the morning my first glance is at the skyline. All through the day I see it at intervals, and it never tires. It gives a sense of repose and stability which compensates the more immediate tensions set up by the galaxy of trees to the south and west, with varying forms and varying shades of green. On the one side, the complexity of growing life; on the other, the stability of earth.

There is no sense of loneliness, as there might well be in some spot uninhabited except by wind and stones. The animals are neighbors in a sense. There is a field mouse who scurries away into the grass from the house whenever I come, as if he felt guilty—as well he might, for he takes the prune stones from the table and scatters them in the most unconventional places. There is a red squirrel who will sit on a stone for a score of seconds, changing posture every two or three so quickly that the eye cannot follow. There is a small bird that flies to the outside of the window, clings to it for a little while, climbing up a bit, then flies off. A field mouse makes his house in one of the piles of sod on the border of the ploughed field. The deer went wading in the wet ground near the road at dawn, and scampered off when I appeared, their white tails bobbing up and down in the half light. The porcupine follows a daily routine. He surrounds the house at night, hunting for the entry I have blocked with a stone. He nibbles at the tallow on my paper flower pots and knocks some of them over. He goes to the old chicken yard and gnaws on a piece of bone. He takes a roundabout route to the stables, climbs up the back way, and gnaws at the horse stall. Then he goes by his accustomed path down to the brook for a drink, and stays away till the next night. A small garter snake inhabits the ledge above the chicken yard where there is a good view, and wriggles reluctantly away, looking back, when I come with the buckets, then climbs out and watches me dip the water. And within the last few days there has been the added company of the small green shoots of corn, which grow perceptibly day by day; the double leaflets of lettuce, and the complex little buds of beans pushing through the earth. Though I have not made them grow, without me they would not have grown, and I feel a link with them.

There are other neighbors beside the vegetable and animal ones. There is a weekly chat with the postmaster, who doubts if I can make anything grow up here. There is a near neighbor, two miles off, a Miss Hanford, who comes for weekends with friends and stands on the terrace wearing blue trousers, smoking a cigarette and looking very weekendish. She has heard that either a Quaker colony or a group of English refugees was coming to Hilltop. There is Mr. Muzzy, the friendly keeper of the general store; the titanic garage keeper of West Townshend who sings as he speaks and lends you the tools to do your own repairs with; and his old mechanic who looks like Caspar Milquetoast and whose wife taught in our little No. 4 school fifty years ago. In Bondville there are the genial houseparents of the youth hostel, Mr. and Mrs. Browning, full of interest in our project; young Al Slade, jack of all trades, who gave me a lift when I got lost in the woods and came out on Stratton Road; and the Browns who came once to Pendle Hill, including a Miss Brown who, being from New York, tried to teach young Slade how to milk a cow.

There is in the place the possibility of achieving what God must have intended for man; that is, the good life. There is the opportunity to initiate one's children by natural means into the structure of nature and the dignity of labor. There is a chance to live, I think, at peace with one's self, in unity with one's immediate family, in close cooperation with one's friends, and in congenial harmony with one's neighbors. At some point within such framework it should be possible in time, with diligent corporate seeking, to discover in the immediate reality of living, the meaning of the religious life.

THE SUBSTANCE OF PACIFIST LIVING BY ALFRED JACOB

(sample from an essay dated November 1942)

Not everyone believes that we have come to the end of an age, and that the growth of violence in the world during this century represents the beginning of the civil war of humanity. Some there are who hope for a return to prewar normal, or for an advance into a better time to come. But there are others who visualize the present as a moment unlike all others, in which the individual stands on the brink of an known future. Such individuals must think out afresh the meaning and function of their life. They can no longer follow uncritically the standards satisfactory to a decaying society. They feel called to stand on their own feet, exercise their own judgment, answer for the wisdom of their own choices. They are prepared to disobey laws if need be, abandon conventions, and reeducate their tastes. They are searching for the substance of pacifist living.

Pacifism cannot be regarded as simple opposition to this war. Basically it is opposition to those elements in human life and association which inevitably cause wars. Otherwise it would amount to opposing the symptoms while tolerating the disease. Wars, across the centuries, appear to have been caused in many cases by avarice, predatory instincts, fear, exhaustion of resources, intolerance. Latterly they seem to have economic causes which are rooted ultimately in human relations; in the attitude of one man to another—abolitionist to slave owner, king to subjects, employer to employee, lender to borrower. Wherever the human relation falls short of friendship, charity & mutual responsibility, there is a seed capable of growing into a tree whose fruit will be war.

Pacifist living, then, is a life free from the seeds of war; that is to say, free within its own tiny sphere of those elements which, magnified to national proportions, encourage the spirit out of which war develops.

How can this be possible? Is not the very structure of modern social life based on competition, on the exploitation of native races (for coffee, sugar, rubber), on migrant labor (a denial of mutual responsibility), on company police, industrial spies, deceptive advertising, wasteful distribution and armed protection? Can anyone claim to be living pacifically when every penny he spends encourages and sustains these wrong relationships which are the seed of war?

No one can rightly claim one hundred percent consistency in everything he does; yet we may assert that inasmuch as man earnestly tries and intends to withdraw his support from the evils of society, he approaches intentional pacifist living. This appears to be possible only in a fair degree of isolation, a fair degree of economic self-sufficiency, a greatly lowered standard of living, and, in consequence, in a simple, rural environment. Pacifist living at this point becomes identical with intentional subsistence living; and it is precisely this manner of living which, if generalized throughout humanity, would make wars impossible and a high level of well-being inevitable.

C

THE SCHOOL IN
ROSE VALLEY

February 1946 report

PIERS JACOB

General remarks

It has been very hard to get acquainted with Piers as he volunteers no information about himself and has shown no particular interests or enthusiasm through which one might establish contact. He is equally impersonal in his relationships with the other children; he apparently likes them and is liked by them—but I discovered quite recently that he did not yet know all of their names! He seems happy, is always pleasant, cheerful and a "good sport," but either does not need or does not know how to make closer, more personal contacts with people. These last few weeks an interest in science and a livelier give-and-take with the other boys have developed, and may be the first steps in freeing Piers from the too tightly walled little world of his own in which he is living.

Social Studies

Piers is undoubtedly getting much more—if only of general background—from our study of American history than he can possibly give back, either in written form, or orally. He is intelligent and thoughtful, but his lack of academic skills, his difficulty in understanding and following directions given to a group, and the whole problem of adjusting himself to this new, noisy, exciting environment inevitably make the going very hard for him. He is certainly beginning to get himself oriented and should make real progress next semester.

Arithmetic

His mathematical understanding and reasoning ability are *excellent*; he can equal the best in the group when it comes to understanding and applying a new principle. He grasped the whole idea of fractions almost instantaneously and once an idea is grasped, he has it for keeps. He is, however, handicapped by a poor foundation in the elementary processes—he cannot add, subtract, multiply, and divide whole numbers accurately or quickly. Drill in these seemed not to help at all, but rather to make him feel unhappy and "defeated." So, for the present, we are letting him go ahead with fractions, decimals, cubic feet, scale drawings, graphs, etc., which he *can* do well, hoping that as he gradually realizes for himself the need for "firmer foundations" he will see the point of a return to drill and profit by it. This has worked successfully with other children.

Current Events

He is completely uninterested as yet and has much less factual knowledge at his disposal than the other children. He has, however, made one or two good contributions to our discussions.

English

Having some trouble with spelling but doesn't look too serious. Piers needs to listen more carefully—seems easily puzzled or distracted but I think he is quite anxious to do well. We need to work toward greater ease in spelling and writing. Grammar understanding seems to be good.

Joyce Harvey

Art

Hasn't been in art enough for me to be able to comment.

J.H.

Achievement Test Results

Piers made almost no mistakes in these tests; he simply did not get enough done to make higher scores as he works very slowly.

Peg Nowell

D

THE DEMISEE

by Piers Anthony (1958)

Detective Joad was investigating a crime. "Now let's get this straight," he said. "Your name is William Sebastian. You were speeding on Highway Four . . ."

"Officer, I always drive above the limit," the man said piously.

"Quite right. I wish more people had your civic spirit. You saw this man—"

"Well, you see there was this stoplight. You know how frustrating it can be to be caught by a light. It had just turned orange, and I was still a hundred yards away. I knew I didn't have any time to spare . . ."

"I understand. Go on."

"There were some pedestrians at the crossing. One of them was already in my right of way." Sebastian gestured helplessly. "I just couldn't slow down, Officer—I would have missed the light. There was nothing to do but go over him."

"Perfectly understandable. I would have done the same thing myself."

"I'm sure I killed him. I didn't think any more of the matter, until you called—"

"Of course," Joad cut him off. "Now, did you get a good look at him? Could you identify him if you saw him in the lineup?"

Sebastian screwed up his face in thought. "There was hardly any time to look," he said. "He was a tall, blond, pretty husky

259

fellow. He was wearing a kind of candy-stripe sport shirt . . . I really couldn't make out much else."

"That's good enough for a start. We got the blood type from the stains in the road. One of those automatic street cleaners beat us to it and almost eradicated them, but we managed to get enough to narrow down the field."

Joad sent out a call to round up all the men answering the description whose blood checked and who were known to have been in the area at the time. The charge was suspicion of Demise, a capital offense. The three witnesses at the crossing were also brought in.

There were six men in the lineup. Every one of them was tall, blond, husky. Two wore candy-stripe shirts. All were indignant.

"Recognize him, Sebastian?"

"I'm sorry, Officer. It could have been any one of them."

Joad turned to the witnesses. "Can any of you pick him out?"

"Sure," said one. "Think I'm going to? Not on your life."

"That maniac in the car almost clipped *us*," another witness said angrily. "Why should we rat on the one he actually got?"

"Talk!" Joad roared. "I'll book you as accessories."

But they weren't having any. "It's no crime to carry a dead man off the road," the first one said.

Joad tried a different tack. "Don't you people realize a serious crime has been committed? A man has been killed in an accident. *Killed,* mind you. It is the duty of every conscientious citizen to see that he remains that way. What would happen to the country if every man who died could be resuscitated with impunity?"

But the witnesses turned deaf ears to him.

Joad worked himself into a professional rage. "You know that only congressmen and members of the Special Police are exempt from Demise, and properly so. These men are neither. One of them has committed the crime of patronizing a bootleg resuscitator. He has greedily taken back his life, when any honest man would have stayed dead. He is a Demisee!"

"No need to swear," one of the witnesses said coldly.

"All right," Joad said, turning to the suspects. "I suppose all of you have alibis?"

They all did. One man even had two. None would submit to a lie detector examination, or even a physical check for evidence. Citizens, Joad thought with frustration, had too many rights these days. It interfered with the meting of justice.

It looked as though they were at an impasse. "Are you sure there is no other clue you can give us?" he asked Sebastian.

"I can't think of any. It happened just the way I said. I hit him square in the middle. I heard him grunt as he went down, and that was all. I'd have made sure of him, but the light—"

"Wait a minute! You heard him grunt? Why didn't you say so before, you idiot?"

"I beg your pardon?"

"I mean, you've given me the clue. You have a pickup in your car, of course?"

"Of course," Sebastian said in an aggrieved tone.

"Get it. We'll use the transcript to identify the voice. This will break the case!"

When the several transcripts had been compared to the voice on the car's recorder there was no longer any question. Joad thanked his stars that none of the suspects had thought to protest having his alibi recorded. Otherwise the case might never have been solved.

"Send up the Euthanasia Squad," he ordered. "Hold on to Suspect Five. Let the others go. The witnesses, too. We've got our man."

Joad couldn't help gloating while they waited for the squad. "So you see," he said smugly to Suspect Five. "All your machinations were to no avail. You can't beat the law."

The suspect seemed oddly resigned. "I was hoping it wouldn't come to this," he said. "I'm going to have to show you my commission." He produced a card and passed it over to the detective.

Joad's eyes bugged out. "Oh, I'm sorry, sir. I had no idea—"

"Quite all right, Policeman," the other said in patronizing tones. "It was careless of me to walk in front of that vehicle. You were only doing your duty."

The door opened and three husky men appeared. "Euthanasia," one announced. "Who's our man?"

Joad pointed wordlessly to Sebastian.

"This way, please," they said gently, carrying the screaming man away.

"What could I do?" the detective said wearily. "I had already announced that the case was solved. There had to be a Demisee."

"Quite right," the blond man agreed.

EXCERPT FROM EDITOR'S LETTER:

I like "The Demisee," but it seems to me the twist at the end is too heavy for so short a story . . . it seems to me that the story would be simpler and more effective if you merely had the culprit dragged off to euthanasia instead of Sebastian, and end with Sebastian congratulating himself, or being congratulated, on his good citizenship. It might help also if you could work in here some hint as to the reasons (overpopulation?) for this inversion of the laws we're familiar with. If anything of this kind occurs to you, let me have your new ending, to be inserted after " 'We've got our man.' " on p. 4. I'll hang on to the script until I hear from you.

REVISED CONCLUSION OF STORY

"Send up the Euthanasia Squad," he ordered into the intercom. "We've got our Demisee." He turned to the group. "You may all go now, except for Suspect Five. And thank you for your help, Mr. Sebastian." They filed out with alacrity.

Joad couldn't help gloating while they waited for the squad. "So you see," he said smugly to Suspect Five. "All your machinations were to no avail. You can't beat the law."

The suspect was annoyed. "The law may not be where you think. If only you knew the inconvenience your bungling investigation has caused me." He pulled out his wallet and flipped open a special compartment. He extended it wordlessly to Joad.

"Don't think any tricks will get you out of—" Joad began. Then he saw the card, "Captain Hunter of the Special Police . . ." he read aloud. "Oh, I'm sorry, sir. I didn't know—why didn't you say something before?"

"And reveal my identity in front of all those idiots? Perhaps you don't realize, Policeman—"

"My apologies, sir. Of course I understand the great importance of men of your caliber. If there is anything I can do—"

The captain's attitude softened. "Quite all right, Policeman. It was careless of me to walk in front of that vehicle. You were only trying to do your duty. Now I have important business elsewhere."

Joad clutched his arm. "But Captain! You can't leave yet. I've already announced that the case has been solved. You've got to tell them why there is no Demisee . . ."

The man shrugged him off. "I told you before that I can't reveal my identity."

"But Captain! Euthanasia is coming for their man. They have a quota. If I don't have a Demisee to hand over, they—they might even take me—"

EXCERPT FROM EDITOR'S LETTER, FIVE WEEKS LATER

I must apologize for not writing you sooner about the revised ending of "The Demisee." I thought the revision was unsatisfactory—too labored and anticlimactic—but I think the ending can be fixed up editorially without too much trouble, and if you don't object, I'd like to try that.

However, it now appears that my inventory for the next issue is full, and if I hang on to the story, the earliest I could use it would be December. If you'd like to offer the script elsewhere in the meantime, I'll cheerfully send it back, and ask to see it again around mid-November if it hasn't sold by then.

EXCERPT FROM EDITOR'S LETTER, SIX WEEKS LATER:

If has been suspended temporarily, and I am therefore regretfully returning your story. When and if the magazine resumes publication, I'll ask you to resubmit it if it is still available.

[NOTE: The magazine did resume publication, but under new editorship, so the sale was lost.]

EXCERPT FROM CRITIC THOMAS H. UZZEL'S PAID COMMENT ON THE STORY, 1960

Some stunt, the plot of this story! Where do you get such fantastic ideas? There may be a fantasy crime story somewhere among these farfetched inventions but it certainly is not easily visible. Your particular version is handicapped in several respects and somehow I have a feeling that you must be aware of these weaknesses as well as I am.

A usable fantasy can be superrational, in some way fabulous, but at the same time it must be rooted in or based on some truths about human beings and customs. The basis of your plot seems to be to reverse the purpose of the law as it affects traffic accidents. As near as I can make out you interpret the law in your story as the reverse of what it actually is. A driver is punished if he *fails* to kill a pedestrian but goes free if he can prove that he has killed a man. Your Sebastian is in trouble because he can't prove that he killed a man. It is not clear why he couldn't easily find proof but evidently you want the reader to believe that the body was quickly removed by someone without the driver seeing how it was done. Your invention of having one or more dead men appear for questioning at a lineup is a violation of the basic principles of good fantasy; such a thing is impossible in any sense. Your reference to a pickup in the driver's car is beyond me to understand. The suddenly revealed identity of Suspect Five is a wild coincidence. There is some novelty in your extravagant reversal of the purpose of the law but I can't imagine any editor being drawn by the use you have made of your idea.

I don't know whether to attempt any constructive advice about this plot or not. At the center of your inventions, as I understand them, is the well-known problem of finding the corpus delicti to prove a man guilty. Instead of having the several suspected victims appear in a lineup in a live condition, why don't you keep them as corpses? The driver would be unable to identify which of the corpses is the man he killed. What then? The driver might be able to prove that one of the five suspects is his man. This would seem to be proof enough to satisfy even a wacky court, but for your story I suppose the judge instead of sentencing the driver would give him one more chance to drive through a light, kill a pedestrian, and produce the latter's body.

Some story! I have a queer feeling you have been playing some kind of gag on me to see if I would take this story seriously. Well, as a professional inventor of plots, I claim to be able to find a good plot in almost any human situation or any incident. This plot of yours is a pretty severe test of my talents!

E

BASTILLE

by Piers Anthony (1964 experience)

But a university training is the great ordinary means to a great but ordinary end . . .

—John Henry Newman: *The Educated Man*

I might as well have been naked on that stage. I faced the high school class, the cynosure of twenty-eight pairs of eyes. Ordinarily I could have handled it. But this time I was supposed to teach them a subject I did not precisely know myself. Grammar: the conjugations and sordid permutations of the irregular verb, and all I knew was what was in the text before me.

I tried, having the students answer their own questions because I could not always be certain whether they were right or wrong. I fumbled through the challenge of the subjunctive case—or was it "mood"?—able only to say that sometimes it was correct to say "I were" rather than "I was." I knew the proper use of it, but not the technical explanation for it. When a student mentioned the predicate nominative in connection with a participle, and I did not challenge him, the regular instructor observing from the rear of the classroom was able to restrain himself no longer. He plunged in, laying waste foolish questions right and left, cowing the pupils with ready terminology that I could hardly follow. I stood stupidly in front, letting the tide wash over; I could not compete.

How had I come to such a pass? I had resolved never to stand before a class unprepared, yet here I was on the spot, being graded myself on my effectiveness in teaching from ignorance. Already the disdainful glances of the students flicked over me. The only question remaining was to determine to what degree I had been found wanting. There would be seven weeks ahead with this same class; I did not see how I could face it.

At the age of twenty-nine, with four years of college, two of the army, and five of miscellaneous employments behind me, I had elected to enter the field of education. "But I don't know enough to teach!" I had protested to the employment counselor. But he had had the answer ready: teacher training. Across the bay the new university was graduating its first fourth-year students; there I could prepare for a state certificate. There was no doubt. Once I met their requirements, I would be prepared.

I went back to college, picking up fifteen credits the first term with an honor average and forging into the accelerated second term with all my energy. Because I was a writer, my field was English; because my Bachelor of Arts degree was in writing, I needed only theory and methods courses. My doubts were brushed aside. "You'll have no trouble," they assured me. "Maturity is the main problem for a new teacher, and you are past that stage."

I hoped they knew what they were doing. I could see little practical use in their required courses, and I failed to see how I could handle a teaching assignment without much greater command of the subject itself. But after all, they were the educational experts, not I.

I should have emulated the philosopher Descartes, and doubted everything. Now, before a twelfth-grade jury, I was sorry I hadn't.

> *And we are here as on a darkling plain*
> *Swept with confused alarms of struggle and flight*
> *Where ignorant armies clash by night.*

—Matthew Arnold: *Dover Beach*

What was the basic problem? Didn't the university *know* when a prospective teacher was ready? Why couldn't a serious student in his twenties, willing and able to take any necessary courses, prepare himself for a subject he knew he would have to teach?

The answers are not simple. At times there is a sizable dichotomy between theory and practice—and it seems most evident in the field of education itself, the least likely place for it. There has been an academic revolt against the competently trained but inadequate teacher; current thought is that it is better to teach *well* than to have complete mastery of the facts while failing to get them across to the student. The result has been a virtually complete domination of theory and method, to the exclusion of content. Having veered away from Scylla, education has drifted into Charybdis.

Take grammar: The university did offer a course in this subject on an optional basis, though it was expected that a writer who had sold commercially would already have sufficient grounding in its principles. I took the option: I enrolled in the only course available, Structure of American English. I found it confusing. Conventional grammar, the professor assured us, was passé; in a few years it would be forgotten entirely. Structure was the coming thing. This was a complex edifice built on phonetics—the science of sounds—and moving up through phonemics, morphemics and graphemes. Once digested, it did make a certain internal sense—and since I had never been able to comprehend conventional grammar, I was glad to try this new science. I passed the course.

But when I got to the high school for my practice teaching experience, I discovered immediately that they neither taught nor cared about structural grammar. The terms I knew were inapplicable. I could not refer to a participle as a "structure of modification" and be intelligible to the students, who naturally hadn't been to college to assimilate the new order. My training in structure had not helped at all for the conventional system; a gerund was still Greek to me. Had the concept been expressed I could have named it in structural terms, but the vocabulary itself meant nothing. I spoke a different language.

This was why I felt naked in that classroom. Unable to appreciate what I did know, the students assumed I knew nothing. So did the regular instructor.

Was my experience a fluke? Hardly. No courses in conventional grammar were offered at any of the colleges and universities in my area, and no *other* kind was taught in the high schools. There was no formal way for a teacher to master his subject on his own. The colleges and the high schools were quietly at war, and the one caught in the crossfire was the student teacher: me. Neither side would compromise, so the carnage continued.

I was inclined to wish a pox on both their houses. I had learned my writing trade well enough to sell fiction to professional magazines without ever having to master the formal rules for either species of grammar. A champion runner does not need to know the technical names for the muscles, ligaments, and bones of the legs in order to perform; a person does not need to recite the name of a grammatical structure to use it in speech or writing properly. So the subject seemed scarcely relevant, and perhaps the time spent on it was a waste of the student's time. Surely there was some more direct and comprehensible way to clarify the student's use of language! Why encumber it with extraordinary artificiality?

That was only one example of the problem of teacher training. I was to encounter others head-on.

> *I was ever a fighter, so—one fight more,*
> *The best and last!*

—Robert Browning: *Prospice*

These things, then, constituted my seven-week chore: grammar, which in effect I did not know; composition, interminable to grade and highly subjective; Victorian literature, about which I knew almost nothing. My future as a teacher depended on my performance in these few weeks, and I was off to an abysmal start. But I was ever a fighter. I arranged to have my grandmother, a former teacher, tutor me two evenings a week in conventional grammar; a dozen years before she had tided me through high school by tutoring me in German, which I had been on the verge of failing. I studied literature on my own, foraging in the library and elsewhere for references. I found a programmed text, *English 3200*, that was terrific. Meanwhile I cut my losses by avoiding grammar in the classroom. "I cannot snow you with the terms," I told them, embarrassing the regular instructor by the unintentional implication that that was what *he* was doing. He stopped observing soon after and left me to my own devices; it was better for both of us.

I proceeded to composition, grading papers on a crash program in order to have them ready in time to take the place of grammar in the class sessions. Here I was competent; I did know the elements of effective expression. I would read the better class papers out loud and have the students discuss them. Sometimes I used an overhead projector to show a paper on the screen, and marked corrections for all to see and discuss. But here again I ran into complications.

Classes have personalities. This is separate from the characters of the individuals comprising them. One or two students will dominate the class, or there will be a general aura about it. This can be pleasant or unpleasant; it depends.

My morning class was quiet and aloof. It did not respond. When I read what I thought was an interesting paper, I was met with silence. If I said something significant, more silence. It drove me crazy; nothing I could do could arouse that class, and I felt certain that I was failing it in some indefinite way. I hated to face that class.

The afternoon class was exuberant. It always responded, particularly to humor. Here the problem was control. I could not keep that room quiet. Students popped up and ran around the room freely; balls of paper flew; birdcalls echoed continually. It was fun in its fashion, but it made a bad impression when visitors passed by the door.

There seemed to be no one program that would fit both classes. I was apt to run out of material in the morning, and out of time in the afternoon. Compositions seemed to bore the morning class, and to incite the afternoon class to near mayhem. I hoped things would improve when we got to literature.

One of the essays assigned to the afternoon class was on the topic of intern teachers: How did the students feel about being guinea pigs for such training? I was nervous about assigning it to the morning class. But the result was an education in itself. There were some penetrating criticisms of my manner of teaching and command of the subject. I was not doing well. I would have to fight harder.

Four legs good: two legs bad.

—The sheep: George Orwell's *Animal Farm*

My pet project for the classes was the unit on *Animal Farm.*

This novel was a penetrating commentary on the nature of Communism (or perhaps any grass-roots revolution), written in the form of a fairy tale about a farm run by its animals. Although it was published in 1945, in the same month that the atomic bomb made headlines, and hardly fits the Victorian scheme of things, the instructor and I had agreed that I would present it to all four of his classes, not just the two I had been working with. For the first time I was on really solid footing. I knew what I was doing, and had a subject that I was certain would interest all the students. As it turned out, the regular instructor fell ill, leaving me to handle the full load for a week, and the unit was exactly what was called for.

My university supervisor, who was responsible for my grade for practice teaching, paid a visit on the day I was introducing the unit to a new class. Such visits were unannounced; the object was to see how I was doing on a routine basis. That made it a gamble, from my point of view, and it was a gamble I lost. There had been a bomb scare that morning, causing the entire school to wait outdoors for forty minutes while a search of the grounds was made, and disrupting the entire schedule. I had not been certain whether I would be handling that class that day. The abrupt appearance of the supervisor unsettled me more. I stood there before the class on my two legs and made blunders that had him blushing. It seemed I would never make good!

There was another matter that the university authorities apparently declined to recognize: legs. Seventeen-year-old girls are by no means inadequately endowed, and they tend to be careless about the way they sit in the classroom. When I addressed a girl, I was apt to be presented with a notable expanse of leg, thigh, and sometimes more, which put me off my literary stride. At times I wished that such girls' intellectual attributes, as shown by their papers, matched their physical ones. I was told that half the girls would be married within a year of leaving high school, and I knew that half of all marriages ended in divorce; I could appreciate why, on both counts.

Animal Farm went reasonably well in all four classes. I believe most students enjoyed it and learned something about both literature and international politics. Some of the papers on it were quite ingenious, and of course we discussed in class the parallels to the later Communist takeover of Cuba. The Bay of Pigs fiasco fitted beautifully, since the main characters of the book are pigs. One paper in particular stood out: it was eighteen pages long, compared to the one-to-three pages normally turned in, and was of high quality. This was by a girl I shall call Mary—and more must be said of her.

Before my full-time internship there had been a two-month period of one-day-a-week class observations. These soon became one-day-a-week teaching sessions. I would assign a paper one week and discuss it the next. In the interim I might take a selection to my university class, to show *my* teacher and fellow education students what I was working with. This was in accordance with the agreements worked out between high school and university.

I used a system of my own for grading, since I felt that a single letter grade was insufficient. I graded on the mechanics: syntax, punctuation, spelling; and content: organization, thought, effectiveness. I put both grades on the paper, so that the student could see in what manner he fell down, and be able to concentrate on eliminating his weak points. Some had excellent ideas but were poor in the mechanics; others wrote fluently, but had nothing of import to say. On the whole I was satisfied with my grading innovation; it worked well.

One day at the university class I showed a paper that had received a failing grade, for the mechanics. Another internee challenged me: she felt I was being too harsh. "What would you call an 'A' paper?" she wanted to know. I rose to the occasion: I brought out a straight "A over A" paper and read a sample paragraph. The point was made. There was a remarkable difference between the two.

In fact, the class suspected there was too great a difference; the second paper was almost professional in tone. "Are you sure that student did it herself?" I was asked. This made me pause. How could I be sure? It would have been easy to plagiarize; many high school students have tried it.

I reported the suspicion to the high school instructor. He took the author—Mary—aside and put the question to her. Next day she presented him with an extemporaneous essay addressed to me on the subject of plagiarism. I had not made the accusation; I had been more like a messenger in this case. But she associated it with me, and was irked. The paper was clever, forceful, and hilarious. It demanded armed guards at the doors, written affidavits, and nonintellectual wording to ensure that all student work was original.

That essay was passed from hand to hand among the members of the school faculty, and chosen as the first selection for the forthcoming school literary magazine. Certainty it negated the question of Mary's need to plagiarize. She had enough talent to make such an act meaningless. I read the essay to the class and complimented her on it. This was how I met her, so to speak; she had been an anonymous body, before.

Now she had caught fire again with the *Animal Farm* assignment, and had done a superlative job. I wrote a long comment on her paper—I always tried to give personal comment, and the students seemed to appreciate this—my note three pages itself. I pointed out the few areas she had missed, and quoted other examples that I thought would help her. This paper, too, was A/A. It was a pleasure to work with such a student, sarcastic though she tended to be. There are complexities in the lives of every person a teacher little understands, but the bright ones show it more.

There was meaning for everyone in *Animal Farm*. Initially the men had stood on two legs, and represented evil and oppression. The animals stood on four, and were good but oppressed. This was the prime demarcation: four legs good, two legs bad—the final word stretched out into a sheep's bleat: Ba-a-a-ad! Once the animal revolution had thrown off the yoke of men, the pigs began to run things. Eventually the pigs even began to walk on two feet . . .

In like manner, I found that the ingenious theory of the university courses, the promising challenges, faded in practice. The "improvements" in teaching were rising to two legs.

> *Oh, yet we trust that some good*
> *Will be the final goal of ill.*
>
> —Alfred, Lord Tennyson: *In Memoriam*

With my interest in writing, particularly of the creative variety, I encouraged my classes to write imaginatively. "Dream with me," I urged them. "Imagine yourself writing a short story, and having it published in the school magazine. Friends congratulating you on your success. Doesn't that appeal to you?" One hand showed in the morning class: "No," he said. The afternoon class, as always, responded more readily. I felt that they, at least, would make the effort.

When the papers came in, the morning class—the one I thought I had been unable to move—had one of the finest collections of creative writing I had seen from a high school group. Not failure, but success lay before me. I judged that this class was very likely to place a greater proportion of pieces in the school magazine than any other class in the school. But as it turned out, my afternoon class exceeded it, and the two together placed a majority of all the pieces published there. Fewer than sixty students of mine had outperformed the remaining two thousand!

And one of the first to place was the boy who had told me he wasn't interested.

But problems continued. The afternoon class, always unruly, grew steadily more so. Toward the end of each week it was almost impossible to keep it quiet. During the concluding minutes on Friday I didn't even try. I talked to individuals about their papers and let the rest chatter; they were just waiting to get out.

I turned to discover the school principal listening at the door. I realized how the situation must appear to him: chaos. I started to tell him that the class was not always like this, but the words did not come out quite as intended. It sounded as if I were publicly condemning him for listening in. He turned about and departed, and I wondered what I might have done to my future.

Another day I allowed my attention to be distracted from the class as a whole—there were always details of administration to attend to, interminably—and turned to discover two boys in a fist fight! I dived in, fearful for my glasses, and broke it up. But once more I wondered what such loss of class control would mean to the assessment of my own performance.

There were subtle differences with my supervising instructor, the regular high school teacher. He was known as a hard grader; he spoke almost with pride of his tests that flunked the majority. He was determined that no unfit student should be passed on to college. But I differed; if my students failed, I felt that the real failure lay in me, in my teaching. I wanted to take the unfit student and make him fit: in a word, teach. The instructor saw the class as a selective process, to separate the sheep from the goats. I wanted only to convey the most information, let the grades fall where they might. It did not bother me if a poor student passed; perhaps he was actually learning more than the good one, who knew the material before taking the course. The result was that my grades were more generous, and I believe the instructor saw this as a weakness on my part.

I also believed in the option. I felt that students would study harder and learn more if they had some choice in the subject matter, and in the manner it was presented. The regular teacher observed with silence. He generally made the decisions for his classes. When we came to literature, I noted that one of my favorite pieces was missing from the text. Thomas Babington Macaulay was represented only by some small essays. So I described to the morning class the background for his long heroic poem *Horatius at the Bridge*: The Etruscan army was marching to sack ancient Rome, and there was nothing but the river Tiber to stop it. If the Romans could just chop down the bridge in time, Rome would be saved—but it was obvious that the van of the Tuscan army would reach the bridge before the demolition was complete. Therefore brave Horatius volunteered to stand at the bridge and hold off the enemy, to gain time. "Do you want to listen to it?" I inquired. "I will have to test you on it, if I take up class time—" This was the crucial point. Would they choke down the extra work?

The vote was close, but finally, by a margin of five, they accepted it. Next day I read the poem to them, pausing frequently to explain the action. I heard sounds in the class, fidgeting, books being shifted—it wasn't going over. But when I finished, disappointed, they corrected me. They had after all enjoyed it—at least, compared to the usual fare. Once more my omen of failure had been premature. My option had worked.

> *Lo, all our pomp of yesterday*
> *Is one with Nineveh and Tyre!*
>
> —Rudyard Kipling: *Recessional*

The month of literature went comparatively smoothly. At least there was a solid foundation to build on. I read the essays and verse, and discussed them in class. The subtleties were largely wasted on the students, but at least they were being exposed to material that they might appreciate one day. I took five minutes to go into the savage histories of the doomed cities, Nineveh and Tyre: "If all this is implied in two words," I said, "think how much must be in Kipling's whole poem! Think of the warning he was giving to Britain—a situation now coming to pass." They listened passively.

The afternoon class quickly picked up new passwords. The

birthplace of Thomas Carlyle—Ecclefechan, Scotland—turned out to be a word to conjure with, and stray questions were likely to be answered by this term. "Offal" was another, taken from one of the Macaulay essays. I quizzed both classes frequently on the material. Grades were high, but I feared this was rote, and that they did not really understand it. I tried to keep up with the boring vocabulary quizzes; as nearly as I could tell, the students were not gaining materially from these exercises, but they were required. Students would learn only the first definition in the dictionary, which might not be relevant—or worse, assume they knew the word, and misuse it in a sentence. "He was *affronted* with many problems." "This *phenomena* was new."

But the hump was over. I had survived my internship, and perhaps done some good in the process. I would be a teacher.

Then came Nineveh.

It began simply enough. I found a note taped on the back of my car: DANGER STUDENT DRIVER. I removed it and said nothing; teachers are subject to this sort of thing. Next day I came home to find my house dead: no power, no water. Frantic calls determined that requests for suspension of service had been made in my name, which the services had honored without question. This time I notified the school authorities.

Then a van pulled up to deliver a hospital bed. My wife turned it away, and learned that a female voice had placed the order. Likewise the prior calls: a female voice. The following night the bell rang and a man stepped in, a case of Ancient Age on his shoulder: ordered in our name. Later that evening it happened again: another store, another case of whiskey. And a third time—and not every person was pleased to learn it was a practical joke. I called the police, and shortly a man was at my house. When I was talking to him the phone rang: an angry woman's voice telling me that she had seen all the liquor trucks coming to my address, and that it was shocking. "Hold the line a moment," I said. "There's a gentleman here I think you should talk to." I beckoned to the officer, but she hung up before he could answer. I knew it had been no neighbor. My neighbors did not make calls of that nature, and a genuine observer would have noted the police car now in my drive. And of course the liquor had been brought in private cars, not trucks.

Later it occurred to me that the prankster—for surely it was she on the phone—probably thought one of the liquor deliverers was present. He might have recognized her voice. No wonder she had hung up in a hurry!

The police were sorry, but could offer no help. There was no way to determine which student was responsible. It could be any one of them, or the girl friend of one.

Next, I received letters in answer to my "inquiries" to several lonely-hearts bureaus. Did the prankster realize that I was long since married? Surely so, for the voice had more than once identified herself as "Mrs. Jacob," using my mundane last name. It was almost as if she liked that appellation.

Then there was a story submission in my name to one of the science fiction magazines I wrote for, *Galaxy*. It was accompanied by a typed letter, with my signature forged at the bottom. "To begin with," it said, "I am an accomplished writer . . . I know, of course, that you don't get works like this very often, and I'm quite sure that it will be published in your next issue without fail . . . unless you felt that it should be submitted to a more worthy magazine. . . . Now for a few comments, to help you better understand *Terror on Planet X* for the great work that it is. . . . Note the subtle use of sex. . . . Yes, this is my pinnacle of achievement—but I realize I am human and can make errors. I will appreciate any criticism you might have to offer, providing it is intelligent criticism . . . I realize I have great talent . . . make me an offer and I will try to work something out for you."

The thought that such a missive could have passed through the hands of an editor appalled me. Yet it was accompanied by a rejection slip. Of course the package could have been faked up; rejection slips are printed forms that can be attached to anything. So I wrote a letter to a friend who knew that editor, Frederik Pohl, asking her to verify whether the package had gone through Pohl's office. I didn't want to write to *Galaxy* about a nonexistent event. She verified it. The editor remembered it. The damage had indeed been done. Since this mischief had been crafted to damage my professional reputation, it was no longer merely a nuisance; it was forgery and libel.

I read the story, "Terror on Planet X." It was true to its title: deliberately cheap science fiction. What a horror, to have my name attached to this juvenile mess! But as I read it, and saw the infernal humor, a great light dawned. I had seen that style before.

Mary!

There were other episodes, but they were merely inconveniences. I drafted letters apologizing to those inconvenienced, declining membership in book and record clubs, and explaining the situation to Fred Pohl at *Galaxy*. He responded sympathetically, having encountered such things before; he told of one young man who had been tricked into believing his story was so good he was being offered a job as editor of the magazine; Pohl had had to set that person straight when he showed up at the office. Some joke! For me, there were some seventeen episodes in all, but apparently all had been initiated in a four-day period ending with the "neighbor's" call to me. At that point she had been scared off, but the fallout had taken much longer to clear. I turned in her name to the authorities, but was advised that her family was prominent locally and so the matter would probably be buried. It was.

> *Better by far you should forget and smile*
> *Than that you should remember and be sad.*

—Christina Rossetti: *Remember*

My last week was absorbed in preparations for the examination I was to give my students, the final observation by the university supervisor, and a day back on the university campus taking tests of my own. When I was to be graded on, myself, I did not know. Every time the university man entered the high school classroom the demeanor of my students changed radically. "We wanted to make it look good for you," they explained afterward. But I had been braced for their normal behavior, and was put off by the change; it was a bit like stepping in an unseen hole. I knew the university man had no real basis on which to judge my performance; he had never really seen me in action. It was possible that none of the university people had seen the real action; no wonder they had an ivory-tower attitude! I talked with another intern, who told me that this man had been playing down her performance to her high school instructor. "Watch out for him," she advised. "He's two-faced." So I tried to question him about his estimation of my performance—after all, a student of any type has a right to know how he is doing—but he avoided the matter. With that, and similar hints from other sources, I had my warning: I would not do well. In many areas internships were not graded as such; an automatic A or B was given if the intern was trying and learning. Certainly I had tried very hard and learned much, but I suspected something other than this was operating here.

Sure enough, my grade came even before my internship was finished. The concluding report from the high school had not yet been sent in; something other than my performance was indeed operating. My grade was a C. In the system of the times, this was a euphemism for substandard performance. I was no longer an honor student. I talked with the high school instructor, who was supposed to have input on my grading, and he said that he had told the university man that he could not fairly call my performance an A, though he would not protest it—but the university man had already decided on the C. So much for that.

I was to discover, when I got my teaching certificate, that despite my having a teacher test score well above the ninetieth percentile, no school in the public system would hire me; eventually I got a job at a private school. I considered going on for a Master's degree in education, but when the university assigned the same man as my adviser, I dropped that notion, and in due course retired to full-time fiction writing. It seemed I just was not suited for a career as a teacher.

But the practice-teaching experience was highly meaningful, and I would not have exchanged that experience for any other. It helped me more than all the other education courses combined. I only regret that so many other students, who might have made better teachers than I did, have been victimized by the system and perhaps had their careers aborted unfairly. The profession of teaching suffers from more than low pay; the pay scale could be quadrupled, and it would remain difficult to get intelligent and motivated people through this gantlet.

How I wish it were possible to lay siege to that ivory-towered Bastille of teacher education and bring it down to earth, as did the French people in Carlyle's history, *Fall of the Bastille*. How much better it would be to dispense with the murky politics of those who refuse to face reality, and let the student teachers issue forth to battle—prepared! Perhaps some future year this will be the case.

The final examination I gave my high school students was rough on them; great numbers failed. I thought it was fair, and stood by it; all the questions had been taken from the pop quizzes that they had done so well on before, and they were getting higher grades from me than they usually did from their regular instructor. I would have preferred to curve the grades—that is, allocate a fair range and center on that, so that the students were ranked in proportion to each other—but complexities of the situation prevented. So the grades were not high. Perhaps I was serving my students as the system was serving me; I hope not.

On the last day of my internship I handed back the papers—and the students handed me a beautiful cake! We had a feast there in the classroom, against school regulations but fun anyway. I suppose they had intended me to take the cake home, but they deserved it as much as I did. I had thought I had failed to move that morning class, but they gave me a send-off I would be happy to remember. The afternoon class was the same. As it turned out, this was not my gateway to a lifetime career in teaching, but it was certainly a significant experience.

In later years, when my own children came into the school system, I watched warily, and had little patience with inferior teaching. Yet I was not surprised, because I had learned the hard way what kind of teachers the system did not want.

NOTE: The following story I did not author, but since it was submitted under my byline and I doubt the real author would care to claim it (or the legal consequences of such a claim) I submit it here as an appendix to this essay. In retrospect, it is rather flattering to think that a girl as pretty and talented as Mary would go to this extreme to make an impression on me. Perhaps it is only right that it finally see print.

Terror on Planet X

It was a bleak, dreary day on the planet Earth. The rockets zoomed to a landing everywhere, and the men were busily working. Zar Malga, test pilot for Interspace Enterprises, was walking hurriedly to the office of his boss. He knew something strange was in the air, and he was very excited. As he came to the office of Ure Kalna, boss of the company, he passed a small dog. "Hi doggie," he said. The dog was a spacehound, and looked up with a wagging tail. Zar walked on into the office. "I'm here boss," he said cheerfully.

His boss looked up. "Oh, Zar ... I have a very important mission for you." The boss went on to explain that he wanted Zar to fly to Planet X, an unknown planet far out in the galaxy. He told Zar that no one had explored Planet X, and that he would be the first. Zar agreed to go, because otherwise his boss would fire him. Besides, Zar was very brave. His boss told Zar that they had a brand-new spaceship for him to fly and Zar was glad! He'd always wanted to get ahold of that T-45 airship! It was so shiny and powerful. Zar ran out of his boss's office to tell his crew.

Zar Malga fastened his seat belt and yelled to his crew to do the same. It was sixty minutes till takeoff time and Zar was getting nervous. His crew consisted of three men and ten women. Zar was very fond of women crews. Besides, it was the year 2007 now, and morals had changed. Everybody believed in Freud. Zar called, "It's almost time for takeoff, is everybody ready?" The crew all yelled "Yes!" in unison. Then came the countdown. 10 ... 9 ... 8 ... 7 ... 6 ... 5 ... 4 ... 3 ... 2 ... —1! Blastoff! The crew clutched their seats as the great silver bird took off into space—off through a trail of fire, off to Planet X!!! Everything was working fine, and Zar decided to relax for a while with one of his crew members. He and she retreated to the back room for a little while.

T-45 was sailing toward her goal. It would be about three days before they reached Planet X if they were lucky. They zoomed past stars and planets, and admired the beauty of outer space. The great ship was traveling at the fantastic speed of two million miles an hour, and they didn't quite know how far Planet X was. They'd just have to wait and see if they hit it. Days and days passed. Zar began to wonder if his boss hadn't been a little off in his calculations. Maybe his boss was trying to get rid of him!! Maybe there *was* no Planet X! These things bothered Zar! Finally he was relieved of worry, as they caught sight of Planet X in the distance. They would be there in another hour. The beauty of space was still there, but the crew was too worried to notice it.

The crew hurried around and gathered equipment, for they had no idea of what the climate of Planet X would be like. They also gathered equipment for research about the planet, because the boss had told them to get information about how he could exploit it. Zar hopped into the space suit his first mate was holding, and instructed his crew members to do the same.

He loaded several ray guns, in case of unfriendly wildlife. Then he brought the great, silver bird in for a graceful landing.

Zar slowly opened the door to the ship. They were actually on the mysterious planet!!! Zar was very thrilled. He unloaded some equipment to test the atmosphere and pressure, and found that wonder of wonders, they were the same (or nearly so) as on Earth. He instructed his crew to wear the suits anyway, in case of some unforeseen emergency. They each took a ray gun and started off to explore the wonders that Planet X might hold.

Zar and his crew had gone but a little way when they saw a gruesome, fantastic sight! There before them was a huge green monster. The monster had large teeth and looked very fearsome. It was over fifty feet long with the head of a dragon. Zar screamed and ran behind his crew. From there he fired at the beast, while it devoured one of his women crew members. Oh, well, thought Zar. Nine left. He fired series after series of powerful frappa rays at the monster, and soon it crumbled under this terrible attack—not even a green monster could stand up under deadly frappa rays. The remaining crew of twelve (not counting Zar; he's the captain) proceeded into a dense rain forest. They had gone a little way when another terror confronted them. This time Zar acted quickly. He held out a crew member to tempt the monster (which was a big snake-like creature) while he had another crew member shoot it with deadly frappa rays. Thanks to the leadership and courage of Zar, there were still eleven crew members to continue with the mission. Zar looked around for things for the boss to exploit, but this was a very dull planet. He found no evidence of intelligent life anywhere.

The planet was starting to get dark when Zar suggested they start for the ship. Then he remembered! He had forgotten a compass. They did not know how to get back to the ship! This was very terrible, since they only had two days on the planet when things would be right for takeoff. Zar was very depressed, and started to cry. One of the women suggested that they camp till light, then they could retrace their steps. Zar thought that was a very good idea, and it cheered him up. They built a camp from some old branches and trees, and settled down for the night. Zar stationed two women to stand guard. Thus, they fell into a fitful sleep.

The rays of the warm sun woke Zar up bright and early. The

women and three men had been up for hours, trying to trace their trail. It had rained a peculiar green rain during the night, obscuring their trail. Zar decided to just keep walking, and hope that they ran upon the ship. The crew finally agreed. They walked through the rain forest, and thought they were on the right trail. There before them was the clearing they had fought the snake-monster in, on their way. Zar directed the women, and they searched the brush for any hidden menace before Zar came. The path was looking increasingly familiar, and the crew was confident that it would find the ship soon. Just as things were looking increasingly good, another monster appeared! This one was a large, hairy apelike creature which stood almost nine feet high. It came at them with a roar, and Zar acted quickly. He threw oil from his radio in the creature's face, while the other members of his crew fired their ray guns at it. Once again Zar had saved the day. The crew hurried to the ship, and boarded quickly before they met up with another monster. Zar closed the cockpit door and prepared for takeoff. He was very disgusted with Planet X—nothing but monsters and rain forests. The boss wouldn't like his report—he might even be transferred to Outer Pluto! Everyone knew that Outer Pluto was the worst place in the galaxy to be, for only men crews were allowed. Zar tensed as the great silver bird soared into space for a graceful takeoff.

It was two hours till landing time on Earth. Their homeward trip had been very uneventful, to give them a rest from their terrible adventure on Planet X. Zar would be glad to get home, even though the boss would not be as pleased with his report. Then, Earth was in view! It would only be a matter of minutes ... seconds ... "Prepare for landing!" Zar shouted. 10 ... 9 ... 8 ... 7 ... 6 ... 5 ... 4 ... 3 ... 2 ... 1!!! The great silver bird gracefully landed in the airstrip of Interspace Enterprises. Zar remained a while after the other crew members had gone. He wanted to think—to reflect on the dangers he had faced in Planet X. Yes, this voyage had truly been,

Terror on Planet X!!!!

F

BOILERPLATES

Spot essays on subjects readers often request, set up on computer for ready access.

AUTHOR:

A number of my readers ask about my personal background. It is pretty interesting or pretty dull, depending on viewpoint. It is interesting because I am foreign-born, had a fouled-up childhood, and became a vegetarian. It is dull because I am now a settled middle-aged married man of comfortable means and vaguely conservative personal tastes.

I was born on August 6, 1934, in Oxford, England. My mundane name is Piers Anthony Dillingham Jacob, the first half becoming my literary pseudonym. My parents were doing relief work in Spain during the Spanish Civil War of 1936–39; since they did not want to take their children into war, my younger sister and I remained in England, cared for by a nanny. When that war ended, we joined our parents in Spain for a year, and I began to learn Spanish. Then my father was arrested, apparently by mistake; rather than admit error, the Franco government expelled him from Spain and took over the supplies of food intended for the hungry children there. In this manner we came to America, where my father's family lived. I had my sixth birthday on the ship, and got a cake made of sawdust, because of the limited wartime supplies. As it happened, the Duke of Windsor, formerly King Edward VIII, was on the same ship; I remember seeing his car unloaded by crane at Bermuda.

All of my formal education has been in America. I spent three years in first grade because I could not learn to read, but later I recovered enough to make it on through college. I attended five schools in first grade, and nine by the time I graduated from the twelfth grade at Westtown School in Pennsylvania. I majored in creative writing at Goddard College and got my B.A. degree there in 1956. I also married a girl I met there, Carol Ann Marble. As a resident alien I was subject to the American draft. I was in the U.S. Army from March 1957 to March 1959, and got my American citizenship while there, then retired to Florida, becoming a technical writer at an electronics company, then a state social worker, then a full-time writer for a year, October 1962 to September 1963. In that period I sold my first two stories. But unable to earn my living as a writer, I returned to school at the University of South Florida and got a teaching certificate in English. I taught ninth and tenth grade English for a little over a year at Admiral Farragut Academy in St. Petersburg, Florida. Unhappy with teaching, I retired again to writing in June 1966, and remain a writer today.

We have two daughters: Penny, born in OctOgre 1967, and Cheryl in Mayhem 1970. Meanwhile my writing was doing better, and despite one of the most volatile of careers that included problems with some publishers because I stood on my rights and required contracts to be honored, I became one of the more successful writers in the science fiction/fantasy genre. We moved out of the city, to the forest in central Florida, and bought horses for our daughters. The Florida landscape became that of the fantasy land of Xanth, and horses in various forms galloped through my fiction. I believe I am now one of the more successful fantasy writers of the day, others being Stephen Donaldson, Terry Brooks, David Eddings, and Robert Asprin. I am, however, continuing to write science fiction, and branching out into other types of fiction, such as horror and historical.

COMPUTER:

After thirty years of typing my fiction on manual typewriters, and seventeen years of writing my first drafts in pencil, in 1984 I computerized. I only did it because they stopped making manual typewriters, but now I am quite happy with the computer. I can't carry it with me wherever I go, as I used to do with my clipboard and pencil text, but it saves me retyping, so is about 40% faster than the old system. My time is worth a lot to me, because I'm not getting younger, so the computer system is well worthwhile.

I use a DEC Rainbow with a twenty megabyte hard disk and a 512 kilobyte memory. This allows me to store the texts of several novels, in case I should need to refer to them or to revise them or make new copies, and of course I also have them saved, in first draft and final drafts, on floppy disks, which I store in a fireproof little safe. I keep a printout of the first drafts, too, so there is very little chance of losing my material.

The monitor screen is amber, because I understand this color is the easiest on the eyes, and indeed I have never gotten eyestrain or a headache from using it. The printer is Dec's LA-100, which prints in dot-matrix. I use the draft mode for first draft and "carbon" copies of my letters, as this mode prints at eight times the speed of the letter-quality mode that I use for the top copies.

I use FinalWord II for word processing (that is, regular text), using its "macro" capacity to change my keyboard to the Dvorak layout with the little modifications I have, such as the "quote" marks on the home row in the unshift position. Because the American keyboard of the Rainbow cannot be adapted perfectly, we changed the machine to one of its 14 foreign keyboards, the Swedish, and then changed that to my Dvorak layout. Thus there is a Swedish influence on my work, though it doesn't show on the conscious level.

I use a "shareware" program for my housekeeping—that is, the handling of numbers of files that accumulate. This is Djinn, and it acts like an ancient magical being, by no coincidence, even saying "Farewell, Master!" when it departs.

Do I recommend computerization for others? Yes and no. Yes if you have a lot of typing to do, and can afford the price; no if you type only occasionally. I still use my manual typewriter for envelopes, or I do them by hand.

IDEAS:

Where do I get all my ideas? I think I am asked this question more often than any other, and this may be true for other writers too. I have several answers. First, I happen to be blessed with an extremely active imagination; I couldn't turn it off if I wanted to. As a child I did want to, and couldn't; my mind conjured monsters that pursued me by day, and horrors I witnessed by night, so that I couldn't sleep without a light. When I became a writer, I turned that imagination to positive things, and the monsters that had terrified me became friends, for they went into my fiction. Now I just love monsters!

Second, I do a lot of adaptation. I turn mundane things into magic things, or symbolic things. I turned the state of Florida into the magic land of Xanth, with the details of the landscape assuming special properties. Everything I see about me can be turned into something magic; this doesn't require a lot of imagination, just some free association. Thus I get credit for more originality than I may have, when people don't recognize the mundane roots of my creations.

But mainly, I take advantage of the notions that come to me unexpectedly. When I had a lot of dental work done, I made notes on the process and turned it into a series of stories about Dr. Dillingham, a spacefaring dentist. When I was appalled by the horrors experienced by Haitian and Vietnamese refugees, I retold their story in a novel, *Refugee*, setting it in space in the future. I try to keep a pencil and paper always with me, so that if some random thought occurs I can jot it down; it's not a matter of thinking up new notions, but of saving the ones I do think of. I suspect that every person has many more ideas than he realizes; if he just hung on to them instead of forgetting them, he would have plenty to write about.

But sometimes I simply need an idea, because I have written myself into a hole and don't know how to get out of it. Then I concentrate, asking myself questions and searching for answers. I may simply talk out loud, as it were, putting my comments in a note to myself, right in the text of whatever I'm writing, using brackets to set them off so that I can edit them out later. Like this: [Here is my hero locked in this cell; can he break out? No, the walls and door are too strong. Can he climb out? No, the walls are slick; he just slides back down. Can he dig out? Well, maybe if the floor is packed dirt, he could wet it down so as to make it soft, and scrape it out, and make a hole under the wall. But he has no water. Um, could he urinate on it? That depends on the type of story this is; some readers don't take to that sort of thing. Does he have any other way to dig? Let's say he finds an old bone, where some prior inmate has rotted away; can he use that bone to dig in the dirt? That's pretty gruesome—but this is a gruesome story. Okay, let's do that.] Then I go ahead and write the scene. In short, some of my ideas come from just plain working at them.

WRITING:

I am often asked what it takes to be a successful writer of fiction. My readers seem to assume that because I am one, I know how it is done. The simple answer is that no one really knows; you just have to sit down and write, and send the result to a publisher, and see what happens. If it sells, you're a successful writer; if the manuscript comes back reeking of vomit, you probably aren't. But for those who need more specific guidelines, I have developed an acronym: IDEAL.

I = Imagination—you need to be able to think up ideas and plots and characters and situations, or to develop them along feasible lines. I am blessed with one of the most active imaginations extant, and it's a great help. But if you don't have imagination, I can't tell you how to get it.

D = Desire—you need to really want to write and to succeed at it, otherwise you'll poop out before you get there. Your desire has to carry you through the long lean times without flagging, so that you never give up hope.

E = Effort—you need to work at it. Writing is not a lazy person's profession; if you think that it represents easy money, go elsewhere.

A = Ability—great ideas, desire and effort will still come to grief if you lack the fundamental skills. You need to be able to tell a story in such a way that others will want to read it. You need to be able to discipline your imagination, to integrate your ideas so that they make sense to the average reader and move him to pleasure, sadness, excitement, outrage, lust, or wonder.

L = Luck—You just have to have your manuscript on the

right desk at the right time, and factors over which you have no control may decide the fate of it.

So there are my five key aspects. There are also a number of things that fans, critics, professors, editors, and other experts urge, and naturally these are not what counts. I have worked out another acronym for these misleading aspects: NO SALE.

N = Name—Many people believe that if you have a Big Name, you can sell your material readily regardless of its merit.

O = Originality—How many times do we see reviewers blasting a novel as being unoriginal! But the truth is, there is very little truly original writing being done, and less seeing print.

S = Style—Perhaps the biggest hobgoblin of them all! Fiction is praised and even given awards for style, but what the experts rave about may be unreadable by real people. My god of writing is Clarity; without that there is nothing.

A = Agent—Many folk think that all you need to sell your work is a good literary agent. It is true that an agent can help, but even the best agent can't sell total junk. Also, an unpublished writer can't *get* a decent agent, so he *has* to do it on his own.

L = Literacy—Now it does help to be literate if you want to succeed in writing, but you don't have to go overboard. Just tell your story as well as you can, and don't try to be artificial.

E = Education—You don't need a college degree in writing. You can educate yourself in the manner that counts: Study the work of whatever successful writer you really enjoy reading. Then try to write likewise.

Let me conclude with one device I have found useful: FISH. This one is not an acronym. Think of yourself as a fisherman. Think of your potential reader as a fish. You want to catch and land that fish; if the fish ignores you or gets away, you're a failure. So you cast your line with the bait on the end, something that is calculated to interest that fish. So the fish bites— and inside that bait is your narrative hook, which prevents it from swimming away. Now you have to keep the line taut, because if you ever let it slacken the fish will slip the hook and escape. So ask yourself constantly *will this hold my reader?* as you write your text—and if it seems dull, change it until it is compelling. Never give that fish a chance, because the moment it has an opportunity to set that book down, you have lost it. If you can keep that line taut until the end of the piece, you've got your fish. And the irony is, at the end, when the fish is flopping exhausted on the bank, *it will thank you*!

BLOCK:

Writer's block, the dreadest of creative maladies! I know of only two writers who don't suffer from it on occasion: Isaac Asimov and Piers Anthony. Asimov writes mainly nonfiction, so always has material to work from; I believe he finds it harder to do fiction. I work almost entirely in fiction; what is my secret? I once did suffer block, but learned to conquer it. I have formed an acronym to summarize the principles of this conquest. The acronym is BLOCK.

B—Brackets. That's right: [brackets]. Squared-off parentheses. These are not normally used in fiction, so serve to distinguish their contents from the regular text. When I'm writing, and come to an involuntary stop, I go into brackets to figure out why. It's like the time I was reading a book while walking through the forest; I discovered I had stopped, so I looked about and discovered that a tree had fallen across the road, blocking me. So I circled it and resumed my walking and reading. Even so, when I'm writing, I can halt without realizing why. So I step into brackets and look about: [Why did I stop? What's blocking this scene? My hero has just taken the girl into his arms and said "I love you," and she is staring at him in shock. Why can't I figure out what she says next? I *thought* she was going to say, "Darling, how I've longed to hear you say that!" So what's the matter? Oh, now I remember: she's married. Brother! Well, can I change that? Maybe it's her twin sister who's married. So I can go back to page 3 and plant that, and—but then why is she shocked? Does she think *he's* married? Yes, that would explain it. Okay, plant another reference, something he says that she confuses.] Then go on with the scene and the corrections. When you retype the manuscript, omit the brackets; they have served their purpose. If you work on the computer, you can do what I do now: set up a macro that will seek and highlight bracketed material, so you can double-check it before erasing it. Because brackets are used for other notes too, such as phone messages (so you don't have to rip out your text to make a separate and unrelated note; that could bring on a siege of block by itself) or other ideas, or even grumbles about things that interrupt your concentration. All in the interest of momentum (see under K, below): keep it moving. But mainly the brackets are for handling problems in the creative draft. They are like the construction forms for pouring concrete; you remove them after the stuff has set, but they're mighty helpful while you're working. [However, I should say that late in 1985 I got a word-processing program that allows me to put my bracket notes in a parallel file; the principle is the same, but I no longer have to have the notes right in the middle of my text. It's like doing them on a separate sheet of paper.] [And in 1987 I got a program that allows me to have my notes in a window on the same screen though in a separate file; that's even better.]

L—Love of writing. I suspect that most hard-core block has its root in a failure of the will to write. Do you really want to write? Some people merely want *to have written*—that is, to have fame and fortune. They really don't like getting down into the muck of creativity and grubbing for notions. Verify your motives; do you like the actual process of writing? No, don't tell me that no one does; *I* do. I'm having a ball writing this essay; it's a challenge. All of writing is like that, for me. If it's not like that for you, then maybe you don't really want to be a writer, and should spare yourself further grief by admitting it, and seeking other employment. If you find it easy to find excuses not to write at any given moment, that's a signal of trouble. This is not a question of talent; the most highly talented genre writer I know of, Theodore Sturgeon, had a lot of trouble settling down to write. I get annoyed by things that prevent me from writing, such as meals and sleep. I seem to be addicted to writing; the longer I go without writing, the more uncomfortable I become. No, I don't take it out on my family; I get off by myself and *write*. This is an addiction whose remedy is easy; as with sex, its fulfillment is its amelioration.

O—Organization. If your whole text up to this point consists of one big bracket saying [I love to write! Why can't I get a handle on it?!], then maybe you just don't have things properly organized. Very well; make up an outline. Who's your main character? What is he going to do? What stops him? Is there to be romance? With whom? Humor? Where, when, how? Theme— *is* there one? Ha—maybe you thought a theme was only for dull English papers. Not so; for you it may be your rationale for writing this piece. What did you want to say that you thought the universe would profit by? You don't know? Then *that's* why you stalled. *You had nothing to write!* And this outline showed up that absence. Dump this text and start over with a notion that really turns you on. This relates to L, above, and C, below: not only do you have to Love Writing, you have to Love This Project, or it's no go. Keep buzzing out outlines or summaries or stray notes in brackets until you find the notion, that, like a diamond in the dirt, suddenly gleams at you. Then make it your own.

C—Change-off. Sometimes all systems seem to be go, but still it doesn't move. It happened to me when I was three-quarters through writing *Omnivore*. It was a good novel, and I liked it and believed in it, but making progress was like lifting a mountain. Coincidentally I tried working on another project, *Sos the Rope*, and that moved so well that I just about finished the first draft in ten days. Then I returned to *Omnivore*, and still it slogged. I realized that it wasn't me balking, it was the material. *O* was sophisticated, intellectual stuff requiring a lot of cerebration; *S* was straight action/adventure. So when I couldn't move on the one type, I could on the other. Thereafter I tried to keep two or three projects, of different types, in readiness, so that I could change off. When Serious didn't move, maybe Adventure would; when Adventure balked, Humor might move. This can make a big difference; you can't be sure what will move until you try it, and different things may move at different times. Or maybe you don't want to write the sort of thing you thought you wanted to. I thought I wanted to write sophisticated, literary material; I discovered that I was much better at commercial entertainment. It was just my luck that the latter paid better. No, don't sneer at commercial writing; I'd rather pay my bills by writing adventure, than by trying to teach high-schoolers to be literate, which is what I was doing before I went to full-time writing.

K—Keep working. Momentum may be an abused term in sports, but it seems to have some value in writing. You are most likely to write well in the coming hour if you have been doing so in the past hour. I find I generally start slow in the morning, then build up power as the day progresses, then fade in the evening. One good hour in the afternoon may be worth two in the morning. *I don't want to interrupt that hot hour.* So I do my best to avoid interruptions, whether of external or internal origin, and keep the material moving, no matter what it is.

Hence things like bracket-notes; fifteen minutes of solving plotting problems is just as good as fifteen minutes of polished text. To encourage myself further, I keep a daily record of my output: one line a day summarizing accomplishment. For example, on JeJune 1, 1985, I wrote thirty-two hundred words of my autobiography, *Bio of an Ogre*, proofread forty pages of *With a Tangled Skein* galleys, and dug out weeds for two hours. (That did fit in one line; I use abbreviations.) I can check my accomplishment for any day of any year, back to mid-1966 when I became a full-time writer. It's a useful record in itself, but it's also an ox-goad of an inducement to make a good showing each day. I also note what *prevents* me from doing well; the record accepts excuses. But I don't like reading back over it and seeing excuses. So I keep working—and I recommend the same system to you. I figure that the chances are good that this BLOCK system will get you over many a hump. It works for me.

MARKET:

So you have written your story or your novel, and you want to market it; what do you do now? I have discussed this in the Author's Note following my novel *Crewel Lye*, but will amplify here.

First you straighten out the errors of spelling and syntax as well as you can. These don't relate to your storytelling ability, but they make you look stupid, which you are not, and are apt to prejudice your manuscript in the tired eyes of the editor. Appearance can be more important than content, so get a friend or someone to go over it with a colored pencil, if you happen to have a problem here. You wouldn't go on a date with dirt on your face, would you? This is of similar importance.

Next, type your manuscript. If you don't know how to type, learn. Two-finger will do; I typed for twenty years two-finger, and sold many a novel so typed, before learning touch on a different keyboard. If you have to, get a friend to type it. Your chances of encountering an editor who will even read a hand-written manuscript are akin to those of a snowball in a furnace. Type it double-spaced, on a single side of each sheet, with wide margins; editors like room to mark up manuscripts, and they only mark those they buy. Put your name or the title of the piece on each page: sometimes pages get separated, in an office full of manuscripts, and the editor needs to know to which one the pages belong.

List the approximate wordage at the front. You calculate this by figuring the number of characters in a typical line—about 60—and number of lines in a page—25 to 28—multiplying these together, and dividing by 6. Then multiply by the number of pages in the manuscript. No, this isn't gobbledegook; you count six characters to an average word (five letters and a space); and partial lines, as in dialogue, count as full lines, because they will take up full lines of printed type. So you will have about 260 or 270 words per page, and if it is ten pages long, that's about 2,600 words. Most writers underestimate their wordage, and some editors will simply pay them based on that estimate, so . . .

Ship it to a publisher loose-leaf: no binders or staples or holes. Use a big manila envelope for a story, or a box for a novel. Enclose return postage, if you want your manuscript back after it is rejected. You *do* want it back, so you can ship it out to the next publisher, and the next. Make sure you keep a copy, in case the original is lost in the mail. *Never send your only copy!* Wait a reasonable time—several weeks or several months, depending on your patience—and if you don't hear anything, send a polite query. If that is ignored—well, when it happened to me, when I was an unsold writer, I sent a return-receipt request for my manuscript back. It's a sure rejection, but it seems to me there are limits to the fecal matter a person should have to eat. But it's up to you.

Ah, but where do you send it? Check your local library for the most recent copy of *Fiction Writer's Market*; that lists all the markets with their addresses, editors' names, requirements, and rates of pay. Pick what you deem to be the best prospect for your type of piece, and send it there. When it returns, send it off to the second-best prospect, and so on. Develop a thick skin about this; don't go into a suicidal depression when rejected, just pack it off to the next and resume faint hoping. Rejections hurt terribly; I still hate them, after having had fifty books published. But they are the hailstones you have to withstand.

One other concern: will the publisher steal your work, perhaps publishing it under some other name without telling you? No; no legitimate publisher would do that. Your work is protected from the moment you create it by Federal statute, which derives from the old common law. You don't need to copyright it yourself; the publisher will do that for you, when it is published, and until then it belongs to you. That's another reason to keep an exact copy at home: so you know you can prove it's yours.

Remember, the odds are against you. Only one aspirant in a hundred ever scores in this endeavor. It took me eight years of trying to make my first sale—for twenty dollars. Even if you make good, you are unlikely to make your fortune from writing; my wife had to work for years to support us while I was struggling to get established. There's just not much easy money here. So do it mainly as a labor of love, or as a gamble, and make sure you can afford to lose. But do keep trying; for some few, the lightning does strike. It happened to me, eventually.

I wish you the best luck; you do need it.

PIERS ANTHONY

Bibliography of American editions

Through Age 50 (50 titles)

Chthon Ballantine pb 1967; Berkley pb 1975, pb 1982 (incomplete)
Phthor Berkley pb 1975; Ace pb 1987

Sos the Rope Pyramid pb 1968
Var the Stick Bantam pb 1973   *Battle Circle* Avon pb 1978
Neq the Sword (British only)

Omnivore Ballantine pb 1968; SFBC 1969; Avon pb 1975
Orn Avon pb 1971; SFBC 1971
OX Avon pb 1976; SFBC 1976

Macroscope Avon pb 1969, Gregg hc 1986 (Audio cassette from Newman)

Prostho Plus Berkley pb 1973; Tor pb June 1986

Race Against Time Hawthorn hc 1973; Tor pb 1985

Rings of Ice Avon pb 1974, 1987

Triple Detente DAW pb 1974; Tor?

Steppe Tor hc 1985; pb 1986
Hasan Borgo pb, hc 1977; Dell pb 1979; Tor pb 1986

Cluster Avon pb 1977
Chaining the Lady Avon pb 1978
Kirlian Quest Avon pb 1978   Cluster
Thousandstar Avon pb 1980   series
Viscous Circle Avon pb 1982

God of Tarot Jove pb 1979; Berkley pb 1981
Vision of Tarot Berkley pb 1980   *Tarot* Ace pb 1987
Faith of Tarot Berkley pb 1980

Mute Avon pb 1981

A Spell for Chameleon Del Rey pb 1977
The Source of Magic Del Rey pb 1979   *The Magic of Xanth*
Castle Roogna Del Rey pb 1979   SFBC 1981
Centaur Aisle Del Rey pb 1982; SFBC 1982
Ogre, Ogre Del Rey pb 1982; SFBC 1983
Night Mare Del Rey pb 1983; SFBC 1983
Dragon on a Pedestal Del Rey pb 1983; SFBC 1984
Crewel Lye Del Rey pb 1985; SFBC 1985

Split Infinity Del Rey hc 1980, pb 1981
Blue Adept Del Rey hc 1981, pb 1982   *Apprentice Adept*
Juxtaposition Del Rey hc 1982, pb 1983

On a Pale Horse Del Rey hc 1983, pb 1984   *Incarnations of*
Bearing an Hourglass Del Rey hc 1984 pb 1985   *Immortality*

Refugee Avon pb 1983, Gregg hc 1986
Mercenary Avon pb 1984, Gregg hc 1986   *Bio of a Space Tyrant*
Politician Avon pb 1985, Gregg hc 1986

Anthonology (stories) Tor hc 1985, pb April 1986

Collaborations:
The Ring with Robert E. Margroff Ace pb 1968; Tor 1986
The E.S.P. Worm with Robert E. Margroff pb Paperback Library 1970;
    Tor 1986
But What of Earth? (unauthorized collaboration with Robert Coulson)
    Laser 1976; corrected edition Tor?
Pretender with Frances T. Hall Borgo 1979; Tor pb [?] 1985

Kiai! with Roberto Fuentes Berkley 1974
Mistress of Death with Roberto Fuentes Berkley 1974
Bamboo Bloodbath with Roberto Fuentes Berkley 1974 } OP
Ninja's Revenge with Roberto Fuentes Berkley 1975
Amazon Slaughter with Roberto Fuentes Berkley 1976

KEY: hc = hardcover; pb = paperback; SFBC = Science Fiction Book Club; OP = Out of Print; ? = date of publication not yet set